Emerging Risks

Emerging Risks

A Strategic Management Guide

Edited by
CATHERINE ANTOINETTE RAIMBAULT
and
ANNE BARR

LONDON AND NEW YORK

First published 2012 by Gower Publishing

Published 2016 by Routledge
2 Park Square, Milton Park, Abingdon, Oxfordshire OX14 4RN
711 Third Avenue, New York, NY 10017, USA

First issued in paperback 2016

Routledge is an imprint of the Taylor & Francis Group, an informa business

British Library Cataloguing in Publication Data
Emerging risks : a strategic management guide.
  1. High technology industries--Risk management.
  2. Strategic planning.
  I. Raimbault, Catherine. II. Barr, Anne.
  658.4'012-dc23

Library of Congress Cataloging-in-Publication Data
Emerging risks : a strategic management guide / [edited] by Catherine Raimbault and Anne Barr.
     p. cm.
  Includes index.
  ISBN 978-1-4094-4593-7 (hardback)
  1. Risk management. 2. Strategic planning. I. Raimbault, Catherine. II. Barr, Anne.
  HD61.E44 2011
  658.15'5--dc23

                                                                    2011048044

ISBN 13: 978-1-138-27178-4 (pbk)
ISBN 13: 978-1-4094-4593-7 (hbk)

Contents

PART II   STRATEGIC MANAGEMENT

List of Figures

List of Tables

Acronyms

AAS	Atomic Absorption Spectrometer
AFOM	Association Française des Opérateurs Mobiles
ALARA	As low as reasonably achievable
ANFR	French national frequencies agency
ANSES	French Agency for Food, Environmental and Occupational Health & Safety
APHP	Assistance Publique – Hôpitaux de Paris
ASIP	National Agency for Shared Health Information Systems
BAT	Best Available Techniques
BCP	Business Continuity Planning
BI	Business Interruption
CAS	Chemical Abstracts Service
CASG Nano	Competent Authorities Subgroup on Nanomaterials
CCNE	National Consultative Ethics Committee for Life Sciences and Health
CEFIC	European Chemical Industry Council
CEN	European Committee for Standardization
CLH	Classification and Labelling Harmonization
CLP	Classification, Labelling and Packaging
CMR	Carcinogenic, Mutagenic and Reprotoxic
CNC	Condensation Nuclei Counter
COREB	Coordination du Risque Epidémique et Biologique
CREAL	Centre for Research in Environmental Epidemiology
CSA	Chemical Safety Assessment
CSR	Chemical Safety Report
CSR	Corporate Social Responsibility
DILGA	Délégué Interministériel pour la Lutte Contre la Grippe Aviaire
DOS	Denial of Service
DU	Downstream User
EA	European Co-operation for Accreditations
ECHA	European Chemicals Agency
ECIIA	European Confederation of Institutes of Internal Auditing
EDA	European Defence Agency

EFSA	European Food Safety Authority
EINECS	European Inventory of Existing Commercial chemical Substances
ELF	Extremely Low Frequency
ELINCS	European List of Notified Chemical Substances
ELPI	Electrical Low Pressure Impactor
EMF	Electromagnetic fields
EMR	Electromagnetic radiation
ERO	European Risk Observatory
EU-OSHA	European Agency for Safety and Health at Work
FDA	Food & Drug Administration
FERMA	Federation of European Risk Management Associations
FFTelecoms	French Telecoms Federation
FIEEC	Federation of Electrical, Electronic and Communication Industries
GHS	General Harmonized System
IARC	International Agency for Research on Cancer
ICNIRP	International Commission on Non-Ionizing Radiation Protection
ICT	Information and Communication Technologies
ICTA	International Center for Technology Assessment
INRS	Institut National de Recherche et de Sécurité (National Research and Safety Institute in France)
IP	Internet Protocol
ISO	International Organization for Standardization
LCA	Life cycle assessment
M2M	Machine to machine
MFL	Maximum Forseeable Loss
MRI	Magnetic Resonance Imaging
MWCNT	Multi-Wall Carbon Nanotubes
NCW	Network Centric Warfare
NFC	Near Field Communication
NGO	Non-Government Organizations
NICT	New information and communication technologies
NIOSH	National Institute for Occupational Safety and Health
NIR	Non-Ionizing Radiation
NNI	National Nanotechnology Initiative
NORA	National Occupational Research Agenda
NRBC	Nuclear, radiological, biological or chemical
NTIC	New Technologies of Information and Communication

OECD	Organisation for Economic Co-operation and Development
POP	Persistent Organic Pollutants
PPE	Personal protective equipment
REACH	Registration, Evaluation, Authorization and Restriction of CHemicals
RFID	Radio-frequency identification
ROS	Reactive Oxygen Species
RT	Relational technology
SAMU	Service d'aide médicale d'urgence
SAR	Specific Absorption Rate
SCENIHR	Scientific Committee on Emerging and Newly Identified Health Risks
SCM	Supply chain management
SDS	Safety Data Sheets
SEC	Securities and Exchange Commission
SEM	Scanning Electron Microscope
SIEF	Substance Information and Exchange Forum
SVHC	Substances of Very High Concern
SWCNT	Single-Wall Carbon Nanotubes
TEM	Transmission Electron Microscope
THF	TétraHydroFurane
UNEP	United Nations Environmental Programme
UNFWCC	United Nations Framework Convention on Climate Change
US EPA	US Environmental Protection Agency
VMI	Vendor-managed inventory
WBCSD	World Business Council for Sustainable Development
WEF	World Economic Forum
WHO	World Health Organization
WHS	Workplace health and safety
WWI	Woodrow Wilson Initiative

Acknowledgement

Gower Publishing is grateful for the support of AXA Group who provided the translation from the original French-language text for the Preface, Introduction and Chapters 2, 3, 5, 7 and 8

List of Contributors

About the Editors

Catherine Antoinette Raimbault (Project initiative and management, contributions to the introduction, the chapter on electromagnetic fields and the chapter on strategic management). Consultant in responsible innovation and emerging risks management, founder of Eurekarisk Conseil. Email: ca.raimbault@eurekarisk.fr

Catherine Antoinette Raimbault, founder of Eurekarisk Conseil, is a consultant in responsible innovation and the management of emerging risks. Her services aim to help organizations to anticipate and design their future activities by integrating emerging risks into corporate strategy. She also advocates the implementation of enterprise-wide risk management to proactively address risks and opportunities.

Her activities target the top management of organizations, strategy and R&D directors, chief risk officers, insurers and international organizations.

She became a key interlocutor of international networks through her strategic role in innovation and development in London and Paris, with some of the Lloyd's brokers, TRMiller, Marsh and consulting firm China–Britain Trade Group.

Her background is in International Business Management/MBA, St Xavier University of Chicago – Marketing, Chartered Institute of Marketing, London – International Risk Insurance, Enass, Paris – IPLV, Université Catholique de l'Ouest, and she is an Associate in Risk Management (ARM) and Vice-President of CARM, the French association of Associates in Risk Management.

Anne Barr (Project management, contributions to the introduction, the chapter on electromagnetic fields and the chapter on strategic management). Consultant in risk management and liability risk engineering, founder of LREM Conseil. Email: anne.barr@liabilityrem.com

Anne Barr, founder of LREM Conseil, is a consultant in risk management and liability risk engineering, servicing entities in charge of risk in medium to large companies as well as corporate insurance and reinsurance underwriting or engineering departments.

While helping her clients to better assess and control their risks, she has grown to believe that emerging risks have an important role to play in the management of strategic risks. She has initiated a watch on some of these issues and participated as a speaker in several conferences and seminars on the subject.

She is a partner of the companies Euro Risk Limited, based in Zürich, specialized in Enterprise Risk Management, and Optirisk, based in Paris, specialized in loss prevention.

Her professional experience has focused on corporate risks in the companies Factory Mutual, SCOR and AXA Corporate Solutions, where she respectively held the functions of loss prevention consultant, senior underwriter, liability expert and then as an independent consultant since 2007.

Her background is in Environmental Engineering, with an ARM certification (Associate in Risk Management). She is currently a member of the Liability Commission of the AMRAE – the French branch of the Federation of the European Risk Manager Associations.

The Contributors

Prof. François Bricaire (Contribution to biological risks). Head of Infectious and Tropical Diseases at Pitié-Salpêtrière Hospital Group. Email: francois. bricaire@psl.aphp.fr

Prof. François Bricaire is Head of Infectious and Tropical Diseases at Pitié-Salpêtrière Hospital Group in Paris. He is a professor at the university Paris VI, and is a specialist in Infectious and Tropical Diseases and Internal Medicine.

He is involved in the fight against bioterrorism and is in charge of emerging infections, including contagious and epidemic infections.

He is a member of the High Council of Public Health and a corresponding member of the National Academy of Medicine.

He is the author of several books: *Les Nouvelles Épidémies – Comment s'en Protéger* (Flammarion, 2009), *Le Bioterrorisme* (Elsevier, 2003), *La Pandémie – La Grande Menace* (Fayard, 2005).

He has been made a Knight of the Legion of Honor and an Officer of the National Order of Merit.

Maj. Gen. (2s) Daniel Brûlé (Contribution to New Information and Communication Technologies (NICT)). Consultant, expert in defence and security.

Maj. Gen. (2s) Daniel Brûlé is a consultant and expert in the fields of defence and security.He conducts prospective, operational and technical studies for companies involved in military equipment programmes.

In risk engineering, he is a partner of APSYS, a subsidiary of the company EADS, and provides expertise in terms of studies, consultancy and training to identify, assess and mitigate human, organizational, technical and economic risks.

He spent an operational career within the French Army and multinational military organizations. In addition to the responsibilities of command, support of forces engaged in overseas operations and teaching–engineering, he was in charge of the works on preparing for the future and was head of risk prevention and environmental management for the Army.

Ultimately, he was inspector general with the functions of command, intelligence and training of the Army.

Maj. Gen. Daniel Brûlé is a graduate of the French War College. He is Commander of the National Order of Merit and the Order of the Legion of Honor.

Jean-Louis Chaptal (Contribution to New Information and Communication Technologies (NICT)). Director and founder of CSQUARE company. Email: jlchaptal@wanadoo.fr

Jean-Louis Chaptal, founder of CSQUARE, is a consultant for businesses development and local governments for innovation in technologies, components and systems related to micro-electronics for ICT applications. His services are in assisting companies for R&D, developing strategic plans, defining and developing new products.

A graduate of both Institut National des Sciences Appliquées (INSA) and Institut d'Administration des Entreprises (IAE), he is an engineer who has developed considerable expertise throughout his career in the field of semiconductors, firstly at Motorola and later at Freescale.

For several years he assumed responsibilities as operational director for the development of innovative solutions for consumer applications: mobile phone, digital television, wireless communication technologies and automobile.

In recent years he served as the R&D director for Motorola, and was also in charge of a joint research laboratory with CNRS for six years.

His recent research has been conducted in electromagnetic compatibility (EMC), new materials alternative to silicon-type GaN, the high power switches for hybrid vehicles and nano materials for integrated inductors.

Aside from his consultancy work, he is an active member of the scientific council of several business schools as well as of the board of the University of Mirail, the Comité Consultatif Régional pour la Recherche et le Développement Technologique (CCRRDT) of the Midi Pyrenees region, the Cancer-Bio-Health centre in Toulouse and the Galien commission on e-health.

Michel Dennery (Contribution to the foreword). Deputy Chief Risk Officer, Audit & Risks Division, GDF SUEZ.

Michel Dennery is a civil engineer and Associate in Risk Management with an operational management experience of more than 20 years in gas and electricity networks, working for EDF and GDF SUEZ. He also served as the head of the media relationships department as well as the purchases and procurements department of EDF.

Throughout his career, in his various positions, he always thought in a risk management way, as in crisis communication while dealing with media, and while implementing Quality, Safety and Environmental (QSE) management in operational activities. He was one of the contributors to EDF's very first risk management methodology during the 2000s to operate a real management through risks.

While in charge of implementing risk management for purchase and procurement, he developed a new supply chain to reduce risks and increase its performance.

He has been heading the risk management department of GDF SUEZ since 2006, before the merger of both companies. For him, every manager is a risk manager, and enterprise risk management is key for good risk taking. He says: 'Striving to better manage risks is one of the best ways to ensure ones performance. Risk management is a good way to anticipate the future.'

He is also Vice President at FERMA, the Federation of European Risk Management Associations, and former President of CARM, the French Association of Associates in Risk Management.

Jean-Paul Fort (Contribution to chemicals/REACH). Consultant on business risks, JPF-Conseil. Email: jeanpaul.fort@orange.fr

Jean-Paul Fort is an independent consultant in industrial risks. He offers services to risk managers of large companies as well as to industrial risks underwriters of insurance companies. He also teaches and gives lectures on industrial risks. After various functions in the chemical industry in France, the United States and Brazil, he was the Risk Manager of the Rhodia chemical group for ten years.

He graduated as a chemical engineer from Institut National des Sciences Appliquées (INSA) in Lyon (France) and received a PhD from the University of Montreal (Canada). He is an active member of AMRAE, the French Risk Managers' Association where he leads several task forces.

Dr Alexei Grinbaum (Contribution to the conclusion with a philosophical approach). Researcher at CEA-LARSIM. Email: alexei.grinbaum@cea.fr

Alexei Grinbaum is a researcher at Commissariat à l'Energie Atomique Larsim: Laboratoire des Recherches sur les Sciences de la Matière (CEA-LARSIM) located in Saclay near Paris. His main interest is in the philosophy of physics and the foundations of quantum mechanics.

Since 2003, he has been working on the ethical and social aspects of nanoscience and nanotechnology. His early publications in this area focus on the uncertainty of technological progress and the problem of governance, including a critique of the precautionary principle ('Living With Uncertainty: Toward a Normative Assessment of Nanotechnology', *Techné* 8(2):4–25, 2004), and on public perception of nanotechnology ('Cognitive Barriers in Perception of Nanotechnology', *Journal of Law, Medicine and Ethics*, 34(4): 689–694, 2006). His later work bears on the question of narratives of nanotechnology ('The Nanotechnological Golem', *Nanoethics*, 4:191–198, 2010; 'Nanotechnogical Icons', *Nanoethics*, 5:195–202, 2011).

He is a coordinator for France of the European Observatory of Nanotechnology, where his principal contribution is the Toolkit for Ethical Reflection and Communication on Nanotechnology (http://www.observatorynano.eu/project/catalogue/4ET).

He is a frequent speaker at public debates on nanotechnology and science and society conferences both in France and internationally.

Jean-Noël Guye (Contribution to the preface and to the chapter on strategic management). Senior Advisor to Group Risk Management – AXA (Paris, France). Email: JNGRiskConsulting@axa.com; Direct Axa contact: david.cadoux@axa.com

Jean-Noël Guye, after a 'seven seas' career in the oil and gas industry, joined AXA to develop specialized underwriting of very large marine and offshore risks. Since 2005 and up to 1 October 2011, he has been heading AXA resources in identifying, quantifying and managing Emerging Risks with multinational experts from Underwriting and Risk Management departments. He is instrumental with Group Corporate Responsibility in implementing Principles for Sustainable Insurance within AXA business entities. He has represented AXA within various organizations: UNEP FI (Insurance/Climate Change working groups) – OECD (part of Pilot Group for Future Global Shocks Project) – Chief Risks Officers Forum, Emerging Risks Initiative and Sustainability Risk Management working group.

Education: Master Mariner and Marine Engineer, Ecole Nationale de la Marine Marchande- Le Havre.

Olivier Hassid (Contribution on country risks). Managing Director of the Security Offices Managers' Club, CDSE. Email: olivier.hassid@cdse.fr

Olivier Hassid is currently the Managing Director of the Security Offices Managers' Club, the French association of security directors, bringing together the largest national firms. He was in charge of security matters within the Cabinet Office before joining Brinks as Deputy CEO until 2007.

He holds a PhD in economics from the University of Paris 1, Panthéon Sorbonne and has been teaching since 2005 at the University Paris 10 Nanterre and the ESC Reims.

He has written numerous books and articles on security: *Crisis and Risk Management* (Dunod, 2011), *Risk Management* (Dunod, 2008), *Enterprise Security to Prevent and Manage Risks* (Maxima, 2010). He heads the Safety & Strategy review.

Dr Alain Lombard (Contribution to nanotechnologies). Toxicologist, Allotoxconsulting. Email: allotoxconsulting@yahoo.fr

Dr Alain Lombard is a European Registered Toxicologist. His career started in 1973 as Research Assistant at the Pharmacology Laboratory of the Faculty of Medicine of Nancy. Then he joined SEARLE R&D Laboratory France at Sophia Antipolis as Toxicologist and Animal Unit Manager and worked for two toxicological non-governmental organizations (NGOs) under contract; as Toxicologist at CIT–Evreux, and, as Toxicologist-Business Development Responsible at Hazleton France, Lyon. Finally, he served 15 years as Industrial Toxicologist at ARKEMA France (ex ATOFINA, ATOCHEM) and Business Unit Scientific Advisor. He represented the company at national and international meetings and organizations (CEFIC, ECETOC, EDANA, IMA, JRC, WHO). He also supported the in-house chemical plants in industrial hygiene as Head of the Industrial Hygiene Unit.

- 2007–present: ALLOTOXCONSULTING, Manager of the consulting company in Toxicology: Company expertise in Nanotechnology HSE.

- 2006–2008: AFSSET/ANSES, French Agency for Food, Environmental and Occupational Health & Safety: Expert member of the Working Group and co-author of the book *Nanomaterials and Occupational Health.*

- 2006–present: AFNOR-ISO, Toxicologist expert, member of the Nanotechnology WGs.

- Two books and one booklet:
  - Author of the chapter related to Nanomaterials in the book *Sécurité et Prévention des Risques en Laboratoires de Chimie et de Biologie* (Safety and Risk Prevention in the Chemical and Biological Research Laboratories), in press 2012.
  - Co-authors of the Booklet 'Guide de Bonnes Pratiques: Nanomatériaux et HSE' (Good Practices for Nanomaterials and HSE) for the French Chemical Union (UIC-FFC), 2009.
  - Co-author of the book *Nanomaterials and Occupational Health*, ANSES 2008.

- Presentations on Nanotechnologies to students and professionals:
  - Scientific Advisor at Vivagora for the programme CoEXNanos, sponsored by the French Ministry of Environment (2010–2011).
  - Training session (seven hours) on 'Nanomaterials: HSE and Societal Risks' at Techniques de l'Ingénieur- Paris (twice a year from 2009 to date).
  - Co-animator of the three-monthly meetings for industrial companies 'FFC-morning sessions Nanotechnologies and HSE' at the French Federation of the Chemical Sciences, Paris (from 2006 to date).
  - Conference (four hours) at the training course of the French Association de Toxico-Chimie (annually from 2006 to date).
  - Twenty five conferences: (one to two hours) on 'Nanomaterials and Risk' for Industries, Unions, Students and Consumers Associations (from 2004 to date).
  - Coordinator of the chapter on Nanotechnology for the French National Research Agency (2005).

Lidija Milasinovic (Contribution to country risks). In charge of studies and strategic monitoring, Consultant on country risk issues. Email: lidija.milasinovic@gmail.com

Lidija Milasinovic is a consultant on country risk issues. She is currently in charge of studies and strategic watch for a social protection group. Previously she was responsible for the recruitment of senior executives and she developed a new practice, 'sustainable development', for an international head-hunting office. In 2009 she co-authored several studies for a publishing company dedicated to the security sector.

She holds an MA in sociology and organizational management from the University Paris 7 Denis-Diderot and an MA in competitive intelligence from EEIE in partnership with the ISC Paris.

Gérard Sengier (Contribution to electromagnetic fields (EMF)). Consultant in health, safety and environment (HSE) risk prevention. Email: gerardsengier@ orange.fr

Gérard Sengier is a consultant in health, safety and environment (HSE) risk prevention.

Trained as an architect and coordinator of Sécurité Protection Santé (SPS), his career in the building sector, the retail industry and mobile networks has been focused on the experts' security, hygiene and working conditions.

Eric Wieczorek (Contribution to the supply chain risk). Expert in supply chain risk management, Owner of Supply Chain Risk Management Consulting, LLC, USA. Email: SCRMConsulting@gmail.com

Eric Wieczorek is the owner of Supply Chain Risk Management Consulting, LLC (SCRM Consulting). Prior to SCRM Consulting, he was Managing Director of Supply Chain Analytics at Dempsey Partners in Philadelphia, PA, USA. In that role he was responsible for all supply chain risk analysis assignments involving the firm's major corporate clients.

With more than 16 years of experience, including eight in pharmaceutical supply chain and risk management, he has also conducted supply chain risk studies for a vast number of industries, including pharmaceutical, chemical, manufacturing, defence, transportation, mining, technology, airline, distribution, retail, financial institutions, marketing, and so on.

He holds a Masters of Business Administration in Risk Management. He has considerable experience in supply chain analysis and business interruption risk quantification, having performed business interruption exposure valuation studies during his tenure as a risk manager for a major global pharmaceutical manufacturer and many other fortune clients as a consultant.

As an Associate Director of Risk Management at Bristol-Myers Squibb in their Princeton, NJ location, he managed the development of their first global supply chain risk analysis by combining internal knowledge of supply chain management and cutting-edge exposure valuation accounting. He has also held posts in the insurance industry for Reliance National and Towers Perrin in Philadelphia.

With the collaboration of **Patrick Leroy** to the chapter on strategic management. Email: patrick.leroy@roquette.com

Patrick Leroy is the Risk and Insurance Manager of Roquette group with a worldwide presence and a €2.5 billion turnover.

He has worked for the major insurance brokers and promotes best in class services to large companies to help them to 'manage' their risks.

Associated in Risk Management (ARM), he is fully involved in AMRAE (Association of French Risk Managers). He is the current President of the Liability Commission in the AMRAE association.

Foreword

'The unpredictable is highly likely', Edgard Morin, the French sociologist and philosopher, once declared long before the Fukushima nuclear accident caused by the tsunami and the cataclysmic earthquake which struck Japan on March 11, 2011. This natural, industrial and economic disaster showed that despite the technology, organization and discipline specific to Japan, and although they reacted with calm and self-control, risk management can never be taken for granted.

Had there been any stress-scenarios? Undoubtedly, but they were carried out in a normal or near normal situation, in the true sense of the word as in a probabilistic sense, and in an imaginable and psychologically bearable context. Can we just continue to live solely in constant fear of the imminence of such an earthquake or in reminiscence of the burial of Pompeii?

It would simply be unbearable. Rooted, the people remain, rebuild and come to life again. We all take the risk. And the more extreme the risk is, the more we take that risk on the grounds that it is recognized as very rare. A kind of denial of risk then accompanies in part this risk taking.

When the event occurs, is it necessarily an emerging risk? Indeed not, but it is experienced as such. Real new risks arise from causes that are themselves new. In this perspective, changes in technology bring their share of emerging risks as their use expands. Others come from a lower tolerance to disasters. Health risks such as diseases are one example. Still others come from new ways of life: when living in villages, with small urban concentration, the effects of natural catastrophes were considerably less.

Trade globalization, immediacy of information dissemination and expansion of the daily life universe to the 'global village' also create new risks, or an awareness of new risks. The voxpopuli has been spreading like wildfire through NTICs (New Technologies of Information and Communication). The media play their role as town criers, but with a global coverage. The politician in fragile position, acting as a surrogate emblematic wise man, should strive to reassure and heal the wounds caused by the emotional tide. Brutal facts are thrown into stark pasture at mealtimes and during television news programmes echoing the rumours of the web.

The world has changed. Is the time so far off when popular wisdom held: 'one must endure what is inevitable and unavoidable', and when 'people took the time to greet each other at greater length'? No, nowadays we create new virtual real contacts with a single mouse click, we control infernal machines with a touch screen and we perform open heart telesurgery.

This technological might creates a sense of power, which anaesthetizes any endurance as much as conscience, and dictates to put a stop to it the next instant. The paradox of risk management is set: more risks have to be taken whilst risk tolerance tends to be lower.

New risks emerge along with technical, architectural and legal innovation, some buried under disasters reemerge to our conscience, and others arise out of the excess of requirements linked to progress. They can all catch us off guard. This book accompanies corporate risk managers through the discovery of some emerging risks. 'Forecasting is not an easy task, especially when it is concerning the future' as Pierre Dac, a French humourist, would state.

They will obviously not find THE answer but possible leads to be fitted to their activities, once fully comprehended. The worst risk is always the one that we do not know or refuse to acknowledge. With these analyses, studies and testimonies, corporate risk managers will be in a position to fulfill their role: anticipate the unexpected.

Michel Dennery
Deputy Chief Risk Officer, Audit & Risks Division
GDF SUEZ

Preface

In an industrial world undergoing accelerated development (new technologies, new processes, products and services), we have to reconcile two objectives that are sometimes contradictory: the goal of ensuring a very high degree of citizen safety and security (the precautionary principle) and that of supporting the ongoing development of innovation which, ultimately, can give rise to risks, either known or emerging.

Known risks are more easily identifiable, quantifiable and 'modelizable' because we have access to critical data. Their temporal horizon is generally limited to the short term, which might be defined as six months or even a year, but some – such as the consequences of asbestos or the sweeping changes caused by the increase in life expectancy – can still be felt 30 or even 50 years down the road!

Emerging risks are new or developing risks. They are new because they are related to the rise of new technologies (like nanotechnologies) and developing because they are linked to new social habits (Internet, mobile phones, and so on). Sometimes they are already developing but have not yet manifested themselves because we lack the requisite distance (potentially, risks linked to exposure to electromagnetic fields). In some cases, they have existed for some time but evolve differently due to a change in perception or jurisprudence (asbestos, biodiversity).

In the absence of data and statistics, the potential losses are as difficult to quantify in terms of magnitude as in terms of frequency.

The knowledge challenge is nonetheless critical on several levels. First, to prevent the recurrence in the future of a phenomenon similar to asbestos, for example, and its cortege of considerable loss in terms of human life, illness and financial damage. Also, to prevent the occurrence – via the interconnection of many emerging risks – of crises whose impact is global, in which the supply chain becomes a major point of weakness when a political, financial, epidemic or other type of event affects an area of the globe that is a part of this chain. Finally, to address acute societal perceptions and fear of risk by seeking to go beyond simple information and instead educate stakeholders with respect to these new or growing risks.

The challenge is considerable, but the time has undoubtedly come to reposition these emerging risk issues within organizational strategy, as part of the Enterprise Risk Management framework and the new rules of governance.

The time has also come to organize the way these risks are monitored and to apply a specific, reliable and robust process for the management of such risks, based on the traditional risk management process framework but with features specific to emerging risks:

- Risk identification: the term detection is more appropriate when it comes to emerging risks.

- Risk assessment: work is more likely to proceed by scenario rather than by modeling, due to the lack of available and reliable statistical data.

- Risk management: the use of pooling with other risks and prevention are more frequent, due to the absence of tried and tested techniques for transferring these risks.

Within business organizations, the risk management department – when it exists, mostly in larger organizations – or more commonly the structures in charge of risk, are the ones ensuring that the risks facing the organization, or that it will have to face in the future, are correctly identified (at the source), anticipated, assessed and then managed dynamically. In general, this department or structure does not manage these risks directly; rather, its role is to ensure that the operational echelons of the organization, which are in daily contact with these risks, are well aware of them and have the tools needed to manage them. In a sense, the entity in charge of risks constitutes a second line of defence upstream of operations, and is tasked not only with thinking about the unwanted developments of known risks, *but also about the development of new risks, whose potential consequences are still little quantified or difficult to quantify.*

Top management has to make a commitment to supporting the activity and organization of monitoring these risks. It will be kept informed and sometimes called on to arbitrate among the emerging risks that appear to be the most critical given the internal and external contexts in play. These priority risks will then have to be taken into account in the decision-making process relative to the organization's strategic challenges.

Via the various issues that are discussed in the course of this work and their respective contributors, we can see the emergence of a number of areas of expertise, each of which will have their role to play in the process of assessing and managing the risks of tomorrow: toxicologists, consultants, researchers, physicians, and so on. These competencies, the quality of the underlying expertise and the existence of a dialogue among scientists, risk managers and executive management could become one of the key factors in the success of achieving optimal management of the impacts of the rapid and major changes that are now part of our environment.

Jean-Noël Guye
Senior Advisor to Group Risk Management,
AXA (Paris, France)

Introduction

Anne Barr and Catherine Antoinette Raimbault

Definition of Emerging Risk

EU-OSHA – the European Agency for Safety and Health at Work – defines an emerging risk as being any risk that is both new and increasing:

> *By new we mean that:*
> *the risk did not previously exist; or,*
> *a long-standing issue is newly considered as a risk due to a change in social or public perceptions; or, new scientific knowledge allows a long-standing issue to be identified as a risk.*
> *The risk is increasing if:*
> *the number of hazards leading to the risk is increasing; or,*
> *the exposure to the hazard leading to the risk is increasing; or,*
> *the effect of the hazard on workers' health is getting worse.*

Consequently, a risk will be considered emerging if:

- A risk that did not exist before appears as a result of the emergence of a new technology (nanotechnologies, new information and communication techniques and so on) or a change in lifestyle and/or a mode of production.

- The existence of a risk that previously was undetectable is brought to the surface thanks to breakthroughs in scientific knowledge.

- An issue is transformed into a new risk as a result of changes in the perception of society. The map of risk perceptions that was produced by Slovic in 1987 already positioned electrical fields, pesticides, genetic engineering and asbestos as risks that were unknown, unobservable, new or that had lagging effects.

Choice of Risks

While knowledge will be one of the drivers of the twenty-first century, it will be just as important to have access to information that is accurate, objective and transparent. Our approach here is not to provide an encyclopedic overview of all emerging risks; instead, we propose to take stock of the state of knowledge with respect to certain key issues and set forth a few proposals for management.

This approach is meant to be both forward-looking and pragmatic – not only in the service of the organization's strategy and risk management but also of all players involved in economic development.

Due to volume constraints, we have limited our discussion to a selection of key issues, taken up below, which respond in particular to the criteria set forth in the OSHA definition: evolutions of a technical or scientific nature, or related to changes in perception or exposure.

We have opted to exclude climate, due to the large number of works on this issue that have already been published. The climate risk is no longer considered to be exclusively an ecological issue, but now involves global economic players in the new climatic governance, one of the major challenges of which is to diminish the impacts of climate change. In terms of references, and given the importance of the challenges for a number of organizations, the major commitments and initiatives related to the fight against global warming have nonetheless been listed in the appendix to this chapter.

NANOTECHNOLOGIES, THE TWENTY-FIRST CENTURY'S INDUSTRIAL REVOLUTION

A world where everything – or nearly everything – is possible poses a challenge that nanotechnologies just might be able to meet. In this world of the infinitely small, the standard unit of measurement is the nanometre (one nanometre is equal to one billionth of a meter) and matter is handled on an atomic or molecular scale.

This is what makes the nanosciences fundamentally multidisciplinary, with applications that have transformed or that will transform any number of sectors, including medicine, sports, automobiles, construction, cosmetics, textiles, food processing and weapons. Nanomaterials are now firmly rooted in our daily lives, and colossal investments are being made by manufacturing leaders in this market, which shows enormous potential for economic and financial development. Investment in research into the impact of their use on human health and the environment, although it exists, has lagged far behind the growth in applications of these technologies. But the fact remains that these technologies are not risk-free. In addition to concerns surrounding nanoparticles, which are found in cosmetics and processed foods, to cite but two examples, ethical and societal questions are also being raised, particularly with regard to personal privacy.

The scope of application is so broad that it has become absolutely critical to mobilize the global scientific community as a whole, with the participation of industrialists to improve our knowledge of both the materials and the risk.

INFORMATION AND COMMUNICATIONS TECHNOLOGIES SERVING THE INFRASTRUCTURE OF THE FUTURE

The appearance of New Information and Communications Technologies (NICT) has played a major role in the spectacular development of our knowledge-based society. They have utterly revolutionized the way we work and live, further strengthening their social and economic impacts.

This formidable technological leap also played a part in the revolution that has taken place in the world of work, with applications for the industrial sector (telecommunications, transportation, aerospace industry, the environment, and so on); for the educational field, with the school of tomorrow; for the media, with new channels of distribution, and so on. It has also reduced isolation and promoted territorial development. Today, it represents an important challenge, for example in the field of remote medicine, a practice that will help an aging population receive homecare.

Undeniably, NICTs have made human beings dependent on them and their use raises serious concerns. The electronic management of health and the use of monitoring and digital identification (ID) technologies have given rise to questions about protecting the right to privacy. The social divide will be even wider for those who are unable to keep up with this digital evolution. The excessively rapid obsolescence of equipment and the production of electronic waste pollution constitute serious environmental impacts. Computer hacking, denial of service and other problems affecting information systems at the global level are important factors of systemic risk that need to be taken seriously.

For this reason, and in order to keep track of the constant changes occurring in the dematerialized world, it is important to establish a new set of rules encompassing security, privacy and ethics.

ELECTROMAGNETIC FIELDS CONTINUE TO MAKE WAVES

Nowadays, we are exposed to the omnipresence of the various sources of the electromagnetic fields that surround us, sources which exist in both natural and artificial states. This exposure has intensified with the arrival of new artificial sources, such as high voltage lines, mobile telephony, antenna relays and new wireless technologies.

This electromagnetic fog, which is also called electro-smog, is a complex ensemble of waves of various frequencies, which run the gamut from low to high frequencies toward the X and Gamma rays. The impact on human beings depends on the frequency and the intensity of the electromagnetic field, and exposure depends on the characteristics of the source and the distance between the source and the exposed individual.

Numerous studies have been launched to assess the impact of electromagnetic fields on human health. All of them appear to converge on the need for additional research. However, early warnings have already led to the adoption of precautionary measures with respect to certain new technologies.

Given the gigantic stakes involved in the development of these technologies, this controversial subject is a challenge in terms of both knowledge and education, and also underscores the need for well-managed tools that can help us to identify and measure these risks.

CHEMICAL PRODUCTS/REACH, A MAJOR ECONOMIC AND ENVIRONMENTAL CHALLENGE, AS WELL AS AN EXAMPLE OF EMERGING RISK MANAGEMENT

Enacted into law in June 2007, REACH is the European Community regulation for the registration, evaluation, authorization and restriction of chemical substances (the acronym REACH stands for the **R**egistration, **E**valuation, **A**uthorization and Restriction of **CH**emicals). This regulation serves several objectives, among them: to improve our knowledge of chemical substances and preparations, to improve our ability to manage the human health and environmental risks related to their production and use, and to enhance both innovation and the competitiveness of the European Union (EU) chemicals industry.

To ensure effective enforcement of this regulation, the European Commission formed the European Chemicals Agency (ECHA), which is based in Helsinki. Businesses are required to adhere to a multi-step procedure that runs from inventory and pre-registration to licensing. Some 30,000 substances among the most frequently used, manufactured or imported are targeted, out of the approximately 100,000 in existence. REACH is completed by Classification, Labeling and Packaging (CLP) and General Harmonized System (GHS) regulations.

The interest of this subject lies in the method and framework created to approach an emerging risk, which offer a number of aspects that are relevant for other areas. REACH establishes a schematic diagram of the life cycle of chemical substances, which spans from research to production through to their end use as products.

The burden of proof is now on the manufacturer, who owns the risk, to demonstrate that its products are innocuous and to anticipate which substances promote or support sustainable development. Part of this burden of proof entails tracking the evolution in our knowledge of the effects of chemical products on human health and the environment.

Without question, REACH is the forerunner of an innovative and transversal dynamic of risk management. In fact, REACH is now a source of inspiration in the area of chemical substance regulation for many countries located outside the EU.

BIOLOGICAL RISK, ETERNAL MUTATION AND INTERNATIONAL MONITORING

The biological risk has been present throughout the course of human history, leaving in its wake a series of major epidemics but also important breakthroughs in medicine. It is dreaded because it can represent a threat in perpetual mutation for all of the planet's economic and political systems. Both its permanence and its highly specific characteristics make constant research and close surveillance necessary.

In addition to being indispensable to life itself, biological agents are present everywhere. Most of them present no danger to humans, and some are even used in the manufacture of food products, in the production of vaccines, and even in the process of cleaning up pollution spills. Conversely, others can trigger illnesses and diseases in humans that are more or less serious. They are transmitted via a chain that counts five links. Preventing the biological risk is a question of breaking this chain as far upstream as possible.

The biological risk is generally presented as having a dual typology. First of all, the biological risk of natural origin, which encompasses constant, emerging and re-emerging pathologies such as the flu and tuberculosis. The other type of biological risk covers accidental or caused pathologies, such as nosocomial infections, mad cow disease, legionella and so on. Risks that are provoked or caused, intentionally or through acts of bioterrorism, can entail several different contagious diseases like smallpox, the plague and anthrax poisoning. An early warning system in the event of a massive attack on the population is impossible in light of the deferred appearance of the symptoms associated with these phenomena.

The evolving and insidious nature of the biological risk, which has no borders or frontiers, its potential for dissemination, and the difficulty in early detection call for the creation of preventive measures and systems as far upstream as possible, as well as for ongoing collaboration on a global scale in areas such as health and safety, so that diagnostic and therapeutic responses can be developed for the benefit of all.

THE SUPPLY CHAIN, AN ESSENTIAL LINK IN TOP MANAGEMENT PRIORITIES

The supply chain is defined as the entire series of linked movements related to the supply and sourcing of goods and services. This is a global concept that does not end with supply/logistics per se. Its scope of action is transversal and encompasses all of the processes that link commodities to final consumers. It lies at the very heart of the activities performed by any business enterprise, and efficient supply chain management (SCM) is an importance source of leverage that contributes to the global performance of the organization. In fact, one small malfunction in a supply chain link can have an impact within the organization as well as provoking a snowball effect along the entire chain, extending outside the organization.

In an increasingly global world, the interdependence of all players and the growing complexity of the supply chain can turn out to be significant sources of disruption and instability. Globalization has created opportunities, but it has also helped to create an environment that is increasingly competitive and tense. The lack of control exercised by the organization or a direct supplier over multiple intermediate suppliers and subcontractors, most often located in far-off countries, has led to an increase in the risks related to supply sources, as the recent Fukushima disaster has so painfully illustrated.

By outsourcing, enterprises have lost control over their destiny. To counter this lack of control over the supply chain, some companies have opted not to return to a full-scale vertical integration model, but rather to reintegrate some of the vital links in the chain. They are also adopting collaborative approaches aimed at developing cooperative partnership relationships with their suppliers and their clients. By bringing together and involving all of the players in the task of maintaining stability in the supply chain, the risks associated with the silo method of operation are eliminated, promoting resilience and ensuring a better balance between the need to manage costs and deliver quality service to the client.

Businesses must adopt global management of the supply chain risk in order to manage the sequential risk and make supply chain management a source of competitive strength.

COUNTRY RISK, AN EVOLVING RISK, SUBJECT TO TENSION

Financial globalization and its phenomena of contagion, globalization of trade and the new areas of tension tend to reshape the country risk landscape.

In recent years, the notion of country risk has undergone change. Increasingly, it integrates financial and macroeconomic issues, in particular the counterparty credit risk, the monetary risk and the systemic risk, as well as the socio-cultural issues that exist alongside the traditional political risk.

Against this backdrop, new power relations have come into being, and in doing so have reshaped the contours of the geopolitical and geostrategic map.

New forms of cooperation and joint action have sprung up between various countries, in some cases morphing into bona fide bodies of governance. Examples include the G8, G20, G2 (United States and China), the BRICS (Brazil, Russia, India, China and South Africa) and the BASIC Group (Brazil, South Africa, India and China), which was formed at the Copenhagen Summit in late 2009 for the purpose of discussing the future of the Kyoto Protocol.

The world will also have to rise to the challenge of new regions of tension linked to new strategic issues related to the sourcing of water, food, commodities and energy, as well as to new challenges raised by global warming, the proliferation and disarmament of nuclear weapons, the Arab uprisings, and so on.

The new battlegrounds have taken over cyberspace, piracy and kidnapping–ransom, new biological arms and other forms of terrorism.

Faced with these new modes of attack and future global challenges, the related risks of the supply chain, crisis transmission and security will lie at the heart of the debate.

In sum, management of the country risk is an excellent example of a global approach to risks and challenges at the strategic level for both governments and businesses.

PART I

Major Risks and Issues

Nanotechnologies

Alain Lombard

Nanotechnology is a field of research and development involving the manufacture of structures, devices and systems from process allowing structuring materials at scales smaller than one micrometre at the atomic, molecular or supra-molecular levels. At this size, material can reach new physico-chemical properties and behave differently from the same material at the micrometre scale, which make them particularly interesting.

Nanotechnology has been defined as 'engineering at a very small scale' by the Institute of Nanotechnology in 2007.

Research and industrial production of nanomaterials has been exponentially increasing over the past ten years. Estimated worldwide public funding for nanotechnology research could amount to a total of nearly US$1.1 billion by the end of 2011.

It opens up undreamt-of possibilities for industrial and medical applications. The projected market size of products incorporating nanotechnology could reach US$27 billion by the year 2015.

Thus, we can consider that the advent of nanotechnology is a major shift in the technological and industrial development of the twenty-first century.

However, a large degree of uncertainty has yet to be clarified, with regards to the safety of nanomaterials on health and the environment and the social impact of the development of nanotechnology for society at large.

What is the Nano-world?

The nano-world is the continent of the infinitely small. It is at molecular level, where the laws of physics change and evolve towards quantum mechanics.

The unit of measurement is the nanometre. The prefix 'nano' comes from Greek and means 'very small'.

It expresses the billionth of a metre, or 0.000,000,001 metre (10^{-9}), a million times smaller than a millimetre.

Comparably, a nanometre is 500,000 times thinner than a ballpoint pen trace, 50,000 thinner than the thickness of a hair.

Definitions of 'nanomaterials' refer to materials with at least one dimension of nanometre size, less than 0.1 micron or 100 nanometres (100 nm) or nanomaterials larger than 100 nm that acquire a specific physico-chemical property, compared to the bulk material, related to the decrease of their size. The chemical composition of these nanomaterials is mineral or organic. They can be from natural sources (sand, dust, smoke from forest fire and volcanos eruptions) or from industrial sources. The multitude of definitions related to nanosciences and nanotechnology is currently under review at international level to establish widely shared and recognized terminology and definitions.

According to the International Organization for Standardization (ISO), nanomaterials are divided into nano-objects and nanostructured materials.

DEFINITIONS OF THE NANO-OBJECTS

Nano-objects are materials with at least one dimension in the nanoscale, less than 0.1 micron or 100 nanometres (100 nm):

- nanoparticles (including spherical fullerenes), also named ultrafine particles;

- nanowires (nanotubes and nanofibers); and

- nanoplates (ultrathin coatings).

A fullerene is a molecule composed of carbon that can take the form of a sphere, an ellipsoid, a tube (called a nanotube) or a ring. Fullerenes are similar to graphite, composed of sheets of hexagonal rings linked, but containing pentagonal rings and sometimes heptagonal, which prevents the sheet being flat. The diameter of a sphere formed by 60 atoms of carbon is less than one nanometre. Nanotubes are formed by one or several concentric tubes. They are formed of carbon atoms arranged in hexagonal array and two half-molecules of fullerene at each end. Fullerenes tend to form aggregates of varying sizes (25–500 nm) in solvents (water, ethanol and acetone).

The nanowires are nano-objects with elongated dimensions ranging from a nanometre to several tens of nanometres for the section and from 500 to 10,000 nanometres in length. The nanotubes can have a length of more than five microns (5μm) and a diameter of 0.7 to 1.5 nm (single-walled nanotubes) or 2 to 50 nm (multi-walled nanotubes). It is now possible to manufacture very long nanotubes. Nanotubes can be formed by other chemical elements than carbon: nanotubes in polystyrene and in PTFE (polytetrafluoroethylene) may also exist (ANSES/AFSSET 2006).

Nanoplates or nanomaterials from scale 2 are materials for surface coating that can be created from one to multi nanolayers to provide the surface with mechanical properties (hardness), or related to water properties (hydrophobic, hydrophilic, non-stick), or thermal properties (heat resistance, insulation), or chemical properties (anticorosivity), or biological properties, or electronic properties, or magnetic properties and or optical properties. These coatings are produced by physical or chemical deposition on a surface. Multilayers can be developed to provide some physico-chemical properties specific to electronics and to integrated circuits or, in the field of surfaces, hardness for tribological applications (ANSES/AFSSET 2006).

DEFINITION OF THE NANOSTRUCTURED MATERIALS

Nanomaterials with a size larger than 100 nm may also acquire nano-specific physico-chemical properties, compared to the nanoscaled bulk material.

This category includes several sub-categories:

- nanostructured powders (nanostructured aggregates and agglomerates);

- nanostructured core-shell particles (polymeric nanocomposites and nanoalloys);

- nanostructured composites (nanostructured onions, nanostructured capsules, and nanostructured plates);

- nanodispersions (nanosuspensions, nanoemulsions and nanofoams);

- nanoporous materials.

Another example is the bio-nano-objects which are an association between organic or mineral nano-objects and biological molecules.

An Exponential Growth

In recent years, the scientific, industrial and military world has embarked on the research and production of nanostructures and nano-objects. Many research programmes are underway in Europe, the United States and Asia to develop applications that will give them a technological edge over other countries. Several hundred million euros are spent annually on research and development.

The United States is the global leader in investment in this area as well as in scientific production and research & development (R&D). R&D expenditures amounted to 1.2 billion euros in 2006, and research for military applications can be estimated at around 500 million euros. The United States was the first to develop a coordination structure called the 'National Nanotechnology Initiative' (NNI) in 1996, with an effective launch of their administration in 2001. Its budget amounted to 1.26 billion euros (1.64 billion dollars) in 2010.

American and European public research budget in nanotechnology are comparable. The public effort in R&D in nanotechnology is substantial in Europe, including France. The financial effort of France in the field of nanotechnology places the country second in Europe behind Germany. Between 2001 and 2005, over one billion euros of public money has been invested to develop research in the field of nanoscience and nanotechnology. In 2007, public spending was around 280 million euros.

The UK, like many other countries, has invested heavily in nanotechnology. The UK has not articulated an overarching national strategy on nanotechnology that can rank alongside those from the likes of the US and Germany. The UK public funding for the period 2009/2010 amounted to 83.20 million pounds (130 million euros) (The Nanotechnology Mini-Innovation and Growth Team (Mini-ITG) report, 2010).

France and Europe generally appear well placed in the field of scientific production in nanotechnology. The number of academic publications in Europe is almost identical to that of the United States, but the difficulty lies in the ability to convert this work into products and value (conversion of knowledge into patents and creation of innovative companies). The United States is the country that publishes most (18 per cent of publications are American, 11.4 per cent Japanese, 8 per cent and 5 per cent German and French). France ranks fifth in the world in terms of number of publications on nanosciences. Two-thirds of patents in this sector are held by Asia (China, Japan and South Korea), significantly outpacing the United States and Europe. Germany accounts for two-thirds of European patents followed by France and the United Kingdom. Applicants are primarily industrial at 70 per cent, mainly multinational corporations (Le Cedef, 2009).

The market forecast for nanotechnology was exaggeratedly estimated in the year 2007 to trillion dollars. According to Nanowerk:

> The report 'Nanotechnology: A Realistic Market Assessment' released by Bcc Research Market Forecasting in 2010 estimates the worldwide sales revenues for nanotechnology to be 26 billion dollars in 2015. Yes, that's illion with a b, not a tr – in 2015. According to this report, the largest nanotechnology segments in 2009 were nanomaterials, with sales reaching 9 billion dollars in 2009. This is expected to grow to more than $19 billion in 2015. Sales of nanotools, meanwhile, will experience high growth. From a total market revenue of 2.6 billion dollars in 2009, the nanotools segment will increase at a 3.3% Compound annual growth rate (CAGR) to reach a value of 6,812.5 million dollars in 2015. Sales of nanodevices, on the other hand, will experience moderate growth. This market segment was worth 31 million dollars in 2009 and will increase at a 45.9 percent CAGR to reach a value of 233.7 million dollars in 2015. 26 billion dollars in 2015 is in a different universe than the previous record forecast of 2.95 trillion dollars. It won't make for eye-catching quotes in business plans,

grant applications and political speeches, but it feels a lot more honest'.
(Nanowerk News, 2010).

The development of nanotechnology could generate direct employment to over 2 million people.

According to the French AFSSET in 2006 (now called ANSES), 1,400 types of nanoparticles were commercialized in significant quantities in the world.

The annual world production of nanomaterials is about seven to ten million tons of carbon black (the main constituent of tyres). For titanium dioxide: 4.4 million tons of small particles and 3,800 tons of nanoparticles (used primarily in paints, and cosmetics, and buildings). About 300,000 tons of silica are used as a constituent of 'green' tyres. Several tens of tons of carbon nanotubes are used in the automotive industry and reinforced composites.

According to the Woodrow Wilson Institute (WWI) 'Consumer Products Inventory of Nanotechnology Products' 2011, 1,317 finished products are listed in the consumers market. This represents an increase of 400 per cent since 2005. The WWI collects names of products that claim to use nanotechnology.

A recent survey made by the Dutch institute RIVM (National Insitute for Public Health and the Environment) in 2011, on 22 products, to analyze the content of nanomaterials in consumer products, concluded: 'Nanomaterials were not found in a number of products with a nano claim, or products contained another than the claimed nanomaterial. In addition, nanomaterials were found in some products without a claim.'

TYPE OF NANOMATERIALS AND APPLICATIONS

Nano-objects

- Metal nanoparticles:
  - nanoclays for structural composites;
  - ZnO and TiO_2 UV absorbers in cosmetics, plastics, and coatings;
  - CeO, silica and alumina or Chemical–Mechanical Polishing slurries (CMP) CeO for fuel catalysts;
  - TiO_2 for photocatalytic coatings, glasses, filters and also in solar cells;
  - silica and alumina nanoparticles for coatings in paint;

- Li compounds for batteries;
- nanosilver for antimicrobial activities in fabrics and composites;
- Pt, Pd, Ni, Co, Rh particles, in chemical catalysis;
- Cu, Ag; sensors in conductive layers in displays; printed electronics, especially with Surface-Enhanced Raman Scattering (SERS) or plasmonics-based sensors;
- aluminium nanoparticles for 'energetics'.
  - □ The global market in 2010 was estimated at 1.8 billion euros.
- Carbon nanotubes:
  - Multi-Wall Carbon Nanotubes (MWCNT) most important volume for conductive and structural composites;
  - Single-Wall Carbon Nanotubes (SWCNT) in composites and in memory, sensors, thermal management, conductive display layers, (Electro Magnetic Interference/Electro Static Discharge) EMI/ESD coatings.
    - □ The estimated market in 2010 was worth 200 million euros.
- Fullerenes:
  - in composites, mainly for sporting goods;
  - as antioxidant additives for cosmetics;
  - in organic solar cell components;
  - in fuel cells;
  - uses as lubricants
  - novel therapeutics drug carrier.
    - □ The market in 2010 was estimated at 50 million euros.
- Nanowires:
  - for conductive layers for displays;
  - in sensors;
  - in solar cells;
  - in logic devices.
    - □ A small market in 2010 estimated at 13 million euros.
- Dendrimers:
  - for drug delivery, therapeutics, and diagnostics;
  - applications in personal care, coatings, composites, inks, and adhesives.
    - □ Estimated market in 2010: 33 million euros.
- Quantum dots:
  - biolabels and in vitro diagnostics devices;
  - optoelectronic applications like LEDs, displays, solar cells;
  - inks and paints for identification or brand protection.
    - □ The market in 2010 is estimated at 30 million euros.

Nanostructured materials

- Nanoporous materials:
  - primarily silica in aerogel materials for insulation, as well as in optics, electronics, catalysis; polymers for separation media; polymers;
  - silicon, or carbon for drug delivery systems;
  - carbon, polymer, hydroxyapatite, in medical device coatings.
    - ☐ Estimated market in 2010: 540 million euros.
- Nanostructured metals:
  - in hard coatings or structural components in aerospace, automotive, pipelines, sporting goods;
  - as chromium-free anti-corrosive coatings.
    - ☐ Estimated market in 2010: 150 million euros.
- Polymer nanoparticles:
  - engineered nanoscale particles of latexes, urethanes, acrylics, and so on used or studied for coating and composite formulations.
- Drug nanoparticles and nanoscale reformulations:
  - coated nanoparticles of actives or encapsulation in liposomes, micelles, emulsion, and so on, widely applied to food and personal care and in drugs delivery.
- Nanoscale films:
  - sub 100 nm layers of polymers, metals, ceramics which are self-assembled or deposited on surfaces from SC wafers to glass to fabrics.

Hazards and Risks

Human exposure to nanoparticles has always existed in the natural environment (pollen, dust or fumes of any kind including volcanic dusts). Thus, minute quantities of Fullerenes in C60, C70, C76 and C84 (molecules in the form of a sphere of 60, or 70 or 76 or 84 assembled carbon atoms) are produced naturally in the soot during organic matter combustion and in the heat lightning through the atmosphere.

Ambient air contains large quantities of nanoparticles having a diameter of or greater than 10 nm either of natural origin (sand, smoke, pollen and so on) or emitted by human activity (car traffic, combustion, barbecues and so on).

There are over 10 000/cm^3 nanoparticles in a quiet room without any activity and more than 500 000/cm^3 nanoparticles in the streets with high traffic activity.

Correlations were made between urban particulate pollution, including a large number of very fine particles and nanoparticles, and modification of various parameters of lung function and cardiovascular systems of the inhabitants of these areas.

In the working world, exposure to nanomaterials has also been evident for decades: that is, fumes emitted by metallurgical furnaces, welding fumes, thermal decomposition, also the manufacture and use of carbon black, and amorphous silica, and so on.

The nature of the risks associated with exposure to nanomaterials of staff involved in research and industry is little studied, often due to technical difficulties to characterize and control the nanomaterials and also lack of budget.

Nowadays technical developments of nanomaterials have been made, most of the time, without worrying sufficiently about potential health risks resulting from, more or less controlled, occupational or environmental exposures.

These issues concern both the workers in the nanotechnology sector, who may be exposed to significant concentrations of nanomaterials, and also the general population whose exposure to these nanomaterials is usually more indirect, by way of contacts with devices containing nanomaterials.

The risks related to nanomaterials are correlated to several relevant endpoints:

- the physico-chemical characterization and classification of nanomaterials which are indicators of potential penetration into the body and of potential interactivity with the body components (size distribution, shape, surface area, composition, surface chemistry, surface charges, crystal structure and so on);

- the biological effects on cells, tissues and organs;

- the detection and characterization of exposure of employees or users;

- the validity and effectiveness of available means for collective and individual protection.

With some exceptions, exposure to nanomaterials from natural occurrence seems to be globally well tolerated by the human body and animal, as they became accustomed to it during the evolution of species. Some nanoparticles or ultrafine particles seem to be only passing through the body and to be quickly eliminated without any interaction. On the other hand, manmade nanomaterials, created to develop new specific physico-chemical reactivity vis-à-vis other particles or other organic molecules, can be stored in the bodies and interact with cells and biological fluids such as proteins or cellular DNA to alter the functioning of the affected organ.

This creates new hazards which are not assessed yet, as a result of the current difficulties in assessing the relationship between physico-chemical properties of nanomaterials and their degree of reactivity, or their biological and toxicological effects on cells and organs.

POTENTIAL EXPOSURE TO NANOMATERIALS

The airways are the major route of penetration of these nanomaterials into the body. However, studies indicate, under certain conditions, a possible dermal penetration and a significant absorption from the gastrointestinal tract of some nanomaterials.

Generation of aerosols of nanomaterials

The generation of aerosols of nanomaterials is dependent on the particle size, the particle concentration and other characteristic parameters such as the shape, the density, the state of electric charge, the chemical composition, and so on.

Nanomaterials have a strong tendency to clump together and stick to other dusts, capturing air pollutants from organic, or inorganic and biological origin. Thus, they can be well dispersed in the air as individual dusts or grouped in clusters or aggregates. These physical modifications may change their destiny in the airways.

The events leading to the issuance of nanomaterials in the air are often fleeting or unstable, inducing variability of concentrations and particle sizes, in space and time, making exposure difficult to assess and to monitor.

Characterization of exposure to nanomaterials

In occupational hygiene, the risk from exposure to 'dust' has long been evaluated based on their mass concentrations (mg/m^3) in the air inhaled by the workers.

In the case of nanomaterials, the relevant parameters are no longer only the mass concentrations in the air, but also the number of nanoparticles and/or specific physico-chemical characteristics such as: the developed surface area, the surface state (with, in particular, the role of the presence of metals or electrical charges at the surface), as well as other factors such as the state of agglomeration or the presence of biological contaminants.

The characterization of the exposures to nanomaterials cannot be made by applying such old conventional methods of exposure control. The exposure control methods have to be adapted, because the behaviour of nanoparticles aerosols in the air is modified as compared to micronic aerosols. Micronic aerosols have known 'aerodynamic' behaviour based on size, shape and weight, while for nanoparticles the behaviour in the air is rather compared to a 'gaseous diffusion'.

Therefore, characterizing exposures to nanomaterials is appealing to a specific instrumentation which differs from that usually used in occupational hygiene for micron-sized dust.

At the methodological level, a global analysis throughout the entire lifecycle of nanomaterials is essential to understand all aspects of potential exposures in the laboratories, the factories, the global population or the environment.

For example, the general population is potentially exposed by inhalation, skin contact or ingestion through the direct use of consumer products containing 'free' nanomaterials in a form of aerosols, or 'bounded' nanomaterials in a liquid matrix, creamy matrix (paint, cosmetics) or solid matrix (polymers, plastics, fabrics, or concrete).

Current detection and protection devices for nanomaterials

The detection of nanomaterials in the work environment is an indispensable step for the development of mass production of nanomaterials.

Questions: What happens in the workplace for the employees who are working with nanoparticles and nano-objects? Are they currently exposed? What is their level of risk?

Some tools for the detection of nanomaterials already exist, and can be used in laboratories, industries and environment.

At the industrial level, a few specific devices are marketed in Europe and in the United States but the performances are uneven and the prices are prohibitive for routine use. Some are portable; others are intended for stationary measurements. The specificity and selectivity of these devices vary. The scale for measuring the particle size ranges from 5 nm to 500 nm for a device and 6 nm to 10 000 nm for another.

The techniques used for these devices are varied: Atomic Absorption Spectrometer (AAS) coupled or not to other devices, Condensation Nuclei Counter (CNC), Electrical Low Pressure Impactor (ELPI), Scanning Electron Microscope (SEM), Transmission Electron Microscope (TEM).

In practice, it is very rare for a same sample collected in the air to obtain similar values by using several different equipments. This increases the difficulty of controlling exposures. Since it is difficult to characterize the levels of nanomaterials in the air, it is necessary to use adapted personal protective equipment (PPE), for the protection of the workers against nanomaterials exposures.

The European programme NANOSAFE (2008) tested the existing protective equipment. The results show that all the tested gloves (gloves in nitrile, latex, neoprene, and vinyl) provide an effective barrier against penetration of aerosol nanoparticles; gloves in vinyl being the most protective. Concerning the clothes, it was also shown that the best protection is obtained with clothing outfits in non-woven fibers (Tyvec®) that are airtight. Clothing made from cotton should be avoided as they do not protect. The high-efficiency masks in fibers (HEPA or FFP3) have a good filtration of nanoparticles. Surprisingly, the most penetrating nanoparticles are not the smaller ones, but those with a diameter around 150 nm to 300 nm. Electrostatic masks are more effective, the most penetrating nanoparticles have a diameter of 30 nm, but after two hours of use the penetration of nanoparticles through the electrostatic masks increases to 1 per cent, due to moisture conditions in the masks produced by respiration.

With regard to population and environment, it is very difficult to have a clear idea of the nature of exposures in terms of quality, intensity and duration, related to consumption habits and dissemination.

It is possible to adapt, for professional monitoring purposes, certain devices for detecting nanomaterials and also individual and collective protection, to population exposure controls and the environment exposure controls.

For a mass exposure, the current devices for protection, detection and analysis in the air are no longer adapted to these nanoscale structures.

In the absence of a more precise characterization of exposures, epidemiological studies are not relevant to prove the actual potential risk faced by man and the environment.

Thus, while the development of nanotechnology is accelerating, we have to invent new specific ways to assess, to control and to prevent this hazard as a result of nanotechnology.

Questions: Will our society be able to respond quickly to these questions before the onset of health problems or environmental problem? Is there going to be a scandal like asbestos exposures or the production of contaminated blood?

HEALTH EFFECTS OF NANOMATERIALS

Drawing comparisons with the known effects of air pollution by micro particles raises the fears of similar or worse health effects from engineered nanomaterials (Murphy et al., 1998).

However, very little data is currently available. The published studies show the penetration and the dispersion of nanomaterials in the body, and the possible interactions at the cellular level (Lombard et al., 2005). This preliminary results call for precaution.

Toxicological data already available is few and disparate, and furthermore, it is constantly evolving.

Two types of nanomaterials, nanoparticles and nanotubes, have been investigated. Their behaviours are different in the biological environment, particularly as regards the transfer into the body and the production of cellular responses. Differences were also observed related to the size and to the surface properties of nanomaterials from the same chemical composition.

Penetration and distribution from the respiratory tract into the body

As an ultrafine dust, nanoparticles are deposited in the upper respiratory tract and in the lung (especially in the deep lung) at higher rates than that of micrometre-sized particles.

The aerodynamic behaviour does not follow the laws that govern micron particles. Thus, the finer nanoparticles (1 nm in diameter) are deposited mostly in the nasopharyngeal region (90 per cent), intermediate size particles (5 nm diameter) are deposited uniformly throughout the respiratory tree; the larger particles (20 nm in diameter) are found mainly in the alveoli (ICRP, 1994). Physical activities of the exposed persons increase the deposit in the lung according to the volume of inhaled air.

Experimental studies conducted by G. Oberdörster et al. in the 1990s have shown that titanium dioxide (TiO_2) nanoparticles may penetrate the lung epithelium and move into the lymphatic channels, with gradual accumulation in the closest lymph nodes. This penetration is favoured by the size and number of particles, and the intensity of inhalation. Results of a comparative study with primary particles (size 20 nm) of TiO_2 and carbon black, showed that these nanoparticles do not penetrate the alveolar interstitium similarly: approximately 50 per cent of the dose for TiO_2 and only 4 per cent for black carbon (Oberdörster G. et al., 1992).

Following this trans-alveolar passage, systemic distribution through the bloodstream was also highlighted, as well as storage in the kidney, testis, thymus, lungs and brain. E. Oberdörster (2004) and G. Oberdörster et al. (2004) showed that nanoparticles could reach the brain by following the path of the olfactory nerve. From this work, it was hypothesized that penetration of nanoparticles in the body may follow the nerve pathways, as do viruses.

It was observed an accumulation of 1.4 nm nanoparticles in the placenta of pregnant rats and in small quantities, in the fetus. This could indicate a crossing of the placental barrier (Kreyling et al., 2006).

According to Mercer et al. (2011), 56 days after pharyngeal deposition in mice, Single-Wall Carbon Nanotubes (SWCNT) have migrated into the lungs and entered the pleural surface.

Baker et al. (2008), in a comparative repeated inhalation study in rats with C60 fullerene nanoparticle (55 nm) and microparticles (930 nm), showed that the pulmonary clearance time (half-life) was respectively 26 and 29 days.

The capture of nanoparticles in the blood would be made first in the liver by Kupfer cells, then secondarily by macrophages in the pancreas, and other cells. The elimination process would be in urine by renal filtration, or in the faeces.

In vitro studies show that nanoparticles of small size (smaller than 10 nm) and carbon nanotubes can enter cells and be found in the cytoplasm.

Sadauskas et al. (2007), showed in studies, by intravenous or intraperitoneal injection of gold nanoparticles of 40 nm and 2 nm in mice, that cell penetration is made by endocytosis (uptake by the cell membrane), especially for nanoparticles of 2 nm.

Nanoparticles and carbon nanotubes can also enter sub-cellular structures: mitochondria, responsible for cell energy production and cellular respiration (Li et al., 2003), and the nucleus (Chen and von Mickecz, 2005).

Panté and Kann (2002) showed that macromolecules with diameters below 39 nm can transit in a bidirectional manner between the cell cytoplasm and nucleus.

Porter et al. (2007a,b) has released electron microscope images showing the presence of fullerenes and carbon nanotubes in the cell nucleus. This intra nuclear penetration opens access of nanomaterials to cellular DNA and the possibility of actions on cellular genes. These transfers into the cell organite and the nucleus may well induce disturbances in cellular respiration, increased oxidative stress and have an interference with the replication of DNA and DNA repair.

Dermal penetration of nanoparticles and carbon nanotubes

Fears have been expressed that the nanoparticles of TiO_2 and ZnO used in sunscreens can penetrate the body through the skin and exert a localized or systemic toxicity.

Some studies indicate an induction of genes expression of keratinocytes of human neonatal epithelium in culture by nanomaterials including a sample of SWCNT (Cunningham, 2007).

Some 'in vivo' human studies show no passive transcutaneous passage (Plüfcke et al., 1999; Mavon et al., 2007), while other studies have shown a transcutaneous passage of TiO_2 (Hoet et al., 2004; Oberdörster, G et al., 2005). This transfer may occur by mechanical friction on the skin or when applied to damaged or abraded skin (Trommer and Neubert, 2006) and also through the hair follicle (Mahe et al., 2009). Transdermal penetration of carbon nanotubes is not reported.

The nanomaterials used in cosmetics are nanostructured aggregates with a size around 500 nm or more. They do not easily penetrate through the healthy stratum corneum and do not reach the living cells of the epidermis, while small nanoparticles (10 nm) do. Nohynek (2007) concluded that nanoparticles used in cosmetics do not pose a risk to human skin or human health.

The results of the dermal studies are controversial, and many authors concluded the need to investigate further the passive dermal absorption through human skin of small nanoparticles (<10 nm) (Crosera et al., 2009).

Nevertheless, one could believe that no massive systemic dermal exposure would be feared.

Gastrointestinal absorption of nanoparticles

A high daily intake of nanoparticles and microparticles (100 to 3,000 nm) would be through the gastrointestinal tract. The estimated absorption ranges from 10^{12} to 10^{14} particles per day in the Western world, mainly silicates and titanium dioxide coming from food and toothpaste (Lomer et al., 2004). Nanoparticles are poorly transferred through the gastrointestinal tract and are rapidly eliminated in faeces (Hagens et al., 2007).

The passage through the digestive barrier would be possible by the cells 'M' covering Peyer's patches and lymphoid follicles, and intestinal epithelium (Lomer et al., 2004).

Pulmonary effects of carbon nanotubes

In addition to the chemical composition of the particle, the parameters 'number of particles' and 'surface reactivity' and 'reactive surface' should be regarded as being involved in the toxicity of nanoparticles too.

Oberdörster and colleagues hypothesized that the incidence of lung tumours observed in some animal studies may be related to the total surface of particles in the lungs, more than related to the total number of particles. This indicates that the total surface of particles in contact with the organism is an important parameter to consider in assessing the toxicity of nanoparticles.

Crystallinity is involved in the 'surface reactivity' through its ability to produce free radicals (Dick et al., 2003). In addition to the crytallinity, the 'surface reactivity' is increased by the presence of impurities or of bioavailable metals at the surface of the crystal (Aust et al., 2002).

Warheit studies in 2006 showed that the pulmonary effects of ultrafine particles of TiO_2 are also dependent on the composition of the surface reactivity and the crystal structure.

The intratracheal instillation in rats of SWCNT caused inflammation, epithelioid granulomas and pulmonary fibrosis (Warheit et al., 2004; Lam, 2004). The inflammatory effects are especially due to the presence of chemical impurities (nanofibers, carbon nanoparticles and metal catalysts) related to the production of nanotubes (Lam, 2004).

The work of the team of Shvedova of the NIOSH (National Institute of Occupational Safety and Health) in 2005, suggests that the mechanism of fibrosis caused by purified nanotubes (without any metallic or organic or bacterial impurities) involves not an inflammatory process resulting from a prior activation of lung lymphocytes, but the direct activation of lung fibrocytes. The local synthesis of collagen fibres by fibrocytes would be effective from the seventh day after instillation. Fibrosis is prominent six days after exposure (Shvedova et al., 2005).

There was concern that carbon nanotubes have similar behaviour to asbestos because of their similarity in shape and size (very small diameter <100 nanometres and lengths of several millimetres). It appears that these flexible nanotubes agglomerate in balls in the air sacs being thus unable to pass through it easily and reach the pleura. This agglomeration increases their persistence in the lungs and facilitates the induction of fibrosis and inflammatory phenomena.

Donaldson et al. (2008), in an intraperitoneal preliminary study in mice, indicates a cytotoxic effect of SWCNT similar to that of asbestos.

Hubbs et al. studies (2009) in mice show that SWCNT have penetrated the pleural surface, and as a result are rekindling the comparison with asbestos.

Systemic effects (whole body effects) of nanomaterials

Nanomaterials that enter the body, reach the 'target organs' where they can store and exert their toxic potential.

- Neurotoxicity: nanoparticles could reach the brain along the olfactory nerve route (Oberdörster E., 2004; Oberdörster G. et al., 2004).

  Long et al. (2006) highlighted the impact of form P25 Titanium Dioxide (TiO_2) on cell cultures of microglia (brain macrophages). He noted the presence of nanoscale particles and intra-cytoplasmic aggregates sequestered in the cell bodies of microglia after six and 18 hours of exposure. These nanoparticles do not cause cell death at concentrations of 2.5 ppm and 120 ppm (ppm = parts per million, that is, mg/m_3), but induce immediate biological responses at size <5 nm and continuous secretion of Reactive Oxygen Species (ROS) by the microglia at 120 ppm (a non-toxic concentration of nano-sized titanium dioxide) and an interference with microsomal energy production.

- Immunotoxicity: the nanoparticles binding to proteins can induce immunotoxic reactions. Studies in healthy subjects show that the pulmonary inflammatory reactions induced by nanomaterials can influence the development of allergic pulmonary diseases (Nygaard et al., 2004; De Haar et al., 2006; Alessandrini et al., 2006).

- Vascular effects: the assumption was made that the passage of nanoparticles into the bloodstream in significant quantity may lead to thickening of blood and platelet aggregation (Radomski et al., 2005; Nemmar et al., 2007) and also localized inflammatory effects. This would increase the risk of atherosclerosis and thrombosis in blood vessels that might lead to risk of myocardial infarction.

  Vascular toxicity was evaluated in mice after pulmonary instillation of high concentrations of carbon nanotubes (0.5, 1, 2 mg/mouse). Dose-dependent alterations of mitochondrial DNA in the aorta, with an alteration of inflammatory mediators in cardiac cells, were observed 7, 28 and 60 days after exposure (Li et al., 2004). In vitro studies show that human aortic endothelial cells exposed during two hours with carbon nanotubes results in an increase in mRNA for many genes and a dose-dependent oxidation of low density lipoproteins. These results suggest that carbon nanotubes can lead directly or indirectly to atheromatogenosis predisposition, thus creating points of forming cell clusters, gradually obstructing the blood flow in blood vessels (Li et al., 2004).

- Cellular toxicity: nanoparticles can bind with cellular proteins, produce Reactive Oxygen Species (ROS) and exert a localized oxidative toxic activity.

  Miyata et al. (2000) showed that fullerenes release ROS by photo-irradiation, which can cause cellular damages.

- Mutagenicity: it was shown that nanoparticles can penetrate the sub-cellular structures of mitochondria (Li et al., 2003) and the nucleus (Chen and von Mickecz, 2005). These transfers into the mitochondria could lead to disruptions in cellular respiration, and increased oxidative stress, and produce interferences with the DNA replication and DNA repair in the nucleus.

  Borm et al. (2004) showed specific interactions with DNA (DNA adducts) of nanoparticles generated by combustion, or particles of diesel fumes or carbon black. The nanoparticles are chemically bonded on some DNA bases (DNA adducts) causing changes in the structure of DNA and inducing modification of the behaviour of the cell where genetic changes occurred.

According to the French HSE Agency (AFSSET/ANSES report, 2008):

> *There are few and sometimes contradictory results on the genotoxicity of nanoparticles. For example, nanoparticles of titanium oxide are not genotoxic 'in vitro' in the Ames test and chromosomal aberration test according to some authors, while other authors demonstrate the opposite by using a panel of 'in vitro' genotoxicity tests on human lymphoblastic cells (micronucleus test, comet and chromosomal mutations). Similarly, the C60 fullerenes are proved non-genotoxic on hamster lung cells (Ames test and chromosomal aberration test) exposed to concentrations up to 5000 µg/ml, whereas they are genotoxic in human lymphocytes (comet assay) exposed to low concentrations (2.2 µg/l). It is impossible to exclude that nanoparticles can have genotoxic, mutagenic or carcinogenic effects.*

ENVIRONMENTAL EFFECTS OF NANOMATERIALS

The ecotoxicity of nanomaterials has been the subject of controversial studies.

Questions were raised about the causes of pathologies observed in fishes (damaged cell cycle, neurotoxicity, hematopoietic cells changes), that could lead to systemic diseases.

E. Oberdörster (in 2004) tested fullerenes on five aquatic species: three micro-crustaceans and two freshwater fishes. She did not show any lethal effect on the five aquatic species at concentrations tested with fullerenes dispersed in water, but fullerenes have led to sub-lethal toxic effects in daphnia and fishes and some chronic effects in Daphnia including low mortality, delayed molting and delayed reproduction with reduced clutch size. Cons toxic effects were observed on minnows and daphnia with fullerenes dissolved in TétraHydroFurane (THF). She also observed an increase of oxidative stress in trout exposed to carbon nanotubes.

Smith et al. (2007) showed that the Single-Wall Carbon Nanotubes are respiratory toxicants in trout even if these fish can regulate the oxidative stress and osmotic disruption caused by the SWCNT.

However, carbon nanotubes are hydrophobic and form micrometric-sized aggregates in the presence of water. The cluster size is independent of salinity or temperature (Cheng et al., 2004). This cluster limits the cellular penetration of nanotubes and consequently its toxic potential.

Numerous studies indicate that there would be no ecotoxicity of TiO_2 nanoparticles, but a high ecotoxicity of ZnO particles regardless of the nanoparticle size.

The question of the fate of nanomaterials in the environment is posed, due to their use as a 'free-form' (emissive) or 'bounded-form' (less emissive) in widespread distribution of manufactured products. For example: nanosilica in tyres, nanoTiO$_2$ in cosmetics sunscreen, paints, concrete, food, and so on.

Each year, a significant part of these nanomaterials that are mass produced is emitted into the environment and comes into contact with flora and fauna through the air, water and soil.

Question: What are the effects of nanomaterials on the microbial flora in the environment?

The oxidative effects of the fullerenes do not have any decisive action on the environment (US Department of Energy Nanoscale Science Research Center, 2008), but silver nanoparticles keep their bacteriostatic properties against bacteria. Therefore, environmental concerns have been raised about the disruptive action of nanosilver in the activities and balance of the microbial ecosystems, and specifically in the activated sledges of the waste water treatment (Alvarez et al., 2008)

Bradford et al.'s study (2009) in estuarine sediments shows that there is a decrease in the global bacterial population, without any impact on the genetic diversity of bacterial assemblages.

The hypothesis has been suggested that nanoparticles can penetrate the plants through the root system and concentrate in several organs of the plants (leaves and roots). However, there are limited studies on the overall effect of nanoparticles on plants and wildlife, but some studies prove that there are toxic effects on wildlife and a potential for bioaccumulation in various organisms (Handy et al., 2008).

Questions arise on the lifecycle of nanomaterials, their fate and their inactivation by environmental elements. Fears are expressed on their possible bioconcentration along the food chain, and consequently on the possibility of their being incorporated into human food, thus creating a risk of harmful effects to humans.

The life cycle assessment (LCA) is not only essential as regards the potential toxicological and ecotoxicological effects in the different stages of the lifecycle of the products, but also regarding the use or total consumption of materials and energy.

EXPLOSION HAZARD OF ORGANIC AND INORGANIC NANOMATERIALS

The vast majority of powders ranging in size from a few microns to several tens of microns, are combustible and can lead to explosions, often called 'dust explosions'; it is expected that clouds of nanomaterials may react in the air as fine dusts do. Theoretically, it is possible that the thresholds of ignition of nanomaterials' atmospheres are similar to those of conventional explosive gas. In addition, the manipulation of particles causes the formation of static electricity in processes, which is more difficult to evacuate as the critical thresholds of ignition are low (Proust, 2004). Thus, nanomaterial explosion may destroy part or all of the process. Moreover, a large quantity of nanomaterials propelled by the blast of the explosion may be released into the atmosphere. The potential toxic effects of nanomaterials, coupled with the physical effects, at the time of the explosion, may be aggravating the overall risk (NANOSAFE, 2008).

Summary of Potential Effects of Nanomaterials

Several well-conducted studies confirm that there is 'a specific nanoscale effect' but that this effect is expressed differently depending on the characterization of the nanomaterials.

However nanomaterials are able to:

- cross the alveolar wall and migrate through the lymph and blood into the whole body (to the liver, the pancreas, the kidney, the testis, the thymus, the brain and the placenta);

- cause lung inflammation by the formation of Reactive Oxygen Species (ROS);

- increase the viscosity of the blood and blood clotting and may cause thrombosis;

- cross the cell membranes and migrate into the cell organites and the nuclei;

- cause cell cytotoxicity or cell disfunction;

- have immunotoxic and genotoxic effects;

- induce risk of dust explosion.

Ecotoxicity is not demonstrated but studies indicate some ecotoxicological effects. Lifecycle is not known.

Waste Treatment

During the lifecycle of nanomaterials, elimination is the last, but important step.

Swiss researchers have estimated that 95 per cent of nanoparticles used in commercial products such as cosmetics, paints, and detergents are found in sewage treatment plants during the stages of manufacture, use and end of life (Mueller and Nowack, 2008).

No single nanomaterials removal technique from wastewater or drinking water achieved 100 per cent efficiency in dealing with emerging nanoscale environmental pollutants. This means that a certain percentage of nanomaterials passes untreated, and potentially can adversely impact on the aquatic, terrestrial or human life forms (Musee, 2011).

There is a particular need to address the potential impact of nanomaterials along the lifecycle of a product, from manufacture through disposal ('cradle to grave').

Waste treatment of nanomaterials is difficult because neither the characterization nor the volume nor the dangers of such waste are known. This makes it difficult to develop legislative and policy frameworks that can address potential new forms of waste streams, or find best fits of current regulations in dealing with them.

For the nanotechnology to be sustainable, nanowaste streams must be effectively managed. Some guidelines are published by official bodies within the Health, Safety & Environment (HSE) management of nanomaterials (Industrial Hygiene and Information Management, 2008).

In principle, the European IPPC Directive (Directive 2008/1/EC) concerning Integrated Pollution Prevention and Control (OJ L 24 of 29 January, 2008) could be used to manage the environmental impact of nanomaterials and related issues at Integrated Pollution Prevention and Control (IPPC) installations, through the integration of these considerations into the reference documents on Best Available Techniques (BAT).

The US EPA (Environmental Protection Agency) has established a voluntary programme to handle this new issue, based on a precautionary approach that applies primarily to certain types of 'free' or 'bioavailable' nanomaterials.

This is applicable to:

- pure nanomaterials (for example, mineral nanoparticles or carbon nanotubes);

- materials contaminated with nanomaterials;

- liquid suspensions containing nanomaterials;

- solid matrices including nanomaterials that are friable or where the nanostructure is easily detachable from the matrix and can be detached easily to enter the air, water or soil.

This approach does not apply to nanomaterials called 'bound' that are firmly embedded in a solid matrix (concrete, polymer and so on) and therefore cannot be released without strong mechanical action (cutting, grinding, filing and so on). However, the sustainability of this matrix must be called into question.

The final processing of nanomaterials depends on their nature. It must be done by specialized companies. Many nanomaterials are made of metal and can be treated as such. Others are organic and can be easily destroyed by fire.

As a last resort, vitrification at very high temperatures can be used to inactivate a variety of nanomaterials.

In the absence of certainty about the safety of nanomaterials, the wastes containing nanomaterials must be considered hazardous and must be handled with precaution.

Thus, the implementation of control procedures and the use of more efficient protective equipment, for the employees handling and processing these specific wastes, will either limit or eliminate the risk of exposure.

A certification of waste treatment plants treating nanomaterials and a specific training of employees ought to be considered in this context.

For the protection of people and the environment, controls of the emissions into the environment have to be implemented to prevent releases of degradation products from nanostructured materials.

Question: Should we create controlled landfills plants for nanomaterials as is the case for asbestos and highly dangerous substances?

Regulatory Activities

There are currently no specific regulations in Europe that take into account the nanoscale structure of nanomaterials.

Indeed, chemicals are identified by their chemical formula, and their registration number EINECS (European Inventory of Existing Commercial Chemical Substances) for existing substances before 1981 or ELINCS (European List of Notified Chemical Substances) for substances registered after 1981, or in the USA by the CAS Number (Chemical Abstracts Service). These identifiers refer to the chemical nature of substances regardless of their form. For example: titanium dioxide (TiO_2), which occurs in two, more or less pure crystalline forms, Anatase or Rutile, which have different physical properties, is registered under the same identification number, regardless of the nature and size of particles.

The European REACH programme (Registration, Evaluation and Authorization of CHemicals) automatically covers the nanoscale form of a substance, since the physico-chemical properties must be described, the toxicological properties related to this specific substance form must be verified and the Chemical Safety Assessment (CSA) must take into account all type of exposures to demonstrate good risk control. The specific properties of the nanoscale forms involve adding specific information in the registration dossier.

Additional information may include a specific classification and labelling and a risk assessment adapted to the nanoscale form. This information, also including specific operating methods and measures to control exposures and protect employees and the environment, should be available throughout the supply chain of nanomaterials.

However, in order to notify the specific properties, hazards and risks associated with nanomaterials, we need to have the results of adapted test studies. These suitable tests are still lacking because of the difficulty to characterize nanomaterials and to define precisely the reliable methods to study the effects of nanomaterials on health and the environment.

Specific formal test guidelines must be defined to help manufacturers study the real hazards of nanomaterials on the market. The Organisation for Economic Co-operation and Development (OECD) is currently working on these test guidelines.

In Europe, The European Project NanoCode: a multistakeholder dialogue providing inputs to implement the European Code of Conduct for Responsible Nanosciences & Nanotechnologies Research commenced in January 2010. This two-year project is funded under the Programme Capacities, in the area Science in Society, within the 7th Framework Program (FP7). The objective of NanoCode is to define and develop a framework aimed at supporting the successful integration and implementation, at European level and beyond, of the Code of Conduct (CoC) for nanosciences and nanotechnologies (N&N) research as developed by the European Commission.

As part of the application of the 'Precautionary Principle', it is essential to take into account in a chemical substance dossier: the nature of nano pure substances or products containing them, assigning, by default, a high level of danger, and advocating conservative protection measures.

At present there is no discrimination in the registration dossier according to the size of a chemical. A subgroup for REACH 'Competent Authorities

Subgroup on Nanomaterials (CASG Nano)' has been created in 2008 and will edit recommendations for nanomaterials in 2012.

Pending adequate regulation and failing to know the hazards of nanomaterials, we must limit the risks by implementing strict risk management. That is, to impose a strict limitation of 'free' nanomaterials, the use of nanomaterials forms which are non-emitting and not bioavailable, and limited exposures for workers, consumers and the environment through appropriate operating procedures.

Standardization Activities

In recent years, intense activity has been implemented at international and national standardization level, for instance:

- the ISO Technical Committee TC 229;

- the European Committee for Standardization (CEN) TC 352.

And several States Committees that mirror the work of ISO and CEN, for instance:

- the French Commission for Standardization (AFNOR X457);

- the German DKE/K 141Nanotechnologies;

- the BSI Committee for Nanotechnologies (NTI/1);

- the Dutch Standardization Association (NEN), Nanotechnology Commission;

- the American National Standards Institute's Nanotechnology Standards Panel;

- the Chinese United Working Group for Nanomaterials standardization;

- the Japanese Council on Nanotechnology Standards.

INTERNATIONAL STANDARDIZATION: ISO

The ISO Technical Committee TC 229 is organized into four working groups:

- WG 1: Terminology and Nomenclature (Canada);

- WG 2: Measurement and Characterization (Japan);

- WG 3: Health, safety and environmental aspects (USA);

- WG 4: Specification of nanomaterials (China).

Over 35 standards documents are currently under development, and three papers have been published by ISO TC 229:

- ISO/TS 27687 (Technical Specification): Terminology and definitions for nano-objects – Nanoparticle, nanofibre and nanoplates;

- ISO/TR 12885 (Technical Report): Health and safety practices in occupational settings relating to nanotechnology;

- ISO/PRF TS 80004-3 (Technical Specification): Nanotechnology – Vocabulary – Part 3: Carbon nano-objects.

EUROPEAN STANDARDIZATION: CEN

CEN has the same scope as ISO and the CEN TC 352 works in collaboration with ISO TC 229 under the terms of a specific agreement on technical cooperation (Vienna Agreement):

- no duplication of work;

- ability to mutually adopt documents;

- leadership for the development of documents is assigned on a case-by-case basis.

The work under CEN leadership:

- Guide to nanoparticle measurement methods and their limitations;

- Nanotechnology – guide to methods for measurements nanotribology;

- Guide to manufactured nanoparticles and labelling of products containing manufactured nanoparticles.

The activities of CEN TC have been structured in two working groups:

- WG 1: Measurement, characterization and performance evaluation;

- WG 2: Commercial and other stakeholder aspects.

The Secretariat of CEN TC 352 is assumed in part by AFNOR (French Standardization System Association) in 2011.

EXAMPLE OF A STATE COMMITTEE: FRANCE: AFNOR X457 'NANOTECHNOLOGIES AND NANOMATERIALS'

AFNOR represents, promotes and defends French interests in the European (CEN Technical Board) and international (ISO Technical Management Board) standardization steering policy bodies and permanently sits on the governing bodies of the international organization. Today, 90 per cent of the standards drafted by AFNOR are of European or international origin.

The national committee AFNOR X457 'Nanotechnologies and nanomaterials' is mirroring the ISO TC 229 or European CEN/TC 352 working groups to express the national position on the draft standards on nanotechnologies.

The French committee is composed of the following representatives: professional organizations, producers, consumers, laboratories, research centres, labour unions, prevention organizations, administrations and education.

Within ISO WG 3 Health, Safety and Environment, a sub working group – Guidelines for occupational risk management applied to engineered nanomaterials, based on an approach to *control banding* – is led by AFNOR to develop a guide helping HSE managers to take into account issues related to nanomaterials in the workplace.

Discussions are also underway in the Working Group 'Nanoresponsible' on how to address the added value of a product resulting from nanotechnology with regard to the analysis of benefit/risk ratio. This reflection on 'Nanoresponsible WG' is led by AFNOR at the international level through ISO.

Health, Safety and Environment (HSE) – Good Practices Guidelines

Paradoxically, there has been little breakthrough in the field of HSE.

The study of hazards and potential risks of nanotechnologies to health and the environment takes place simultaneously with the discovery and development of new nanostructures. Yet HSE research in nanotechnology is not keeping up with the explosion of technological developments. An extensive literature search in databases of scientific publications in all areas shows that the number of publications relating to HSE is much lower than that of technical publications. A quick estimate in 2009 indicated a proportion of less than 2 per cent.

In the absence of certainty about the hazards of nanotechnology, and ways of detecting nanoparticles for the protection of workers and of the environment, Good Practice Guidelines for limiting the risks have been edited.

Examples of Good Practice Guidelines:

- The European Commission's Code of Conduct for Responsible Nanosciences and Nanotechnologies Research, unveiled in 2008, is a centre piece of the EU's nano policy.

- The French UIC – FFC HSE 'Guide de Bonnes Pratiques, Nanomatériaux et HSE'.

- The German BAuA 'Guidance for Handling and Use of Nanomaterials at the Workplace'.

- The UK HSE 'Managing and working with manufactured nanomaterials'.

- The US NIOSH 'Approaches to Safe Nanotechnology: Managing the Health and Safety Concerns Associated with Engineered Nanomaterials'.

- The international website: http://goodnanoguide.org.

Emerging Risks? A Societal Issue?

The huge technological potential expected from nanosciences and nanotechnology now considers nanomaterials as a non-homogeneous group in which the conventional techniques of handling and protection can be implemented.

Each nanomaterial endowed with specific technical characteristics must be considered as a particular entity, with specific physico-chemical, toxicological and environmental potential, for which specific control and suitable protective measures must be created to protect human health and the environment.

The current lack of knowledge on nanomaterials can be listed as follows:

- the physico-chemical, toxicological and environmental characteristics of each type of nanomaterials;

- reliable characterization and analysis of nanomaterials in the air, water and soil;

- existence of a reliable measure for individual and collective protection related to the specificity of these nanomaterials;

- lack of national and international standards on the subject.

This observation leads us to be cautious in handling and using nanomaterials in industrial production and in consumer products.

Technical and commercial developments of nanoparticles and nano-objects are dramatically increasing, mostly without enough research on possible health risks occurring from more or less under control occupational exposure, as well as the impact of their release into the population and the environment.

Paradoxically there is little anticipation in the HSE area and the dangers and potential risks of nanotechnologies to health and the environment are being studied along with the discovery and development of new nanostructures.

This situation described as 'learning by doing' does not leave much margin of safety or possibility of return, should a major problem occur.

Question: Can we reverse the process, should it slip before it's too late?

It is an issue of social governance and implies analyzing the need of these new technologies for our society as well as the citizen's place in the selection and control of these technical developments that may impact them.

Questions: How to involve the public in the decisions of the technological developments that will impact him at the end? Is this desirable? Is this possible? To what extent?

Questions on legal liability and criminal entrepreneurs: Can we monitor the developments of science and industry? How to define responsibilities and ensure the compensation that would result from industrial accidents or consumption?

Those are the questions facing the government, insurers and investors (IEHN and EGFR, 2007).

Outside the fantasies on 'Convergence NIBC' (Nano-Computers-Biological-Cognitive) and increased human or cybernetic, other questions arise about 'civil liberties of users and consumers'.

Questions: How to control the use of electronic tracers (RFID) or other micro-markers and prevent the establishment of a monitoring system of habits and acts of individuals?

The control of researchers, developers and manufacturers in the future uses and implications of nanotechnology development is questioned: *How far can they go unchecked? Can we trust their scientific, industrial, commercial and societal sense of ethics? How to control their activities without interference with their freedom to create and without risking to sterilize technological developments?*

Many ethics committees have issued opinions that suggest caution in the production, handling and use of nanotechnology, in particular that of the

French CCNE (National Consultative Ethics Committee for Life Sciences and Health) in 2007, which listed nine recommendations still valid today:

1. Ensure that sufficient information is available on the dreaded property of molecular nanosystems designed by man to cross the biological barriers, especially between blood and brain, and be currently little or non-biodegradable, which may have (outside of therapeutic indications), major health consequences.

2. Urgently increase R&D of nanometrology to develop and increase the instruments detecting and identifying nanoparticles that will form the nano-objects and nanostructures, and particularly those that are intentionally created.

3. Emphasize the consequences arising from the imbalance between a lack of development (or publication) of basic research and an acceleration of production of commercial technology applications, an imbalance that may overburden the essential choices.

4. Initiate, in the same issue, multidisciplinary research for designing new nanomaterials while concurrently addressing and taking into account their positive and negative primary effects on the environment, health and biological implications.

5. Give priority to all necessary protective measures for workers in contact with nanomaterials, and to the confinement of research and production sites of these nanomaterials.

6. Provide a relationship of trust through transparency and continuous dissemination of scientific knowledge to the public and private research community by implementing a European legislation requiring mandatory reporting of all new nanostructures including their potential consequences on the biological reactivity.

7. Promote information networking between all agencies in charge of health and safety.

8. Expand the dissemination of scientific, technological and industrial research in nanosciences and nanotechnology.

9. Lastly, be extremely vigilant on the significant consequences as regards individual liberties and respect for human dignity, if identification and interconnection capabilities were developed without information to the public.

The French CCNE concludes:

> ...the ethical issue related to the use of nanomaterials can be classified on two axes. On the one hand the philosophical question raised by nanosystems concerning the creation of a new artificial man-machine, still deemed as a threat to human beings. This important issue in terms of ideas should not overshadow the second and far more urgent question, that is the covert intrusion of nanoparticles in the public, as it focuses more on the technological performance and commercial profitability than on the perception of potential risks. The second question requires the authorities to remain vigilant of any possible rejection by society of these new technologies, as they could be perceived focusing more on the race for innovation than on the respect of the physical and mental integrity of individuals. Monitoring the impact of advances in sciences and technologies is a responsibility that involves society as a whole, and that cannot be simply left only in the hands of economic actors or NGOs. Nanosciences cannot be merely reduced to nanotechnology.

Non-Government Organizations (NGOs) are very active in the surveillance of the development of nanotechnologies worldwide.

Two examples can be quoted:

- International Center for Technology Assessment (ICTA) 2007: NanoAction; Principles for the Oversight of Nanotechnologies and Nanomaterials. '*Proponents of a nanotech "revolution" predict that it will cause dramatic and sweeping changes in every aspect of human life. We believe that a precautionary course of action is necessary in order to safeguard the health and safety of the public and workers; conserve our natural environment; ensure public participation and democratically decided social goals; restore public trust in, and support for, government and academic research; and permit long-term commercial viability. We call for all relevant bodies and actors to take actions to implement, incorporate, and internalize the above principles for nanotechnology and nanomaterial oversight immediately.'*

This document has been endorsed by nearly 70 groups from six continents, www.nanoaction.org.

- ETC Group: Communiqué #105; 'The Big Downturn? Nanogeopolitics' edited in 2010. Since our call for a moratorium, science has cast nano's safety even further in doubt, with hundreds of studies now demonstrating harmful effects from exposure to nanoparticles. Governments and industry have come too far and invested too much to give up on nanotech's promise of becoming a pillar of the twenty-first century's 'green economy', www.etcgroup. org.

Transparency and governance should require public input in nanotechnology-related decisions.

The UK Royal Commission on Environmental Pollution expressed in the document Novel Materials in the Environment: The Case of Nanotechnology, 2008:

> *'New governance arrangements are necessary to deal with ignorance and uncertainty ... We strongly recommend a more directed, more coordinated and larger response led by the Research Councils to address the critical research needs.'*

Waiting for this global organization, a moratorium in the developments and uses of nanotechnologies is often requested by NGOs.

Conclusion

Past experiences have shown that it is impossible to anticipate every possible application of a technology, and some inventions were developed only by the conjunction of science, appropriate technologies and the potential use that can positively result for future users.

All great discoveries have escaped gradually, in stages and over time, from their initial designs to conquer new areas of use. One recent example is the

Internet, that has left the containment level of communication reserved for the US military and academic researchers to become available to the general public worldwide.

The characteristic of nanotechnology is its exponential growth and the rapid generalized release after its discovery, without complete characterization and control, and evaluation of its effects on humans and on the environment.

This leaves room for speculation and concerns about their hazards and risks to users and the general public.

Perplexity and concerns have been highlighted by the various public debates worldwide, to an extent that created very negative reactions, sometimes aggressive, against nanotechnology on behalf of the 'precautionary principle'.

Questions: Can we decide to stop this major technological progress that can provide technical and economic solutions in all sectors of our society, including human health and the environment? What is the price to pay and are we willing to accept it? How to apply the 'precautionary principle' without hampering technical progress?

As always, when our civilization is at a major technological leap, hopes of a better life, but also the fear of the emergence of problems, appears related to the release of these new techniques, for which we cannot even imagine all the developments and benefits, but we can guess they will have to have both positive and negative aspects for the human species and the environment.

What matters is how to predict to what extent these changes will be acceptable and controllable.

These are the critical questions to be urgently raised, as nanotechnology is a challenge for the future that we already have to manage now.

References

AFSSET, Nanomaterials, Health Effects on Man and Environment, 2006.
AFSSET, Nanomaterials, Safety at Work, 2008.
Alessandrini F., Schulz H., Takenaka S., Lentner B., Karg E., Behrendt H., Thilo, J. Effects of ultrafine carbon particles inhalation is allergic inflammation of the lung. *Journal of Allergy and Clinical Immunology*, 117, 2006: 824–830.

Alvarez P.J.J., Li Q., Mahendra S., Lyon D.Y., Brunet L., Liga V., Li D. Antimicrobial nanomaterials for water disinfection and microbial control: Potential applications and implications. *Water Research*, 42 (18), 2008: 4591–4602.

Aust A.E., Ball J.C., Hu A.A., Lighty J.S., Smith K.R., Straccia A.M., Veranth J.M., Young, W.C. Particle Characteristics Responsible for Effects on Human Lung Epithelial Cells. HEI Report No. 110, 2002.

Baker G.L., Gupta A., Clark M.L., Valenzuela B.R., Staska L.M., Harbo S.J., Pierce J.T., Dill J.A. Inhalation toxicity and lung toxicokinetics of C60 fullerene nanoparticles and microparticles. *Toxicological Sciences*, 101 (1), 2008: 122–131.

BCC Research Marketing Forecasting. Nanotechnology: A Realistic Market Assessment. Report Code: NAN031D, July, 2010.

Borm P.J.A., Schins R.P.F., Albrecht A. Inhaled particles and lung cancer, part B: Paradigms and international risk assessment. *Journal of Cancer*, 110 (1), 2004: 3–14.

Bradford A., Handy R.D., Readman J.W., Artfield A., Muhling M. Impact of silver nanoparticle contamination on the genetic diversity of natural bacterial assemblages in estuarine sediments. *Environmental Science & Technology*, 43 (12), 2009: 4535.

CCNE, the National Consultative Ethics Committee for Life Sciences and Health, Opinion No. 96, Ethical Issues Raised by Nanosciences, Nanotechnology to Health, 2007.

Chen M., von Mickecz A. Formation of nucleoplasmic protein aggregates impairs nuclear function in response to SiO_2 nanoparticles. *Experimental Cell Research*, 305, 2005: 51–62.

Cheng W.D., Wu D.S., Li X.D., Lan Y.Z., Zhang H., Chen D.G., Gong Y.J., Zhang Y.C., Li F.F., Shen J., Kanz Z.G. Design of single-walled carbon nanotubes with a large two-photon absorption cross section, physical review B. *Condensed Matter and Materials Physics*, 70, (15), 2004: 155401.1–155401.6.

Crosera M., Bovenzi M., Maina G., Adami G., Zanett C., Florio C., Filon Lares F. Nanoparticle dermal absorption and toxicity: A review of the literature. *International Archives of Occupational and Environmental Health*, 82 (9) 2009: 1043–1055.

Cunningham M.J. Gene-cellular interactions of nanomaterials: genotoxicity to genomics, in *Nanotoxicology: Characteristics, Dosing and Health Effects on Target Organs*, edited by Monteiro-Riviere N., translated by Taylor, L. and Francis/Informa Healthcare. New York, 2007: 173–196.

De Haar C., Hassing, I., Bol, M., Bleumink R., Pieters, R. Ultrafine but not fine particulate matter causes airway inflammation and allergic airway sensitization to co-administered antigen in mice. *Clinical and Experimental Allergy*, 36 (11), 2006: 1469–1479.

Dick A.C., Brown D.M., Donaldson K., Stone V. The role of free radicals in the toxic and inflammatory effects of four different ultrafine particle types. *Inhalation Toxicology*, 15 (1), 2003: 39–52.

Donaldson K., Poland C.A., Duffin R., Kinloch I., Maynard A., Wallace W.A., Seaton A., Stone V., Brown S., Macnee W. Carbon nanotubes introduced into the abdominal cavity of mice show asbestos-like pathogenicity in a pilot study. *Nature Nanotechnology*, Jul 3 (7), 2008: 423–428.

European Commission, Community Health and Consumer Protection. Nanotechnology: Preliminary Risk Analysis on the basis of a workshop organized in Brussels on 1–2 March, 2004 by The Health and Consumer Protection Directorate General of the European Commission, 2004.

European Commission, DG Environment, Do Nanoparticles Affect the Health of the soil Ecosystem? Published 16 October, 2008.

European Commission, Communication from the Commission to European Parliament and the European Economic and Social Council 'Regulatory Aspects of Nanomaterials', 2008.

European IPPC Directive, Directive 2008/1/EC on the prevention and reduction integrated pollution, OJ L 24 of 29 January, 2008.

Hagens W.I., Oomen A.G., de Jong W.H., Cassee E.N. and Sips A. What do we (need to) know about the kinetic properties of nanoparticles in the body? *Regulatory Toxicology and Pharmacology*, 49 (3), 2007: 217–229.

Handy R.D., von der Kammer F., Lead J.R., Hassello V.M., Owen R., Crane M. The ecotoxicology and chemistry of manufactured nanoparticles. *Ecotoxicology*, 17, 2008: 287–314.

Hoet P.H.M., Bruske-Hohlfeld I., Salata O.V. Nanoparticles-known and unknown health risks. *Journal of Nanobiotechnology*, 2 (1), 2004: 12.

HSE-UK: Nanoparticles, An occupational hygiene review research; report 274 prepared by the Institute of Occupational Medicine, 2004.

ICRP, Human Respiratory Tract Model for Radiological Protection. Publication 66. Ann. ICRP 24 (1–3), Pergamon Press, Oxford, 1994.

Industrial Hygiene and Information Management, Nanomaterial Safety Plan ES & H Division Publishing SLAC-I-730-008-R002-0A09M August 4 (updated 29 June, 2009), 2008.

IEHN & EGFR, Fiduciary Guide to Toxic Chemical Risk, Investor Environmental Health Network, 1901 North Moore Street, Suite 509 Arlington, Virginia and Rose Foundation for Communities and the Environment 6008 College Ave., Ste. 10 Oakland, CA, 2007.

Kreyling W., Semmler-Behnke M., Möller W. Health implications of nanoparticles. *Journal of Nanoparticle Research*, 8 (5), 2006: 543–562,

Kolosnjaj J., Szwarc H., Moussa F. Toxicity studies of fullerenes and derivatives. *Advances in Experimental Medicine and Biology*, 620, 2007: 168–180.

Lam C., James J., McCluskey R., Hunter R. Pulmonary toxicity of single-wall carbon nanotubes in mice 7 and 90 days after intratracheal instillation. *Toxicological Sciences*, 1 (1), 2004: 126–134.

Li. N., Stout C., Cho A., Schmitz D., Mistra C., Sempf J.M., Wang M., Oberley T., Froines J., Nel A. Ultrafine particulate pollutants induce oxidative stress and mitochondrial damage. *Environmental Health Perspectives*, 111 (4), 2003: 455–460.

Li. Z., Salmen R., Hulderman T., Kisin E., Shvedova A., Luster M., Simeonova P. Pulmonary carbon nanotube exposure and oxidative status in vascular system. *Free Radical Biology and Medicine*, 37 (1), 2004: S142.

Le Cedef: Economy and Finance Distribution Centre, Minister for the Economy, Industry and Labour, Ministry for the Budget, Public Accounts, the Civil Service and the State Reform, 2009.

Lombard A., Boczkowski J., Gaffet E. Environmental determinants: 'Nanoparticles and Health'. Briefing Note for the National Health and Environment: New Perspectives in Research, 2005.

Lomer M., Hutchinson C., Volkert S., Greenfield S.M., Catterall A., Thompson R.P.H., Powell J.J. Dietary sources of inorganic microparticles and their intake in healthy subjects and patients with Crohn's disease. *British Journal of Nutrition*, 92 (6), 2004: 947–955.

Long T.C., Saleh N., Tilton R.D., Lowry G., Veronesi B. Titanium Dioxide P25 produces Reactive Oxygen Species in immortalized brain microglia (BV2): Implications for nanoparticle neurotoxicity. *Environmental Science and Technology*, 40 (14), 2006: 4346–4352.

Mahe B., Vogt A., Liard C., Duffy D., Abadie V., Bonduelle O., Boissonnas A., Sterry W., Verrier B., Blume-Peytavi U., Combadière B. Nanoparticle-based targeting of vaccine compounds to skin antigen-presenting cells by hair follicles and their transport in mice. *Journal of Investigative Dermatology*, 129, 2009: 1156–1164.

Mavon A., Miquel C., Lejeune O., Payre B., Moretto P. In vitro percutaneous absorption and in vivo stratum corneum distribution of an organic and a mineral sunscreen. *Skin Pharmacology and Physiol*ogy, 20, 2007: 10–20.

Mercer R.R., Hubbs A., Scabilloni J.F., Wang L., Battelli L.A., Friend S.M., Castranova V., Porter D. Pulmonary fibrotic response to aspiration of multi-walled carbon nanotubes. *Particle and Fibre Toxicology*, 8 (21), 2001.

Mini – IGT Report. (The Nanotechnology Mini-Innovation and Growth Team) Nanotechnology: A UK Industry Review, 2011.

Miyata N., Yamakoshi Y., Nakanishi I. Reactive species responsible for biological actions of photoexcited fullerenes. *Yakugaku Zasshi*, October, 120 (10), 2000: 1007–1016.

Mueller N.C., Nowack B. Exposure modeling of engineered nanoparticles in the environment. *Environmental Science and Technology*, 42 (12), 2008: 4447–4453.

Murphy S.A., Butch K.A., Pooley F.D., Richards R.J. The response of lung epithelium to well characterized fine particles. *Life Sciences*, 62 (19), 1998: 1789–1799

Musee N. Nanowastes and the environment: Potential new waste management paradigm. *Environment International*, 37, 2011: 112–128.

Nanowerk Research and General News. Nanotech Market Forecasts – What a Difference a Trillion Makes, http://www.nanowerk.com, posted 10 August, 2010.

NANOSAFE. What About Explosibility and Inflammability of Nanopowders? Safety Parameter Characterisation Techniques for Nanoparticles, report February 2008 DR-152-200802-2.

Nemmar G., Hoet P.H., Vandervoot P., Dinsdale D., Nemery B., Hoylaerts MF. Enhanced peripheral thrombogenicity after lung inflammation is mediated by platelet-leukocyte activation: role of P-selectin. *Journal of Thrombosis and Haemostasis*, 37, 2007: 1–27.

Nohynek G. Grey goo on the skin? Nanotechnology, cosmetic and sunscreens safety. *Critical Reviews in Toxicology*, 37, 2007: 1–27.

Nygaard U.C, Samuelsen M., Aase A., Lovik M. The capacity of particles to increase allergic sensitization is predicted by particle number and surface area, not by particle mass. *Toxicological Sciences*, 82 (2), 2004: 515–524.

Oberdörster E. Manufactured nanomaterials (fullerenes, C60) induce oxidative stress in the brain of juvenile largemouth bass. *Environmental Health Perspectives*, 112 (10), 2004: 1058–1062.

Oberdörster G., Ferin J., Finkelstein G., Wade P., Corson N. Increased pulmonary toxicity of ultrafine particles, II, Lung lavage studies. *Journal of Aerosol Science*, 21 (3) 1990: 384–387.

Oberdörster G., Ferin. J., Gelein R., Soderholm S.C., Finkelstein J. Role of the alveolar macrophage in lung injury: Studies with ultrafine particles. *Environmental Health Perspectives*, 97, 1992: 193–199.

Oberdörster G., Sharp Z., Atudorei V., Elder A., Gelein R., Kreyling W., Cox C. Translocation of inhaled ultrafine particles to the brain. *Inhalation Toxicology*, 16 (6/7), 2004: 437–445.

Oberdörster G., Oberdörster E., Oberdörster J. Nanotoxicology: An emerging discipline evolving from studies of ultrafine particles. *Environmental Health Perspectives*, 113 (7), 2005: 823–839.

Panté. N., Kann M. Nuclear pore complex is able to transport macromolecules with diameters of ~ 39 nm. *Molecular Biology of the Cell*, 13 February 2002: 425–434.

Pflücke F., Hohenberg H., Hölzle E., Will T., Pfeiffer S., Wepf R., Diembeck W., Wenck H., Gers-Barlag H. The outermost stratum corneum layer is an effective barrier against dermal uptake of topically applied micronized titanium dioxide. *International Journal of Cosmetic Science*, 21 (6), 1999: 399.

Porter. A., Gass M., Muller K., Skepp J.N., Midgley P.A., Welland M. Direct imaging of single-wall carbon nanotubes in cells. *Nature Nanotechnology*, 2, 2007a: 713.

Porter A., Gass M., Muller K., Skepp J., Midgley P., Welland M. Visualizing the uptake of C60 to the cytoplasm and nucleus of human monocyte-derived macrophage cells using energy-filtered transmission electron microscopy and electron tomography, *Environmental Science & Technology*, 41 (8), 2007b: 3012–3017.

Proust C., Remembrance, INPL, Université de Lorraine, 2004.

Ramsey D., Maynard A., Kagan V.E., Castranova V., Baron P. Unusual inflammatory and fibrogenic pulmonary responses to single-walled carbon nanotubes in mice. *American Journal of Physiology – Lung Cellular and Molecular Physiology*, 289 (5), 2005 : 698–708.

Sadauskas E., Wallin H., Stoltenberg M., Vogel U., Doering P., Larsen A., Danscher G. Kupffer cells are central all in the removal of nanoparticles from the organism. *Particle and Fibre Toxicology*, 4, 2007: 10.

Shvedova A., Kisin E., Mercer R., Murray A., Johnson V., Potapovich A., Tyurina Y.Y., Gorelik O., Arepalli S., Schwegler-Berry D., Hubbs A.F., Antonini J., Evans D.E., Ku B.K., Radomski A., Jurasz P., Alonso-Escolano D., Drews Mn., Morandi M., Malinksi T., Radomki M.W. Nono-particle induced platelet aggregration and vascular thrombosis. *British Journal of Pharmacology*, 146 (6), 2005: 882–893.

Smith C.J., Shaw B.J., Handy R.D. Toxicity of single-walled carbon nanotubes to rainbow trout (Onchorhynchuis mykiss): respiratory toxicity, organ pathologies, and other physiological effects. Aquatic Toxicology, 82 (2), 2007: 161–121.

Trommer H., Neubert R.H.H. Overcoming the stratum corneum: the modulation of skin penetration. *Skin Pharmacology and Physiology, A Review*, 19, 2006: 106–121.

US Department of Energy Nanoscale Science Research Center's Approach to
  Nanomaterial ES & H, Revision 3a – 12 May, 2008.

Warheit D., Laurence B., Reed K., Roach D., Reynolds G., Webb T. Comparative
  pulmonary toxicity assessment of single-wall carbon nanotubes in rats.
  Toxicological Science, 77 (1), 2004: 117–125.

2

New Information and Communication Technologies (NICT)

Daniel Brûlé and Jean-Louis Chaptal

The limitless spiral of innovations renders any newly mastered situation unstable, lending credence to this statement by Goethe: '*Every solution to a problem is a new problem.*' The new technologies and, in our case, those related to information, intervene in social life. They intervene in the equilibrium of societies and play a part in their transformation. At one and the same time, they concentrate challenges of technology and innovation, economy and culture and, increasingly, challenges of safety and governance. The more they combine among themselves, the faster the pace of change, bringing with it a galloping complexity.

In 1994, American policymakers said that '*if the Internet succeeds, we will be able to loop our knowledge; we will be able to conserve the lessons of our experience, constitute tactical and historical databases to shed light on the future*'. Since then, the Internet has become a reality and what we imagined has already faded into the past. Information technologies irrigate more and more areas and push us towards more management, more rationalization of political action with respect to an end: knowledge, well-being, profit, strength, power and security.

Information and Communications Techniques (ICT) in general and the science that accompanies them (ICTS) are sources of *considerable progress*, which gives them a positive and strategic dimension. They provide human beings with abilities that step up the pace of change in their environment and that is good. But at the same time, they are *invasive* and cause new enslavements, deviances and risks. This is why human beings find it difficult to assimilate the transformation and, more or less consciously, they fear the loss of full control over their own liberty.

Hence the perception that there is public concern and that public opinion tends to focus more on the downside than on the upside of progress. Indeed, for every breakthrough it is possible to counter with the downside, synonymous with vulnerabilities, alienation, loss of liberty and irreversible harms for the society and its organizations. Conversely, these questions and these mutations, the risks, both real and perceived, are also sources of progress and constitute opportunities that need to be seized, because the salient challenges are simultaneously economic, technological, political, legal and ethical.

Necessarily limited, this contribution has no other ambition than to offer some food for thought on the remarkable expansion of info technologies and their impact on society and organizations, and to then evoke the challenges and issues that we have found to be significant, particularly in terms of threats (risks) and opportunities that may result from them.

A Common Definition of Information Technologies

We have agreed to use the term Information Technologies (IT) or Information and Communication Technologies (ICT) to describe the set of modern technological solutions used in the *processing* and the *transmission* of information, principally computer science, the Internet and telecommunications.

From a semantic perspective, the notion of *processing* involves the receipt, classification, analysis, storage and exploitation of all types of information, regardless of its form. These actions are increasingly automated thanks to the intensive use of computers associated with specific or generic software. The notion of *information and communication systems* is a collective reference to the human and technical means that include decisional systems or structures and physical communications networks for a given organization. The notion of *telecommunications* encompasses the techniques for transporting information and remote transmission and, by extension, all issue or receipt of signals, writing, images, sounds or information bits by wire, radio, optics, acoustics or electromagnetic systems.

Information Technologies at the Origin of a New Industrial Era

Information and communication technologies (ICT) are at the origin of a *'third industrial revolution'*. The socio-economic upheavals that are accompanying them are comparable to those that came about during the two previous revolutions: the appearance of the motor and the industrial era, and then that of electricity and fossil fuels. There is, however, a difference: *Information technologies (IT) intervene in the field of human intelligence,* whereas the progress associated with the previous revolutions improved tools. The introduction of the computer, followed by the exponential development of the concept of information, is probably the most important phenomenon of modernization witnessed at the end of the twentieth century. Human beings are in the process of living a new experience or experiment: a set of data whose size is incredibly bigger than that we have had access to up to now is instantly accessible on the Internet. And information technologies, which are increasingly present, have led to tangible evolutions in how our societies work, as well as contributing to the transformation of the social body on every level: collective, individual, professional, domestic, public and private.

INFORMATION AND COMMUNICATION TECHNOLOGIES AS ACTORS IN THE TRANSFORMATION OF THE SOCIAL BODY

The ubiquitous nature of information technologies promotes the *transformation of the social body* because connectivity 'at all times and everywhere' and the ability to process and manage billions of bits of information are developing with increasing speed. Information technologies alter the bonds between people and the relationship of each person to him- or herself. Their use is influencing, insidiously but no less tangibly, human evolution.

Recall the words of Erasmus: *'Man is not born, but made man.'* This process of becoming is a metamorphosis of the little human produced by nature into a person capable of knowing how to be and how to do, starting from the convergence of genetic information and his or her environment taken in its totality. So: *'Equipped with computers, will our thought change? We are living a decisive moment in the process that is making us. Worrisome for certain people, this birth thrills others. We are bringing it on without knowing what human it creates, assassinates or magnifies'* (Serres, 2003).

Before the arrival of ICT, we had probably never had as many resources that were so efficient for communicating amongst ourselves and intervening in the state of the world and on ourselves.

INFORMATION AND COMMUNICATION TECHNOLOGIES – PLAYERS IN ECONOMIC AND POLITICAL COMPETITION

The economy is not everything, but from this perspective the contribution of information technologies to business performance constitutes a central question that is widely discussed in research circles. Today, the digital economy is the main factor behind improvements in the ability of developed economies to compete. The services and uses created through ICT are an integral part of the tools for strategic development and enable the exchange of multiple, relevant and even uncertain responses. ICT have an immediate impact, increasing the intensity of activities related to the exchange of information data, stepping up the dynamism of decision making and contributing to productivity. More broadly, they serve as amplifying levers for the functioning and the adaptation of the processes of economic, political and security-related production, within the framework of dynamics that are now crossing traditional frontiers.

INFORMATION AND COMMUNICATION TECHNOLOGIES – PLAYERS IN GLOBALIZATION

The development of satellites, computer technologies and then the Internet has played a huge driving role in the transmission of information without borders and *is a factor in globalization*.

Today, thanks to the mobile phone, calls can be made from anywhere to anywhere at any time. Television and the Internet report global news as it happens. Information technologies are the driving force behind the real-time functioning of the global banking system. Criminality itself is global. Terrorism has no frontiers.

All of the world's Western nations are observing a dynamic of risk perception that is gradually evolving along the defence–security–vulnerability continuum maintained by the phenomenon of network-based communications. In barely 20 years, the defence of national borders – which used to be a necessity – has given way to the need for security without territorial attachments, as new vulnerabilities that must be controlled appear everywhere and in everything. By risking a comparison with the recent past, we can state that information technologies have enabled humanity to go from the local to the global, from the confines of a specific space to spaces without borders and global problems, but without any conceptual control or forward-looking vision.

INFORMATION AND COMMUNICATION TECHNOLOGIES – DISRUPTIVE FACTORS

Today, it is the rapid production of new solutions, more and more *invasive*, which dominates. But it is difficult to avoid evoking the Internet, which is one of our daily tools. This relational technology (RT), which is still relatively new, will continue to undergo metamorphosis in the next few years, and we can't imagine what it will become. *Convergence* towards other uses and other technologies – unknown to us today – is likely to produce *discontinuities and even disruptions* in our social habits as well as in the way we live. *New processes,* like the passage from our current voluntary connectivity to tomorrow's non-voluntary connectivity will come into view, with deferred effects that are hard to imagine.

The Internet will become what users make of it. Joël de Rosnay has gone as far as to state that '*the Internet of 2020 will constitute a disruption of civilization*' (de Rosnay, 2008).

TOWARDS THE INTERNET OF COMMUNICATING OBJECTS

An example of disruption is being put in place right in front of us with communicating objects. They are invading our daily lives and generating an intelligent ambiance. Inert up to now, the physical objects that surround us will soon be able to communicate with one another and with human beings, within a network architecture where the Internet is a relational means. They already exist in the form of multiple types of sensors, increasingly networked and wireless, integrated in mobile telephony, GPS, remote control of security and automobiles, toys, ID cards, and so on.

On average, we use more than ten communicating objects today. Tomorrow, the number will run in the hundreds. The miniaturization of electronics enables us to associate them with an onboard computing power that gives the impression they are intelligent, while also making them invisible in some applications. Thanks to new computing and transmission technologies, they are becoming practically autonomous energy-wise over very long periods and ranging over extended networks.

New solutions are being offered for themes such as voice on IP (Internet Protocol), mobile offices, M2M (machine to machine), security, e-business, identification, wireless, green IT and cloud computing[1] (*cloud computing is an IT organization concept that places the Internet at the heart of the activity of businesses, allowing the use of remote or deported servers and computers to create services that are accessible online*) and the phenomenon of multiplication of social communications networks. And this is how information technologies are enabling the emergence of a new communications paradigm: '*the things or objects network.*'

ARTIFICIAL INTELLIGENCE AND MAN-MACHINE INTERFACES

Artificial intelligence is now combining with new IT capable of self-learning to create man-machine interfaces and simplify the use of objects. Prospects that only recently seemed incredible are now actually appearing: the wheelchair used by someone who is paralyzed could soon be activated by the mind of its user. And biotechnologies could replace the conventional chemical synthesis to offer personalized care and treatment; the customized will replace the ready-to-wear. Already, the refrigerator can automatically send a shopping list, and alarm systems warn caregivers remotely that an aged parent has fallen in his or her living room.

THE ACCELERATION OF HUMAN ACTIVITIES

Communicating objects are also stepping up the pace of our activities. With the arrival of Apple's iPhone, we learned that users can do a lot of things with this concentration of high technologies, sensors, and interoperability and display capacity in a small mobile device with a tactile screen. With this single object, users can make calls, exchange messages, images and data, retrieve archived material, take photos, work on a document without going back to the office, and exploit data needed to make real-time, remote decisions no matter where they are in the world. And this is just the beginning!

Gradually, new features are being added to the communicating object, such as the incorporation of a GPS, an accelerometer connected to a tactile screen to simplify the man-machine interface, the introduction of radio-frequency identification (RFID) technologies, the possibility of making secure financial transactions, and now the Near Field Communication (NFC) technologies, a technology for communication that can be used for distances of less than 10

---

1   This work of C. Wiseman in 1988 (*Strategic Information Systems*, Irwin, 1988) helped popularize the concept of strategic information by involving info technologies in the strategic process of organizations and by suggesting they could be used as a strategic weapon of development and prosperity.

cm, by contactless readers and cards, compatible with RFID-type technologies. We can manage both personal information and read digital fingerprints. The list is unlimited.

These new functionalities have required major software developments to be buried in portable phones. Several million lines of code used by two to three particularly powerful processors are stored in a simple telephone. As with a PC, an operating system (OS) is needed; and several major industrial players are competing in this arena. Google recently acquired Motorola Mobility, and the global smartphone market shifted within months, as most mobile phones are now using Google's Android Operating System. This open OS, no longer owned by a single manufacturer, is expected to lead to a new economic model for developers and operators.

To conclude this panorama, the world and the use of information technologies have been in a state of total transformation for several years now and the phenomenon is accelerating. The fact that this panorama is changing makes an examination of the opportunities it has to offer even more urgent.

Multiple Sectors of Application and Opportunities

Information technologies are the source of our growth and the starting gun in the race for innovation has been sounded around the world, shedding light on formidable opportunities for progress. The intelligent appropriation of ICT by businesses of all kinds, working in networks, will be a prerequisite of their ability to compete and of the creation of both wealth and high value added jobs. Nanotechnologies will play a major role in the added value of the industrialized countries that are able to seize their opportunity.

As a way of introducing this chapter, we can mention seven challenges for progress made possible by information technologies. Each one offers both opportunities and their downside – risks or threats: power over constraints (freedom or dependence), knowledge (intelligence or ignorance), obsolescence (immortality or insecurity), social justice (equality or injustice), social bonds (conviviality or social void), economic prosperity (well-being or crisis), and planetary solidarity (development or devastation).

Information system design is strongly determined by the interaction among different evolutions – societal, strategic, organizational, technological, regulatory and ethical. From a technical perspective, miniaturization linked to the ability to capitalize on information through their storage meets the needs of users, while the physical obstacles to portability and autonomy are being reduced at an increasingly rapid rate.

Mobility has become a *constant and essential requirement of human beings:* it explains our energy for creating solutions and means of communication. Similarly, the human *quest for comfort and well-being* solicit *innovation*, even if the *use value* of the communicating objects is more appreciated than the technological prowess. Influenced by these expectations and by changing lifestyles, the use of products resulting from the application of information technologies accompanies, in a dynamic way, a new reality based on *network logics*, which are clearly imposing themselves alongside and, in some cases, are even replacing traditional territorial logics.

Other emblematic causes are also at the origin of vast opportunities for development, consumption and use of ICT: globalization, the rise of emerging countries, deregulation, demographics and social impacts, the acceleration of economic cycles, industrial redeployments, and new channels of distribution, security needs, dematerialized transactions and on-board intelligence. All of the major sectors of human activity are concerned: industry, finance, defence, security, government, trade and services, putting ICT front and centre as an issue for the economy, industry, society and *sovereignty*.

OPPORTUNITIES FOR THE ECONOMY AND THE COMPETITIVE POSITION OF STRATEGIC INDUSTRIES

ICT sciences lie at the heart of economic and technological progress in all sectors of activity because they permit us to enhance the processes of creation, production and distribution. In the last ten years, they have provided more than a quarter of GDP growth and have accounted for 40 per cent of the total gain in productivity, thanks to the dissemination of innovations to all areas of the economic fabric. Seen from this perspective, the digital revolution is one of the key drivers of technological change and not one of the results.

Information technologies help to enhance the competitive edge of highly strategic industries in which France has strong positioning, including aeronautics, defence, health and energy, with companies like ST-Microelectronic for semi-conductors and Thales for components of onboard systems and calculators (Bull), not to mention other major IT services companies like Cap Gemini and Atos.

While the situation is less positive in the area of software publishing, with just a few companies among the leaders (*Dassault Systèmes*), this industry nonetheless remains one where small players can rapidly become global leaders if they get the right kind of support for their development. France is in a fairly good position in terms of the creation of start-ups (*France Numérique 2012*, a development plan for the digital economy dated October 2008), which means in terms of the direct application of research work. But the difficulty of accessing the European market, which is overly fragmented and which lacks support structures to promote their growth, is a real handicap for innovative companies, which have a hard time attracting the capital they need to industrialize their work.

OPPORTUNITIES IN MANY AREAS OF DAILY LIFE

Social behaviours have undergone substantial change in the course of the past 50 years: the role of women in society, the extension of leisure and recreation, a shorter work week, longer retirements, improvements in the standard of living and so on. One result of these changes has been a significant increase in *mobility*, which clearly has an impact on the demand for and use of services provided by information technologies.

Beyond these visible changes, other modes of life/lifestyles can appear very suddenly and lead to behavioural disruptions, new needs and new information technology solutions that are even more evolved and that will usher in the era of the mobile Internet. Its uses will evolve. The idea of offering free practical information through increasingly mobile terminals that correspond to new lifestyles is already a reality. Travellers arriving in a city will be able to access the cultural calendar of that city, the daily video business news and local news if they have a mobile phone with the Bluetooth function or if they happen to come across a tactile convenience wall, interactive and connected to the Internet. We might also cite the change in the nature of relationships with government administrations, thanks simply to the process of dematerializing routine administrative acts and the appropriation of ICT by those being administered to. Through information technologies, progress has been made in the fields of energy, the environment, security and reliability. There are hundreds of examples that could be mentioned.

OPPORTUNITIES IN TRANSPORTATION

Soon, technologies that haven't even been identified yet are expected to have a profound impact on the transportation sector, both the demand side (remote communication) and the supply side (new services, productivity of various means of transport, shorter travel times). The traffic flow (commuters, material goods, vectors) management function is bound to progress, mainly thanks to information technologies and the solutions they enable.

Changes in behaviour as well as in the functioning of transportation are thus to be expected in the various sectors of transportation. Given the interaction between the transport industry, economic organizations and commuters/ travellers themselves, we can imagine new forms of remote or home officing, deported or shared functions that are specific to certain business areas, a host of remote services that reduce the need for physical mobility and the use of the automobile, but which make extensive use of the solutions offered by information technologies.

OPPORTUNITIES RELATED TO HOUSING AND ITS ORGANIZATION

The location of housing has significant impacts on space consumption and on the environment, as well as on the organization of convenience services and territorial equilibrium (large metropolitan areas, smaller cities, isolated rural areas). From this perspective, mobility remains a powerful driver of *service demands* guaranteed by communication technology solutions: radio, Internet, general and specialized computing, data storage, the transfer of all kinds of data, surveillance and domotics. Against this general backdrop, the dissemination of high speed (cable, ADSL, satellite) and now very high speed (fiber optics or frequencies), as well as education and training that enables equal access to the same services and the same level of information constitute important factors of access to ICT.

OPPORTUNITIES IN THE AREA OF PUBLIC HEALTH

In the area of public health, there are numerous opportunities for the *convergence of several disciplines and technologies* in the service of an ambitious objective: the assurance of equitable healthcare for all.

Telemedicine is one such opportunity. This is a form of cooperation in the practice of medicine that uses information and communication technologies to remotely link a patient with one or more healthcare professionals for the purpose of making a diagnosis and/or administering medical care and treatment. It is a *remote provision of healthcare services* in the specific case where patient and medical practitioner are not in the same place physically. This concept also encompasses a number of other services, such as homecare for people who suffer from chronic illnesses through remote consultations and monitoring, emergency care for people in remote areas who suffer from injuries or illnesses, and so on. It is driven by state-of-the-art information technologies in the form of *secure means of communications* for the transport of medical data and information (text, images, sound) that may be useful in the provision of care.

As recent experiences suggest, telemedicine offers prospects for improvement not only in the daily life of patients but also in the working conditions of healthcare professionals. In the near future, we will be able to observe the emerging phenomenon of telemedicine without borders, in all of its technological, economic, social and ethical aspects.

OPPORTUNITIES ARISING FROM NEW SECURITY-RELATED CONTEXTS

Security, perceived as a major demand of both individuals and the collective, constitutes an opportunity for innovation in the area of information and communication technologies. The world we live in is a globalized universe where people, ideas and goods circulate at the planetary level. The hazards inherent in climate change, the need for energy supply, the challenge of producing enough food to feed a growing world population – the estimate is towards 9 billion by 2050 – these are related issues that will require adjustments to the way we manage risk and uncertainty. And they are rapidly shifting the balance among nations and continents.

Phenomena related to dissemination (of ideas and innovations as well as viruses) are taking on unprecedented importance. The change imperative gives rise in every area to processes of rapid recomposition that are constantly destabilizing social, political and cultural balances, and that tend to force individuals, groups and all human societies to live in a state of perpetual flux, network, uncertainty and competition.

Accordingly, the question of risk becomes a major transversal theme that requires an interdisciplinary approach to the study of risk situations in light of the multiplicity of their impacts and their dimensions. Research efforts that focus on analyzing and modelling these situations, and on devising IT tools for managing the data needed to apprehend their complexity, should obviously be given top priority.

THE DEFENCE, SECURITY AND VULNERABILITIES CONTINUUM

Contained in the French White Paper on Defence and National Security, published in 2008, the major strategic orientations of public expenditure on research and development in these areas concern maintaining critical competencies (ballistic systems, submarine resources), developing technological capacities for information gathering (satellites) and promoting skills in the area of combatting cybercrime and the proliferation of weapons of mass destruction (NRBC: nuclear, radiological, biological or chemical).

France's research policy encourages a transversal approach based on the expression of needs by end users and bringing together players from both the public and private sectors. In the interest of limiting costs, it encourages the adoption of dual solutions for compatible programmes in the civil sector and the armed forces. As purely national solutions prove sometimes to be inoperable, France also commits to collaborations at the European level via the European Defence Agency (EDA) and the European Security Research Programme, and also at the international level through bilateral agreements.

In light of the terrorist attacks, crises and dramas of recent years, citizens expect to be protected. Accordingly, demand exists for the invention of new concepts of security that are novel, easy to use and efficient for the preservation of their physical integrity. Due to the rise in urban living and the mobility of commuters, research into urban security and the control of uncooperative crowds deserves our full attention. It is necessary to invent the tools and technologies for detecting and intercepting remote communications, for identifying individuals, and for controlling and analyzing risks and threats. The national industrial fabric seems to be well-armed in the face of these challenges.

Profound changes in humanity, as well as in organizations and their ways of functioning, are driving the exponential need for new solutions and services in the area of information technologies. As a result, numerous opportunities are opening up to cope with multiple needs and major challenges.

Could the Invasion of Information Technologies into Human Organizations Carry Some Risks?

Technological convergence makes difficult any credible attempt to put things into perspective, as the question of the uses of information technologies has enflamed the entire societal field. Touching on sovereignty, economy and technology all at once, information technologies have a considerable role to play in terms of world balance. In two decades, and without realizing it, we have tilted the balance in favour of a hyper-communicative world.

Not without reason, one might fear that *ICTs are becoming the toolbox for the totalitarianisms of tomorrow*. Indeed, their complexity, their abundance and their invasive nature make them *uncontrollable and dangerous*, as uncontrollable today as environmental issues. Nobody can deny that the capacity for manipulation that they enable – not to mention those which are even more serious, of the 'decerebration' of a portion of humanity due to deviant uses – are threats to both individuals and our society. In this respect, we are living in an ambiguous period where anything is possible.

CHANGING MODELS AND IMPACT ON COMMUNICATIONS

The first step would be to become aware of what might change or not in the development and the expansion of information technologies. The human species has extended its relationships in a way that was unimaginable just a few years ago, thanks to the technical possibilities of mobility and the communications solutions that ICTs have made possible. Is this evolution threatened?

The Internet will remain a relational tool. At the same time, the convergence of technologies will permit the design and distribution of new products, new services and new uses that could, within the next ten years, lead to a *rupture of civilization*, embodied in the passage '*from an economy of mass production to a demand driven economy based on information*' (de Rosnay, 2008). Our traditional models of labour and work, rules of trade, mobility, transportation and travel, lifestyle models and habitats themselves could be called into question, partly due to the convergence of technologies.

IMPACT ON HUMAN BEHAVIOUR

People are already using information technologies in surprising ways. Indeed, millions of users buy, search for information and meet in three dimensional *virtual spaces*. Other universes are coming into focus as a new virtual world, new media and new technologies emerge before our eyes. Today, *Second Life* is the most novel virtual community in existence. More than 9 million people gravitate day and night in a reticular world. Its residents materialize in the form of their avatars, which are faithful or sublimated reflections of their personality: they make money, meet their bankers, get interviewed for jobs, and so on.

The current state of play should change in the near future, as corporate projects emerge for this virtual world. The experiment has proven to be potentially lucrative enough for the major corporate players to get interested and organize events (Nissan, Toyota, Reebok and television channels NBC and MTV). It would appear that this experiment is in its infancy compared with what could be developed in these virtual worlds, where it is becoming possible to construct an infinite number of IT programs that enable games that interact with the entire world, with the Internet as the vector.

Virtualization can lead to a loss of critical sensibility and discernment. It crushes physical distances and timeframes and this can have an effect on our sense of space-time frameworks. The virtual brings *'characteristics that are incompatible with the reality of the living'* (Atlan, 1972, 1992). A new opportunity: these virtual worlds will also need to be secured and protected as too many individuals will lack the faculty of discernment, the critical sensibility or simply the education required to avoid falling into the trap of alienation.

IMPACT ON HUMAN RELATIONSHIPS AND PRIVACY

The solidarity networks of tomorrow announce the advent of a social life that is locally efficient and linked to the global by a series of relationships with numerous external networks. This explosion in network-based communications could serve as the ground floor to a new political model, an alternative way to exercise power, and a new form of post-liberalism. But reality may be otherwise, for example when we observe the invasion of privacy or the new solitude of human beings, a threat that results from the remarkably rapid development of information technologies: the exchange of emails becomes the habitual way that co-workers sitting three desks apart communicate! As this paradox suggests, the greater the possibilities of information technologies, the greater the prospects they open for creating potential models of society and the less they are linked to specific projects.

Other questions, essential ones, will emerge tomorrow. Concerning the notion of privacy or solitary time, for example, every innovation in the area of communication is time consuming. Time spent on the Internet leaves little for reading, writing, recreation or reflection. Silence and tranquility have given way to flows of ephemeral information that can no longer be sorted or assimilated. Do we know for sure that human beings have the physical and psychological dispositions required to assimilate all of the image flows that impinge on them?

IMPACT ON CORPORATE STRATEGY

With their very survival at stake, business organizations will have to seize opportunities or see their growth jeopardized. They will have to leverage the immense resources allocated to NICT research and development efforts. Indirectly, as consumers themselves, they will contribute to the trend towards large-scale production of electronic components, as well as to the race for software and the demand for IT production. ICTs will remain a key pillar of our societies of tomorrow, and those who write software for a living have a very bright future ahead of them. But who today is willing to take a stand on their capacity to elaborate models for tomorrow that are robust, reliable and sheltered from threats?

The question of *security* will also have to be addressed by businesses, in the same way as for all structured social organizations. This issue has already been raised for programmes written for bankers and climatologists, but it will also come up for every aspect of the economy in general. The question of tomorrow's mathematical models will also arise, since it would appear that nothing can absolutely guarantee their robustness given the rapidity with which they will probably be disseminated, interpreted and exploited.

The process of feedback (or analysis ex post facto), a valuable tool for many executives and operational managers, has already been the subject of new questions in light of the possibilities for transferring information in real time and the transparency of interactions among auto-communicative objects. As a result, future management could well be faced with new constraints and imperatives that are already coming into view, with the growing expectation for prospective and early preparations for decision making.

THE CONTRIBUTION OF INFORMATION AND COMMUNICATION TECHNOLOGIES TO THE TRANSFORMATION OF MILITARY CAPABILITIES

The succession of armed conflicts, the pursuit of wars and the threat of terrorism are pushing industrialists to develop new arms integrating high performing *information systems* that implement dual technologies. Equipment designed for projection, network war and surveillance, as well as for airstrikes and projectable commands are the most favoured by this context. As the operations of today are all interarmed and interallied, the interoperability of information systems has become a critical subject.

Made possible by information technologies, the Network Centric Warfare (NCW) concept, which is simply network warfare, is already a reality whose effects were observable as of the second Iraq war in 2003. NCW can be defined as the capacity to *link up* the various operational components and to *retrieve information* thanks to drones, aircraft or satellites, to *disseminate in real time* to designated units in order to strike more rapidly, more precisely and with reduced collateral damage. As a result, the pace of military operations and that of decision making is sharply accelerated.

Thanks to protocols like the Internet and the use of satellite communications, the rapidity and interoperability of communications facilitate the notion of real time in operations. Simultaneously, the increase in the reach and the precision of means of surveillance and protection are leading a radical transformation in the space–time framework of military actions. The importance of operational communications is further amplified. Indeed, it constitutes a critical parameter of the knowledge of situations and hence the choice of the best-adapted modus operandi.

In tactical terms, the stakes are dual: to *understand* the nature of the threat, its intentions, and its positions before taking a side, using the capacities offered by ICTs, and to use the information gathered as the basis for modelling the combat environment and turning the maximum number of risks into advantages before conducting an operation.

In sum, human organizations will take ever greater advantage of information technologies, the Internet and the objects that announce the connection of computers and things... Their impact is considerable. It is necessary to see this as a mutation that hides a deep disruption produced by human ingenuity, a disruption that could escape our control, either accidently or via terrorism. In its extreme form, what threatens our societies is that we risk moving from a well-identified universe to a world that is hazy, which brings with it loss of meaning and reference points.

Challenges for Organizations in Terms of Risks

Our societies are rapidly becoming saturated with the effects of information technologies. It is therefore important for them to become aware of the risks embedded in this third revolution to avoid falling prey to them. So what are the possible risks? What should we do, or rather what should we do to transform these risks into opportunities?

RISKS AGAINST THE SAFETY OF INFORMATION AND COMMUNICATION TECHNOLOGIES AND AGAINST SYSTEM SECURITY

Information and transmission systems are particularly vulnerable and sensitive in terms of security and safety. Viruses, offensive or defensive IT combat, and malevolence are the daily lot of network managers and anonymous users alike. They can lead to additional costs that are exorbitant, both direct ones (the technical maintenance of devices and equipment, the cost of restoring files, and so on) and indirect ones (loss of assets, data and use time).

What risks will affect general safety? The prospect is illusory in this area. As for planning ahead, it is almost impossible to plan ahead for risks or losses. In particular, it is impossible to say with certainty how society will accept them. It is equally impossible to assert what the costs will be and what kind of control the society will be willing to consent in order to reduce the probability of occurrence or repair the harms if they do occur. With the future ICTs, neither information nor the resources needed to analyze it will be lacking. In fact, bits of information already number in the billions. The real challenge will be to acquire the *aptitudes needed to understand them* and also to exercise them with intelligence, to avoid the recurrence of a new disaster like September 11.

RISKS FOR THE ENVIRONMENT

Western countries, taken together, own 75 per cent of all computers, video consoles and mobile telephones on the planet. For the most part, this electronic equipment has a reduced lifespan or shelf life and the volume of electronic waste is increasing by 5 per cent a year in the West. A billion computers have been thrown away in the past five years. The shelf life of these devices is also reduced due to the stepped-up pace of planned obsolescence and new services, new commercial practices and even new fashions. The list of toxic substances present in electronic waste is quite impressive. There are heavy metals (lead, cadmium, chrome, copper and mercury), elements such as selenium and arsenic, brominated flame retardants mixed with plastic to increase the heat resistance of devices. Western society now faces the serious problem of how to dispose of these toxic waste products, an issue that must be considered as part of the general framework of preventing environmental risks and protecting the environment.

A MULTITUDE OF UNDEFINED RISKS OF AGGRESSION

Substantial growth in the number of attacks on information systems is a plausible hypothesis. The Internet is currently construed as a free zone. It is also a *space of non-security* that presumes each user takes adequate measures to reduce risks. Sophisticated one-off attacks (malware is increasingly sneaky and aggressive) and massive attacks via the development of aggression scenarios run botnet attacks using zombie computers that threaten the integrity of information and communication systems.

Attacks propagated via ICTs come from highly structured players who can act on behalf of malevolent secret organizations or rogue governments. These attacks can be carried out on a large scale, like the demonstration of the Russian Army on Latvia in April 2007 or the attempt by the Chinese to block German Government databases in May 2007. And more recently, in April 2011, there was a gigantic attack against Sony's online networks, which a group of IT hackers claimed responsibility for. It forced Sony to unplug tens of millions of clients, whose confidential data was probably stolen. This cast a pall on the security of all IT networks.

We might also observe a similar logic at work in the increase in IT attacks motivated by commercial and competitive concerns, on all types of systems (distribution networks) via software attacks (viruses) or physical ones (the physical destruction of a router) on a command and control information system. We are also aware of the insidious development of threats against governments through subversion and manipulation of information via information technologies.

Consequently, the risk of direct attacks on information systems is bound to become a more common concern to organizations and their executives. In both the public and commercial sectors, the concepts of data hacking, Denial of Service (DoS), theft or the falsification of data will become gradually incorporated into the process of building systems of information. Similarly, in France and probably in other countries, the concept of IT attack and remote communications intercepts will become more frequent in the arsenal of technologies used by governments for economic intelligence and the offensive IT battle (Treaty of Lisbon, 2000) of government structures.

HYPERSECURITY, ENCOURAGING THE EMERGENCE OF AN INSURANCE-BASED SOCIETY

Hypertechnology calls for hypersecurity. Public opinion sometimes seems to be worried about some of the directions being taken with scientific breakthroughs. In addition, public opinion has grown increasingly sensitive to the downside and less so to the upsides and benefits of scientific progress. September 11 and more recent terrorist attacks have accelerated the pace of an underlying trend: the gradual and tolerated erosion of individual liberties within Western society, which constantly demands greater protection and security.

More and more information is being collected everywhere: in connection with transportation, on the Internet, and so on. Societies over-react to threats by soliciting new information technologies to enhance security. It is likely that we are witnessing a trend that announces the emergence of an *insurance-based society*. Information technologies allow us to step up the pace of widespread systems for controlling and monitoring populations. Progress in the miniaturization of communicating solutions, the development of biotechnologies, and the substantial improvement in memory capacity and information processing have enabled their rapid and responsive rollout in the service of security and the level of peace of mind that citizens expect, with the flip side of the coin: surveillance and control of people is omnipresent and, for some, an assault on personal liberties!

In our modern, mainly urban societies, the internal solidarity of the rural culture is giving way to an expectation of outward hyperprotection, otherwise organized and based on intensive use of information technologies. For public policymakers, the challenge will be to address the rising expectations of this level of security with the solution to problems that are increasingly interconnected:

immigration, terrorism, drug trafficking, dissemination, mobility and invasion of privacy.

THE DEVIANT RISKS OF VIRTUAL UNIVERSES

The potential uses of virtual universes are probably unlimited. It is becoming possible to create free technological platforms that are accessible to mere mortals and that enable them to design their environment and use a single navigator or browser that allows them to visit all spaces and interact with other players in a totally virtual environment.

It will be possible to use these platforms for leisure pursuits as well as for work, education, distance learning, the acquisition of skills or apprenticeship. Some of the issues that could provoke concern, for example, are conflicts between traditional economic models – based on scarcity and mass production – and the new future economy, based on niches that interact with one another, supported by flows of users and personalized services. This phenomenon, already underway, will bring new threats to the forefront (viruses, spamming, hackers, frauds, infopollution, traceability, and so on) and new 'new risks'.

Virtual universes occupy more and more space in the real world. The individual runs the risk of being conditioned, without his or her knowledge, and subjected to new perceptions and new representations of his or her own reality. His or her relationship to the world may be called into question. Familiar benchmarks are pulverized: this can once again be referred to as the loss of meaning and the abolition of conventions. These trends may help to explain the paradoxical logic behind the return of individual or group behaviours (gregarious) that seemed to be outmoded and that society will have to take into account.

THE HOLISTIC CHARACTERISTIC OF NEW TYPES OF THREATS

The rapidity of innovations and the widespread adoption of information technologies are changing our social relationships and institutions, while also creating new potentialities and new power balances. We might dread the emergence of a new form of totalitarianism and IT terrorism, because those groups prone to violence are already operating *in networks* presenting specific characteristics that make it difficult to describe or conceptualize them accurately. The use of terms such as terrorist entities, rogue states, obscure powers, anarchists or revolutionary cells are no longer accurate when it comes to providing a full account of the extreme diversity of these groups, their personal histories, their place of residence, their psychological and socio-cultural characteristics or their mindset (motivations, intentions and aptitude to operate).

Information technologies facilitate and accelerate the ability to mobilize players whose behaviour is destructive and who are often not identified and who are isolated, dispersed and without borders, activating them quickly, unpredictably, uncontrollably and irreversibly. Just when our societies are becoming increasingly modern, we are observing a structural instability that is highly influenced by the deviant use of solutions and resources that come from the information technologies.

Positively or by default, there is no longer any risk other than technological: either information technologies reduce or increase our vulnerabilities in the face of randomness, or they create randomness themselves, or they alter the course of events that used to be purely natural. In conclusion, the combination of several independent technological evolutions may engender a disruption with regard to the world as we know it. The question is certainly technical, but also increasingly political. In this disordered universe, it is important to plan ahead.

Regulation? This Question is as Political as it is Technical

For the expert, what follows is only of interest as an incomplete list. Nonetheless, we can try and provide the reader with a few ideas in the area of regulation. Information technologies have become part of the landscape in somewhat haphazard fashion. With a good deal of complacency, developed countries and societies were happy to simply exploit the potentialities. The result is deviancies, weaknesses, risks – known or suspected – all of them the downside of opportunities seized and considerable progress. What this demonstrates is that these phenomena are as political as they are technical. Increasingly, *legal supervision* appears to be a necessary means of governance. When the stakes have been understood to be too high to be left for a business in the private sector to decide what has value and what does not, it is easy to imagine the passage of laws that organize control over the Internet and information technologies in the global sense of the term.

With respect to *content*, Europe – all institutions combined (the European Union, the Council of Europe) – has shown a clear preference for defending freedom of speech and civil rights online, as well as the protection of individuals. The Lisbon Strategy adopted in March 2000 remains the benchmark, marking a major milestone that set a goal for the European Union, that of becoming '*the most dynamic knowledge-based economy in the world by 2010, capable of sustainable economic growth accompanied by a quantitative and qualitative improvement in employment and greater social cohesion*' (Treaty of Lisbon, 2000).

This strategy promises improved economic growth through higher productivity and the creation of new services, in which information technologies play a role. The applications in question focus on *telemedicine, online administration, learning and social development,* especially in rural areas.

The European Union has a strategy for rolling out a high speed infrastructure across Europe and for developing digital transmission networks that are capable of delivering high speed data (at speeds of several Mbits/s). In addition to generating jobs and wealth, this very strong political support for narrowing the gap between rural and urban areas when it comes to access seeks to allow every European to access high speed by 2013 and very high speed by 2020.

The troublesome emergence of the risks related to information technologies has led to a more intense discussion of the need for *regulation of the information market*, in the same way that it is necessary to regulate the financial markets and the environment. It would be silly to deny the values created by information technologies and to ignore individual sensitivity to the idea of the mythical Internet that belongs to one and all. The Internet is a relational resource that has become inevitable, but it is also often a subversive means of disinformation that malevolent governments and organizations or terrorists do not hesitate to use.

With the growing popularity of ICTs, the question of their penal regulation is also an issue in the event of *cyber criminality*. This includes child pornography, the sale of prohibited or counterfeit goods, using the Internet for purposes of prostitution, the practice of phishing, which consists of imitating an online bank, for example, in order to extort user codes and logins from careless web surfers: practices that raise new challenges for those who govern and those who are governed. We might also add the complex question of the legal status of spamming and the pursuit of spammers and other creators of bugs.

In the area of *IT security*, no advanced country can escape its responsibilities. In France, the Hadopi Act, which deals with the law of orientation and programming for the performance of homeland security (Loppsi), is designed to enable the Ministry of the Interior to cover a rather large spectrum and punish cyber criminality. In the United States, Verizon, Cox Communications, ATT and Comcast, US access providers, have warned against downloading protected content under US copyright law. In the UK, the Digital Economy bill, which is expected to come into effect in the spring of 2012, calls for suspending access in the event of online hacking or theft, in accordance with procedures that resemble those adopted under French law.

We are also collectively confronted with a serious problem of *managing electronic waste products*. Since 1997, the Basel Convention prohibits the export of dangerous waste from OECD member countries to non-member countries. Brussels also adopted a directive aimed at prohibiting and limiting the use of several toxic substances in electronic and electrical waste products.

In the area of *public health*, France recognized the value of *telemedicine* and *e-health* in November of 2008. A full chapter is devoted to this subject in the HPST act (a law which concerns Hospital, Patients, Health and Territory, passed on 23 June, 2009). Two legal hurdles are lifted: the principle of prohibiting shared procedures and that restricting the reimbursement of medical care to procedures carried out in the physical presence of the patient. The application decree related to this act has three chapters: a definition of telemedical procedures, provisions to adhere to in the deployment of applications and funding principles.

The immediate impact is reflected in the mobilization of multiple players: industrial players, naturally, which see e-health as a genuine lever of economic growth. Physicians have joined forces in ANTEL, the French telemedicine association, as a way of reducing the dominance of IT professionals on the subject and transforming the association into a learned society, open to all medical fields and ready to produce the expert recommendations needed to guide the practice of e-doctors. Remote surveillance and consultation applications should be given priority in any attempt to actively involve players in the development of telemedicine and teleradiology, which today are the most promising sectors.

A joint European survey of the Federation of Electrical, Electronic and Communication Industries (FIEEC), and the National Agency for Shared Health Information Systems (ASIP), which was released in 2011, relative to ten applications in the fields of telemedicine and tele-health, shed light on important opportunities for the European technological industries. In the interest of playing a major industrial role, Europe needs to view these areas as strategic priorities over the medium and long term, with the active cooperation and involvement of all competent public and private players.

In this technology race, we have to defend an idea of responsible use that has been our own since the first IT and Freedom Act was passed in 1978 and until balanced and global Internet regulation can be enacted, which today appears to be necessary for ensuring the liberty of all with respect to information. The first outlines of this regulation were set forth in July 2009, in the French report on the digital economy in 2025.

Raising Awareness and Strategic Proposals

The cyber world scares people. It is associated with the world of communicating objects, robotics and science fiction. It represents a dramatized projection of human anxieties. The introduction of these objects is viewed as disordered and chaotic, not governed by any particular plan. Tomorrow, an infinite number of sensors and computers might be able to measure an infinite number of parameters related to the private and public domains alike. The question of who owns this information and how they should be used and controlled naturally comes to mind. Some authors insist on imagining – by extending the curve of machine power – that one day super-powerful computers will be able to manage the world in complete autonomy. What can we say about the robustness of systems? What about the robustness of models? Isn't the danger and risk also on the side of those who want to use these new tools for less than noble ends?

Alain Minc imagined a *digital divide* of society (Minc and Nora, 1978). This remains a matter of concern. The phenomenon of the rapid and intense intrusion of information technologies into the lives of people is obviously in the process of occurring, and it is transforming their habits. It may aggravate crises or help to resolve them, as we saw during the banking crisis of 2008, depending on the policy in which they are inscribed. The ICTs bring both the best and the worst, and there is nothing automatic or fatalistic about their effects.

At the national level, which strategy will do the most to enlighten choices in terms of information technology research, innovation and governance?

While global problems emerge, so do opportunities. In raising the question, we are suggesting that these issues should not be left to the market and should instead be handled by governments. Governments, businesses, community organizations and citizens will have to acquire a more in-depth *understanding* of the universe and of human nature, make an effort to understand where they come from and try to imagine what future they are heading for. They should also seek to consolidate models, educate and train in order to ensure an intelligent development and use of ICTs. As a second priority, it is important to address the demands of an increasingly mobile population, without borders, with a responsible attitude toward risks and in search of security, comfort and well-being. It is also a question of taking urgent environmental issues into account while also supporting the national economy.

In light of the above, we suggest four principles that ought to guide this major project:

- fundamental research, which is indispensable to any knowledge-based society; it should be carried out in synergy with world-class research outfits;

- the necessary involvement of the human and social sciences, as they participate in the construction of interdisciplinary interfaces and enrich the public debate;

- the requirement of multidisciplinarity, which leads to the most novel technological breakthroughs and lies at the heart of our major social challenges;

- security and risk management as the solution to a strategic need and a reply to strong societal demand.

The challenge ahead is to ensure that these guiding principles are followed. One last approach completes these principles. It presupposes that everyone becomes aware of their own *ethical responsibility*. Managerial practices often expose decision makers to real behavioural dilemmas. The businesses and organizations that stand out for their social success are those that have implemented a *code of conduct*. The development and use of information technologies in businesses and other organizations requires this *ethical reflection,* part of a three-tiered approach.

The first concerns public powers, which ought to set standards and define what is illegal, antisocial or contrary to moral precepts. The second involves each organization, which must devise and disseminate its own code of ethics. The third concerns managers, who must define and ensure respect for the ethical boundaries linked to their role, as well as inspire those they manage.

Conclusion

Information and communication sciences and technologies are among the nation's top priorities in terms of its strategy for research, innovation and political management. Omnipresent in daily life, they also address constantly growing needs in the area of the modelling, storage and processing of large amounts of data. They enable us to glimpse new and exciting applications in encryption and security, energy management, defence, financial mathematics, modelling, medicine and social networks.

The magnitude of markets, the solutions brought to organizations, individuals and public policymakers in their search for the right balance between the expectations of society, the need for acceptable freedoms and security, gains in productivity and the response to technological and economic challenges in a context of global competition justify a well-thought out public policy promoting information technologies. The rapid rise of information technologies argues in favour of strong initiatives on the part of public policymakers to achieve a real awakening to the opportunities of information technologies that also takes the downside into account.

The world is changing, and so are private and public organizations. Information technologies have become, in a few short years, a key element in the value chain that is shared by all and transversal to the business or the organization.

Beyond public policy, it is up to every organization, public and private, to adapt its strategies in such a way as to manage missions that are constantly changing but nonetheless important for the performance of its activities, its success and its development. Even if there is no direct link between organizational performance and IT expenditure, the constraints and opportunities offered by information technologies should henceforth be part of any corporate strategy.

It is also up to corporate and other leaders to think about actions and acts of management that are most likely to integrate the appropriate information technologies into their core business, by exploiting their virtues and moderating their undesired or counterproductive effects.

The diagnosis, the choice and the rollout of strategy are decisive in ensuring the growth and development of a business or organization. It presupposes developing the ability inside the company to anticipate, reflect and make decisions in the area of ICTs and their use. To conclude, which strategic dimensions should we attempt to highlight?

- Develop the uses of ICTs adapted to the needs of competitive strength, especially in small and mid-sized businesses, as well as in medical and training facilities.

- Search for growth via the use of ICTs and their adapted services in the core business of the organization: multimedia and media of the future.

- Be active in terms of forecasting in the ICT area, which is experiencing dynamic growth: very high speed Internet, mobile Internet.

- Be aware of the challenges related to the mastery of technologies and sensitive uses: Information Systems (IS) security, vulnerabilities, traceability, the role of IS in the definition of strategy.

- Do active intelligence on the assessment of risks related to sensitive data: interceptions, system protection, data security and exchanges.

- Be aware of the impact of ICTs on the management of the organization's human resources and the changes they require.

- Try and understand the issues and impacts of ICT with respect to society: ICTs as vectors of major societal evolutions, ICTs and sustainable development, ICTs and culture.

- Know the regulatory frameworks and ensure their enforcement by adequately trained personnel; the cyber security of the businesses depends on the vigilance of users.

Naturally, some of these guidelines will be easier to apply than others. In addition, all organizations roll out tried and tested practices when they are resituated in their context. By way of conclusion, we have underscored the value of a strategic approach that should take the form of ongoing questions, structured but not mechanistic, propitious to the great freedom and great accountability that are indispensable to progress.

References

Atlan H. *L'Organisation Biologique et la Théorie de l'Information (Biological Organization and Information Theory)*, Hermann, Paris, 1972 and 1992.

Défense et Sécurité Nationale – Le Livre Blanc (The White Paper), Odile Jacob, 2008.

de Rosnay J. *2020. Les Scénarios du Futur (The Scenarios of the Future)*, Fayard, Paris, 2008.

Minc A. and Nora S. *L'Informatisation de la Société (Computerization of Society)*, Seuil, Collection Points, Paris, 1978.

Serres M. *de l'Académie Française (from the French Academy)*, Hominescence, Livre de Poche, Paris, 2003.

Wiseman C. *Strategic Information Systems*, Irwin, Holmwood, IL, 1988.

3

Electromagnetic Fields

Gérard Sengier,[1] Anne Barr and
Catherine Antoinette Raimbault[2]

With the exception of light, the electromagnetic fields (EMF) of natural origin present in our environment are not immediately perceived by our senses. Man has always been surrounded by natural radiation, including certain forms that are necessary to life, but in the past hundred years or so, with the development of electricity and all its industrial and domestic applications, such as telecommunications, radars, and the industrial and medical use of X and Gamma rays, man-made radiation has been added to natural exposure. The proliferation of mobile telephony and the trend for applications using wireless networks have amplified the phenomenon, with the growing presence of wifi terminals and relay antennas in and around the places we live.

In just a few years, an electromagnetic 'fog' has developed around us.

Here are some figures: the number of mobile phone subscriptions is estimated at 5 billion globally (IARC, 2011); the number of base stations was estimated in 2006 (WHO, 2006) at over 1.4 billion worldwide and is increasing significantly with the introduction of third generation technology.

Given the rumours and announcements about electromagnetic radiation (EMR) and electromagnetic fields (EMF), what should we believe? A parallel is often drawn with the asbestos precedent and the precautionary principle is evoked. So, what are the potential impacts on our health? What about electro-sensitivity and the syndrome of intolerance to EMF? A vast quantity of information is circulating, with debates between experts often supporting political argument and pressure from lobbyists.

---

1   Original document in French.
2   Adaptation and update.

Many questions are being raised, fuelling public concern, despite the current vogue for the technologies in question.

In this chapter, we aim to give readers greater knowledge and understanding of EMF and acquaint them with recent reports on the subject.

Electromagnetic Fields

In our day-to-day life, we are exposed to an ever-increasing accumulation of EMF via numerous applications, both in and outside the home, including the following sources:

- Around us: a multitude of antennas on our roofs, pylons, whether mobile telephony relays, radars, radio and terrestrial television transmitters, satellites, analogue transmitters, high-voltage cables, electric cables for trams and trains, and so on.

- Closer to us: electronic toll collection, automatically opening doors, wifi, Wimax, Bluetooth terminals, radio-frequency identification (RFID) chip readers, numerous medical applications, radiology, wireless telephones, mobile telephones, GPS and, of course, household and multimedia appliances.

The proliferation of artificial sources of these EMF could increase exposure and calls for analysis of the effects.

ELECTROMAGNETIC WAVES

Many books and websites describe the wave phenomenon, electromagnetic radiation (EMR), ionizing and non-ionizing radiation.

The most frequently used image is of the circular waves created after a stone is thrown into water. This creates a continuous circular disturbance in the form of waves and, like all waves, they are characterized by their amplitude, length and frequency.

The amplitude is the height of the wave, the length is the distance between the crests of two successive waves and the frequency is the number of waves per second.

In summary, an electromagnetic wave is a disturbance in the EMF surrounding us that moves without changing form and without transporting any matter. It is therefore an ideal means for transporting information!

Light, which belongs to this family, is the only visible type of wave, though there are many other types.

It is the wavelength that makes all difference between light, radio transmission and micro-waves: all these forms of energy cohabit and are part of the electromagnetic spectrum.

THE ELECTROMAGNETIC SPECTRUM

The spectrum extends from static electricity and very low-frequency waves to gamma rays.

- At the bottom of the spectrum: low frequencies, wavelengths between 10 and 100 kilometres = low energy (electrical current, electrical appliances, rail transportation, and so on).

- Near the middle of the spectrum: high frequencies, long wavelength up to microwaves (mobile telephony, radio, television, radar).

- At the top of the spectrum: ionizing rays = high energy radiation (X rays, Gamma rays).

Electromagnetic waves transport energy. The energy increases with the frequency, to the point of becoming dangerous! Consequently, very high-frequency waves, notably high-dose X rays, can burn cells. These are referred to as *ionizing rays*.

The term *'non-ionizing radiation'* (NIR) designates all EMR that, contrary to ionizing radiation, does not have enough energy to modify components of matter and living beings (atoms, molecules).

PHYSICAL MAGNITUDE

Frequency and intensity are magnitudes that characterize electric and magnetic fields, and give them their particular physical properties.

- Frequency is the number of oscillations per second expressed in hertz (Hz). One hertz is equal to one oscillation per second.

- The intensity of an electric field (E) is expressed in volts/metre (V/m).

- The intensity of a magnetic field (H) is expressed in amperes/metre (A/m).

- In magnetic fields, as well as intensity, there is a measurement of the magnetic flux density, which is expressed in Teslas (T) or micro Teslas.

- Wavelength is measured in metres (m), which ranks the various types of waves.

Each wavelength has a precise corresponding frequency. For example, radio waves used to broadcast radio stations and television channels have wavelengths that vary from a few centimeters to several kilometres. FM waves have a wavelength of around one metre with a frequency varying from 87.5 to 108 (MHz).

Possible Effects of Electromagnetic Fields

A study by INRS, (France's National Research and Safety Institute competent in the area of occupational risk prevention) on EMF presents their effects on health, key notions we should be aware of, and measures to assess and prevent this risk (INRS, 2009).

In brief, non-ionizing radiation (NIR), even when of strong intensity, cannot cause ionization in a biological system. However, it has been shown to have other biological effects, such as producing higher temperatures in tissues or creating electrical currents in tissues and cells.

Other reports published show that, for a very wide range of intensities, EMF can have an effect on most physiological systems. A biological effect may have no impact on health when it is within the adaptation limits of the biological system in question.

THE EFFECTS OF ELECTROMAGNETIC WAVES ON HUMANS (DIRECT EFFECTS, INDIRECT EFFECTS AND SPECIFIC EFFECTS)

Short-term direct effects

Electromagnetic waves have the following direct effects: thermal effects in tissues caused by high frequencies, and the effects of electrical currents induced in the human body by low frequencies, electrical stimulation of the nervous system.

Between 100 kHz and 10 MHz, the two types of effects should be taken into account.

Short-term indirect effects

These are fires and explosions (due to a spark or an electric arc), malfunctions in electronic devices (including pacemakers) and a contact current created between a person and an object exposed to the radiation.

Long-term effects

Currently, there is no scientific proof of the long-term effects of low but regular exposure.

Specific effects

Electromagnetic waves can have effects on passive and active medical implants and on pregnancy.

Electromagnetic hypersensitivity and non-specific symptoms

Whatever the type of EMF, certain people complain of 'hypersensitivity' symptoms, such as physical or muscular asthenia, even muscular pain; fatigue, memory loss or apathy contrasting with an abnormal irritability; sleeping problems, insomnia, headaches, feeling drunk, vertigo or dizziness, and so on. Worrying about the risk can in itself cause effects bearing no relation to the real risk. For these symptoms, which are non-specific and reversible, it is hard to confirm the part played by exposure to EMF, whether environmental or professional.

Specific case of mobile telephones

The quantity of power absorbed by the head and the hand is fairly variable and depends on the geometry of the telephone and its own radiation characteristics. It is determined by its Specific Absorption Rate (SAR).

Researchers have identified a number of effects, such as modifications to cerebral activity, response time and the structure of sleep. And research is being conducted on their effects on health.

Risks

Currently, over 1,300 scientific studies on electromagnetic fields have been registered in a World Health Organization (WHO) database (http://www. who.int/fr/), with, in the past 15 years, over 700 specifically covering mobile telephony. In this chapter, we will examine just a few of these reports and opinions on the subject.

INTERNATIONAL AGENCY FOR RESEARCH ON CANCER (IARC) – REVIEW OF THE CARCINOGENIC POTENTIAL OF THE MOBILE PHONE

A Working Group of 31 scientists from 14 countries met at IARC in Lyon, France, in May 2011, to assess the potential carcinogenic hazards from exposure to radio frequency EMF, based on several hundred scientific studies, including recent articles resulting from the Interphone study (see below). The Group conclusions supported the classification of radio frequency EMF as 'possibly carcinogenic to humans', Group 2B according to IARC classification, meaning a limited evidence of carcinogenicity among users of wireless telephones for glioma and acoustic neuroma. Evidence of carcinogenicity was evaluated as inadequate for other types of cancers.

The assessments will be published as Volume 102 of the IARC Monographs (IARC, 2011).

'INTERPHONE' EPIDEMIOLOGICAL STUDY

This WHO study, launched in 2000, assesses links between the use of mobile telephones and the following pathologies: brain glioma *(malign cerebral tumour)*, cerebral meningioma *(benign tumour)*, acoustic neuroma *(benign tumour)* and tumour of the parotid *(malign salivary tumour)*.

It is a research project of the WHO, coordinated by the radiation research unit of the International Agency for Research on Cancer (IARC). A total of 13 countries participated: Australia, Canada, Denmark, Finland, France, Germany, Israel, Italy, Japan, New Zealand, Norway, Sweden and the UK. The studies focused on tumour cases in subjects aged between 30 and 59, with around 2,700 cases of glioma, 2,400 cases of cerebral meningioma, 1,000 cases of acoustic neuroma and 600 cases of tumours of the parotid. The results, published in May 2010, showed no increase in the risk of glioma or meningioma with the use of mobile phones. They also indicated an increased risk of glioma at the highest exposure levels, although biases and error prevented a causal interpretation. This led to the need for further investigation on the possible effects of long-term heavy use of mobile phones.

The Interphone study continued analyzing the use of mobile phone in relation to tumours of the acoustic nerve and parotid gland after the May 2010 results publication.

The Interphone study did not concern exposures for young people. A new project named MobiKids, funded by the European Union and coordinated by the Centre for Research in Environmental Epidemiology (CREAL) was launched in 2009 to investigate the risk of brain tumours from mobile phone use in childhood and adolescence. The project will involve nearly 2,000 young people from 10 to 24 years old with brain tumours and a similar number of young people with none over a study period of five years.

INTERNATIONAL AGENCY FOR RESEARCH ON CANCER (IARC) MONOGRAPH ON EXTREMELY LOW FREQUENCY ELECTRIC AND MAGNETIC FIELDS

Based on several epidemiological studies conducted on groups of children exposed at close range to high-voltage lines showing an increased risk of leukemia, IARC classified these fields in 2002 as potentially carcinogenic for humans (category 2B). This classification signifies limited evidence of carcinogenicity on humans for leukemia in children and no evidence for animals.

SCIENTIFIC COMMITTEE ON EMERGING AND NEWLY IDENTIFIED HEALTH RISKS (SCENIHR)

SCENIHR is a scientific Committee of the European Commission providing opinions on emerging or newly-identified health and environmental risks and on broad, complex or multidisciplinary issues requiring a comprehensive assessment of risks to consumer safety or public health and related issues not covered by other community risk assessment bodies.

SCENIHR's report on the health effects of exposure to EMF (European Commission, Directorate-General for Health and Consumers, 2009), approved on 21 March, 2009, covers all forms of electromagnetic pollution, distinguishing:

- radio frequency (including all mobile telephony, television and radio emissions);

- intermediary frequencies (medical technologies, anti-theft devices or wireless traceability technology such as RFID);

- extremely low frequencies (high-voltage power lines, domestic electricity and household electrical appliances);

- static fields, linked to permanent magnets or continuous currents.

The SCENIHR document is more specifically interested in the biological effects and health risks observed at levels of exposure that are lower than the official limits in most European countries. While concluding that evidence is not sufficient to confirm health risks at these levels, it highlights several gaps in research.

SCENIHR experts recommend that a 'cohort study' be conducted to observe the user population over the long term and another individual dosimetry study to obtain precise assessments of each range of frequencies and individual exposure to radio frequency and hyperfrequency.

SCENIHR draws particular attention to the case of children's exposure, pointing out the lack of epidemiological studies on this category: 'Even if no specific index exists, children and teenagers could be more sensitive to exposure to radio frequency than adults. The children of today will have much greater cumulative exposure than previous generations. Anatomical development of the nervous system is complete at two years of age, an age when children do not use mobile telephones though baby telephones have recently been introduced. However, functional development continues until adulthood and could be affected by radio frequency fields.'

SCENIHR also underscores the lack of data on health risks related to work exposures to strong static magnetic fields such as those generated by magnetic resonance imaging (MRI) equipment or related to long-term exposure to intermediate frequencies that have become increasingly invasive, notably in work environments.

OTHER OPINIONS

ANSES (French Agency for Food, Environmental and Occupational Health & Safety)

This Agency is the result of the merger effective as of 1 July, 2010 of two former agencies, the French Food Safety Agency *Agence Française de Sécurité Sanitaire des Aliments* (AFSSA) and the French Environmental and Workplace Safety Agency *Agence Française de Sécurité Sanitaire de l'Environnementet du Travail* (AFSSET). The potential impact of radio frequency on health is one of the key themes in its 2011 working programme, which follows up steering by AFSSET in the past on collective assessments on the subject.

Radio frequency: The AFSSET October 2009 report highlighted that the majority of studies showing the biological effects of exposure to radio frequency had significant methodological defects (ANSES, 2009). It concluded that 'data from available experimental research do not show any short- or long-term effect of exposure to radio frequency'. This report recommends more extensive research to limit remaining uncertainties and reduce public exposure while specifying that the main source of exposure is mobile telephony.

Regarding relay antennas, the report supports the view that electromagnetic fields do not have any mutagenic effect, do not augment the incidence of cancers, have no deleterious effects on the nervous system, have no impact that is likely to modify the immune system and no impact on reproduction. It also indicates that, at the time of drafting the report, with no conclusion on the Interphone study, the use of mobile telephony did not increase the risk of developing intracranial tumours. Again, according to this report, certain studies suggest there is an increase in the risk of glioma after over ten years of use.

Regarding radars, it was specified that an association between professional exposure to radars of over 2,000 MHz and the risk of lymphoma and leukemia cannot be ruled out.

ANSES encourages epidemiological studies and studies on reproduction and development in children.

Also of relevance is the ANSES (ANSES–AFSSET, 2009) opinion of 26 January 2009 on the effects on health of RFID systems, which again underlines a lack of available data, notably in professional exposure to permanently functioning RFID systems. This opinion also stresses the large number of manufacturers or integrators of RFID systems, of variable sizes and levels of know-how in terms of the need to control safety and health effects on people including effects linked to EMF.

Extremely low frequency: The ANSES (ANSES–AFSSET, 2010) opinion of March 2010, on the 'international appraisal of the health effects of extremely low frequency electromagnetic fields'. These fields are typically those emitted by electrical power lines or any electrical device. ANSES recommends recommencing or pursuing epidemiological studies based on a robust description of exposure to extremely low frequency EMFs, notably through the use of new measurement techniques for individual exposure. ANSES also recommends more research into the possible causes of leukemia in children, more research also into other potential effects of these fields (hypothesis that these fields have implications in neurodegenerative disorders) and studies targeting workers exposed at the highest levels.

ANSES recommends not moving into or creating new establishments for children (schools, nurseries and so on) that are immediately next to very high voltage lines and not installing new lines above establishments of this kind. Additionally, ANSES experts share the conclusions of the international consensus (WHO, 2007), in the belief that the scientific proof of a possible long-term impact on health is insufficient to justify modifying current exposure limits.

Regarding these opinions, the French association for scientific information stresses a lack of respect by ANSES for scientific expertise (open letter of scientific co-rapporteurs of reports to the ministers http://www.pseudo-sciences.org/spip.php?article1394). The national academies of medicine, science and technology, via a group of experts set up to examine health risks from exposure to radio frequency, consider that information in the ANSES report on radio frequencies does not justify a reduction in radio frequency exposure, as recommended by the agency. The scientists denounce these allegations as being prejudicial to scientific expertise.

French Telecoms Federation

The French mobile operators' association *Association Française des Opérateurs Mobiles* (AFOM) and the French telecoms federation *Fédération Française des Télécoms* (FFTelecoms) merged on 3 December, 2010. The extended federation, open to all fixed and mobile operators, ISPs and operators' associations, seeks to create a structured dialogue between all sector parties and permanent debate on issues and changes in the sector.

In November 2010, prior to this merger, AFOM published a guide for parents, relaying the opinion of ANSES relative to the 'calling on parents of teenagers with mobile telephones to inform them of the best usage to reduce their exposure'. The guide also specifies that operators do not target children in mobile telephony promotional campaigns and do not distribute simplified telephones for young children. AFOM has also published a brochure entitled 'My Mobile and My Health', going over key restrictions and recommendations for use (AFOM, 2010).

Medical opinion and group of 20 call for vigilance

In June 2008, 20 physicians and cancer specialists were signatories to a call for vigilance in the use of mobile telephones.

This call was coordinated by David Servan-Schreiber, Professor of Psychiatry at the University of Pittsburgh. Among the main signatories, representing France were Dr Bernard Asselain, Head of the Biostatic Cancer Service at the *Institut Curie*, Dr Thierry Bouillet, Cancer Specialist and Head of the Radiotherapy Services of the Avicenne hospital in Bobigny, Jacques Marilleau, engineer, former physicist at French Alternative Energies and Atomic Energy Commission *Commissariat à l'Energie Atomique et aux Energies Alternatives* (CEA) and French National Center for Scientific Research *Centre National de Recherche Scientifique* (CNRS) in Orsay, Joël de Rosnay DSc; and for Italy, Professor Francesco Berrino, Head of the Department of Preventive and Predictive Medicine at the National Cancer Institute in Milan.

According to the signatories of this call for vigilance: 'Children under 12 should not be allowed to use a mobile telephone except in an emergency, the telephone must be kept at a distance of over one metre from the body during communications by using the loud speaker function, a hands-free kit or an earphone to avoid to the greatest extent holding a mobile telephone, even when in sleep mode'.

Regarding Wifi and mobile telephony relay antennas, Dr Dominique Belpomme, a cancer specialist and President of Association for Research and Treatment against Cancer (ARTAC), said in 2010 (Ouest France, 2010): 'Firstly, wifi in public places and the installation of antennas near public places for children should be banned. People should not telephone with a mobile phone for more than 20–30 minutes per day and should not give mobile phones to children of under 12. 'White zones' should be established for people who are sensitive to waves. And, finally, land use planning should take health issues into account.'

Levels of Exposure

For high-frequency transmitters (emissions from mobile telephones, television and radio antennas),the intensity of the EMF diminishes with distance from the source and, by doubling the distance, the field's intensity halves and therefore the radiation is directional *(sector antenna)*. Measurements show that the intensity of fields is much lower when one is directly below antennas, behind the sector antenna or at an equal distance in front of them.

Radiation therefore depends on the power of the antenna, its distance and its tilt.

Through study of the danger inherent to EMF, limits of exposure after which there are effects on health have been identified. Regulatory limits of exposure have therefore been established using safety coefficients differentiated according to whether exposure is public or professional.

EUROPEAN REGULATIONS

EU Council Recommendation 1999/519/EC of July 12, 1999 on the limitation of exposure of the general public to electromagnetic fields (0 Hz to 300 GHz), proposing limits of exposure for the general public, harmonized at a European level.

This recommendation applies the values proposed by the independent scientific organization International Commission on Non-Ionizing Radiation Protection (ICNIRP). This Commission initially published its 'Guidelines for limiting exposure to time-varying electric, magnetic and electromagnetic fields (up to 300 GHz)' in 1988 (ICNIRP, 1988).

The guidelines are currently under review based on the many scientific studies that have been published since then. The review process is finalized for static fields (ICNIRP, 2009) and in progress for Extremely Low Frequency (ELF) fields. The limit recommended by ICNIRP was obtained by applying a safety factor of 10 for professional exposure and a factor of 50 for the general public to the limit after which there are effects on health. Since 2001, this value has been used in the reference texts of the vast majority of European countries, but some countries (Italy, Belgium, Switzerland, and so on) have applied more restrictive limits. There is continuing political debate at a European level on the potential necessity to modify these values.

Values for limits depend on the frequency band, that is:

- 28 V/m for FM radio FM, 100 MHz band;

- 31 V/m for television, 600 MHz band;

- 41 V/m for GSM mobile telephony at 900 MHz;

- 58 V/m for GSM mobile telephony at 1,800 MHz;

- 61 V/m for UMTS mobile telephony (third generation), 2,000 MHz band.

A process of harmonization of EMF standards worldwide has been initiated by WHO. In the meantime, a worldwide EMF standards database has been compiled by the International EMF Project – http://www.who.int/docstore/peh-emf/EMFStandards/who-0102/Worldmap5.htm.

Directive no. 2004/40-EC of April 29, 2004, on the minimum health and safety requirements regarding the exposure of workers to the risks arising from physical agents (electromagnetic fields).

The deadline for introduction of this legislation was initially set for 30 April, 2008. In October 2007, the European Commission postponed the deadline by four years to allow time for a significant modification to the directive, taking into account the conclusions of research on possible incidence of exposure limits to magnetic resonance imaging (MRI) systems.

For mobile telephones, European standards currently require manufacturers to apply limits in terms of the specific absorption rate (SAR) of the energy, that is, the rate at which energy produced by a device is absorbed by a mass unit of body tissue, expressed in watts per kilogram (W/kg). The standard specifies a SAR index of below 2 W/Kg (average on 10g of human tissue for the torso or the head). Numerous scientific studies demonstrate the harmlessness of these waves at low doses, that is, below the 2 W/kg applied to 10g limit.

MEASUREMENTS

In Europe, measurements for exposure to radio waves should be taken by independent control organizations, accredited by an accreditation body recognized by the European Cooperation for Accreditation (EA). EA is the European network of nationally recognized accreditation bodies located in the European geographical area.

For example, in France, in regulatory terms, Decree no. 2006-61 of 18 January, 2006, on the quality standards required for bodies controlling compliance with exposure limits values, requires that these bodies be accredited by French accreditation committee COFRAC (*Comité Français d'Accréditation*). Measurements are taken according to the measurement protocol established by French national frequency agency ANFR. Results are shown on line on the Cartoradio site (http://www.cartoradio.fr).

NEWS

Resolution 1815 (2011) of the Parliamentary Assembly of the Council of Europe (PACE) on 'The potential dangers of electromagnetic fields and their effect on the environment'.

The Parliamentary Assembly of the Council of Europe (PACE), meeting in Kyiv at Standing Committee level on 27 May, 2011, called on European governments to 'take all reasonable measures to reduce exposure to EMFs, especially to radio frequencies from mobile phones, and particularly the exposure to children and young people who seem to be most at risk from head tumors' (PACE, 2011).

Governments should 'reconsider the scientific basis for the present electromagnetic fields exposure standards set by the International Commission on Non-Ionizing Radiation Protection, which have serious limitations and apply "as low as reasonably achievable" (ALARA) principles, covering both thermal effects and the athermic or biological effects of electromagnetic emissions or radiation'.

The adopted resolution underlines the fact that 'the precautionary principle should be applicable when scientific evaluation does not allow the risk to be determined with sufficient certainty' and stresses that 'the issue of independence and credibility of scientific expertise is crucial to accomplish a transparent and balanced assessment of potential negative impacts on the environment and human health' (Text adopted by the Standing Committee, acting on behalf of the Assembly, on 27 May 2011).

BASE STATIONS

In this regard, in 2011, the European Parliamentary Assembly made the following recommendations:

- 'To pay particular attention to "electrosensitive" persons suffering from a syndrome of intolerance to electromagnetic fields and introduce special measures to protect them, including the creation of wave-free areas not covered by the wireless network.'

- 'Concerning the planning of electric power lines and relay antenna base stations: to determine the sites of any new GSM, UMTS, wifi or Wimax antennas not solely according to the operators' interests but in consultation with local and regional government officials, local residents and associations of concerned citizens.'

(Resolution 1815, 2011).

This applies notably to industrial players currently seeking new infrastructures to deploy fourth generation (4G) technology.

Conclusion

Radio frequency dominates the news on EMFs, with a mass of diverging opinions and numerous communications on the subject. The long-term risks of cumulative exposure to non-ionizing radiation, particularly for young people, cannot be ignored.

Sources of radiation are growing in response to society's needs and increasing demands for new means of communications and new technologies.

Constantly evolving innovations require new research on the associated risks and more communication with regard to increasingly sensitive populations.

All activities affected by equipment and services using EMF will require specific management of this risk, in terms of products, consumers, professionals and the environment, as well as appropriate communication on the subject.

While, for mobile telephony, a pooling of the technical means necessary for communications seems an obvious response, along with a reduction in emission fields, the reduction in emissions should not result in growth in the number of transmitters required to cover a territory. This is a tough issue given the economic and public service implications. It is hard for elected representatives to respond to both the economic pressure for the deployment of networks and the need to protect individuals and their health.

There seems to be a need for an upstream focus on providing both the general public and professionals, in a responsible manner, with information on the risks linked to equipment and usage limits that can be applied. Acceptance and management of exposure can be acquired through knowledge of these electromagnetic fields and how to control their usage. This may be crucial to dealing with the emerging phenomenon of electrosensitivity, and other possible emerging phenomena, including phobias and behavioural issues caused by the addiction to use of mobile telephones and all wireless communication devices.

The first part of the twenty-first century has certainly been marked by a series of natural catastrophes, terrorist attacks and other major troubles, but the growing vulnerability of our major communications systems and their potential impact on our society is an issue that needs to be addressed.

References

AFOM (French mobile operators' association), Le Portable et la Santé/Une Antenne Près de Chez Soi/Votre Adolescent et le Téléphone Mobile – Ondes Radio et Santé/Les Antennes-relais – Fiches Ondes Radio dans le Monde (My Mobile and My Health, Your Teenager and the Mobile Phone, the Parents' Guide), 2010.

ANSES (French Agency for Food, Environmental and Occupational Health & Safety), Update of Assessment of Radiofrequency no. 2007/007 Report of October 2009, AFSSET – http://www.anses.fr, 2009.

ANSES–AFSSET (French agency for environmental and occupational health safety), Assessment of Radiofrequency, Report of 26 January 2009 – http://www.anses.fr, afsset January 2009

ANSES–AFSSET (French agency for environmental and occupational health safety), Summary of the International Appraisal of the health effects of extremely low frequency EMF, Report of March 2010 – http://www.anses.fr, afsset, March 2010.

Cartoradio database http://www.cartoradio.fr.

IARC – Introduction to the IARC Monographs Volume 102, May 2011.

ICNIRP (International Commission on Non-Ionizing Radiation Protection), Guidelines for Limiting Exposure to Time-varying Electric, Magnetic and Electromagnetic Fields, 1988.

ICNIRP (International Commission on Non-Ionizing Radiation Protection), Guidelines on limits of exposure to static magnetic fields. *Health Physics*, 96 (4): 504–514, 2009.

INRS (l'Institut National de Recherche et de Sécurité pour la Prévention des Accidents du Travail et des Maladies Professionnelles) – Les Champs Électromagnétiques (National Research and Safety Institute for the prevention of occupational risks – Electromagnetic fields), INRS web file DW 28, 2009, http://www.inrs.fr.

Ouest France, 'Les ondes en débat à Hérouville' (Debating the EMF issue at Hérouville) 28 January 2010.

PACE (Parliamentary Assembly of the Council of Europe) – Resolution 1815 (2011). The Potential Dangers of Electromagnetic Fields and Their Effect on the Environment. Text adopted by the Standing Committee acting on behalf of the Assembly on 27 May 2011, http://www.assembly.coe.int.

SCENIHR Public Health Europe – http://www.ec.europa.eu/health.

WHO (World Health Organization), Fact Sheet 304, Electromagnetic Fields and Public Health: Base Stations and Wireless Technologies, May, 2006.

WHO (World Health Organization). Fact Sheet N° 322, 'Electromagnetic Fields and Public Health, Exposure to Extremely Low Frequency Fields, June, 2007.

WHO (World Health Organization), International Agency for Research on Cancer (IARC) – Interphone Epidemiological Study, http://www.ec.europa.eu/health, 2009.

WHO/IARC (World Health Organization/International Agency for Research on Cancer (IARC). Press Release no 208, 'IARC Classifies Radiofrequency Electromagnetic Fields as Possibly Carcinogenic to Humans', May 31, 2011.

1999/519/EC. Council Recommendation of July 12, 1999 on the limitation of exposure of the general public to electromagnetic fields (0 Hz to 300 GHz), *Official Journal of the European Communities*, L199, 30/07/1999.

Directive no. 2004/40/EC of April 29, 2004 on the minimum health and safety requirements regarding the exposure of workers to the risks arising from physical agents (electromagnetic fields), *Official Journal of the European Union*, L184, May 24, 2004.

Websites

ARCEP (French electronic communications and postal sector regulator), Le Marché Mobile en France (The Mobile Market in France) – http://www. arcep.fr.

4

Chemical Substances/REACH: The New European Regulation for the Safety of Chemicals

Jean-Paul Fort

The 'REACH' Regulation number 1907/2006 dated 18 December, 2006 (European Parliament and European Union Council) sets a new legal frame for the regulation of the production, marketing and use of chemicals. It is directly enforceable in the EU and a number of associated countries and replaces a large quantity of existing national and European legislation. On 20 January, 2009, Regulation 'CLP' number 1271/2008 relating to Classification, Labelling and Packaging (CLP) of hazardous substances entered in force, which became integrated into the REACH framework.

The acronym REACH stands for **R**egistration, **E**valuation, **A**uthorization and Restriction of **Ch**emicals. Its main goal is to encourage a better knowledge of the properties and risks of chemicals in order to improve the protection of human health and of the environment. In addition, it is designed to maintain the competitiveness of the European industry and its capacity for innovation.

This chapter is just a brief introduction to REACH. For further information, abundant literature can be found on various Internet sites and we advise you seek the help of specialized associations and consulting companies.

Basis Concepts at the Roots of REACH

In a deliberate change from previous legislation, the producers now carry the responsibility for demonstrating that their products can be used safely. In other words, the new legislation involves a transfer of responsibility from the governmental bodies to the European manufacturers or importers.

All substances under REACH are subject to a registration file containing data on physical, toxicological and ecotoxicological properties as well as information on safe use and risks. The concept is 'No Data, No Market', as any marketing of an unregistered substance is prohibited. (As explained below, a system of pre-registration allows for temporary marketing of existing substances until they are fully registered within a pre-set period of time.)

ECHA, the European Chemicals Agency, based in Helsinki is responsible for the coordination and the monitoring of the whole process, with the support of national governmental institutions.

REACH covers substances whether they are manufactured in the Union or imported into the European Union, or whether they are marketed as such or incorporated into formulated mixtures or finished goods.[1]

The greater burden for compliance within REACH is carried by the producers or importers of chemicals. However it does involve the whole supply chain – from the production of the initial substance to its various transformation and uses and until the final destruction of the end products in which it is contained. Hence downstream users of chemicals also have obligations under REACH.

In order to optimize the cost of any requisite testing and at the same time to minimize the amount of testing on animals, the producers and importers of the same substance are required to meet in a Substance Information and Exchange Forum (SIEF) to share their existing information and decide on and share the costs of the additional research to be performed to complete the registration file. A 'Lead Registrant' is named among them to coordinate the basic common file, which is then completed individually and submitted to ECHA by each registrant.

The content of the registration file and the timeframe for registration depends on the volume of the substance on the market and on the hazards to which it is linked.

---

1   The term 'Union' is used here to designate the European Union and the three countries that have joined the REACH process: Norway, Iceland and Liechtenstein.

A Little History Prior to the Implementation of REACH

There are a number of interesting background questions to explore. What was the general picture before REACH? What had already been achieved? What made the REACH project possible? What were the reactions of the various stakeholders in the preparation phase?

We now live in a world where individuals are increasingly intolerant to the risks they do not control. The general public demands 'zero' external risk and authorities attempt to respond with new legislation addressing the safety of consumers and safety in the workplace.

The disastrous effects of the use of asbestos, the work-related illnesses caused by exposure to silica, lead, mercury or benzene amongst others, have focused attention to the risks associated with various products of modern life. In the mind of the general public, the main culprit is the chemical industry and its man-made products. On the other hand, anything 'natural' tends to be seen as good, notwithstanding that asbestos or silica are perfectly natural products without any involvement of any chemistry. It is the fear that an uncontrolled man-made product could have a long-term impact on health similar to asbestos that has prompted European authorities to act in the field of chemicals.

The REACH process could only be achieved by capitalizing on a very large number of previous studies, on a variety of national and international legislation, on international conventions and on harmonized tools for the proper identification of substances, and the evaluation of their properties.

The 2001 Stockholm Convention is one example. It was ratified by a large number of countries and prohibits or seriously limits the use of a list of dangerous products known as Persistent Organic Pollutants (POP) including pesticides such as DDT or Lindane and industrial chemicals such as PCBs. The Convention remains enforceable in Europe.

At the UN Organization level, the new Globally Harmonized System (GHS) for the classification and labelling of chemicals has been created. The European CLP regulation, now integrated into REACH, is derived from GHS.

There are many studies on chemicals and their effects that have been carried out at national and international level, for example, within the OECD and by the Environmental Protection Agency (EPA) in the USA.

One key factor that has greatly facilitated REACH was the existence of two international coding systems for the secure identification of any chemical (keep in mind that the same chemical can be designated by numerous names, not taking into account the various languages). These are the CAS registry numbers (Registry number of the Chemical Abstract Service) and the EC seven digit numbers (European Commission). These numbers have allowed the creation of the EINECS and ELINCS European data bases. EINECS (European Inventory of Existing Commercial Substances) contains the list of substances existing before 1981. ELINCS (European Inventory of Notified Chemical Substances) contains the list of new chemicals, first marketed after 1981. All products in these inventories are retrievable by either their CAS or EC number. Any chemical in a REACH file is designated by both its EC and its CAS number.

During the 1970s, the set of methods for testing the toxicology and eco-toxicology of chemicals were progressively defined and harmonized and have provided chemical companies with the basis on which to file their request for authorization to market new molecules, as required in Europe since 1981. In fact the process now being used for the REACH registration of all chemicals was tested between 1981 and 2008 for new chemicals. Independent laboratories multiplied and have acquired experience in the process. The main drawback for the 1981 regulation has been that the technical file evaluating the new substance was required for a product marketed even in quantities as small as ten kilos per year. This has proved an effective brake on the development of innovative products by the European industry.

In the course of the previous 30 years, the chemical industry had greatly increased the number of risk assessment of its products in order to produce the Safety Data Sheets (SDS) for customers, as required by law. As a result many products have been identified as potentially Carcinogenic, Mutagenic, Toxic for reproduction, Toxic for the environment, Persistent, Bioaccumulative or a combination of these. Reference of it was progressively made in the SDS and the substances were labelled according to the prevailing regulations. However, for the vast majority of existing products, the available data on the potential risk for human health and the environment was clearly insufficient and there was no common standard in Europe.

Until the implementation of REACH, the only way a government could prohibit or limit the use of an existing chemical was to sponsor a survey and provide evidence of the risk caused by the substance. For that reason, the number of complete studies was very limited and the decisions to limit use still scarcer.

In conclusion, at the beginning of this century, the tools were available for identification and testing, and all new (1981 onwards) substances had been tested. What was missing was a thorough evaluation of existing substances. The clear target for REACH was the substances in the EINECS inventory, some of them on the market since the beginning of the industrial revolution in the nineteenth century.

Of the 100 000 plus substances in the EINECS inventory, approximately 30,000 were thought to be produced at a level in excess of one ton per year.

As soon as the objectives of the legislation were apparent, an intense lobbying started, on the one hand by the various chemical industry federations, anxious to minimize the scope and extend the agenda of the project, and on the other hand by ecologists seeking the immediate ban on all products suspected of being toxic.

CEFIC, the European confederation of the chemical industry, as well as the national federations of that industry, were claiming that toughening the current regulations would undermine the competiveness of Europe and promote the transfer of production towards emerging countries.

The initial regulation project was approved by the EC in October 2003. It was first presented to the European Parliament in November 2005 and finally approved in December 2006.

It may be the result of a compromise between two opposite groups of stakeholders, nevertheless, the REACH Regulation is an innovative and far reaching document for improving the protection of human health and the environment; placing Europe well ahead in this respect of its main American and Asiatic competitors.

The various national chemical industry federations and CEFIC quickly understood that it was in their interest to support the process and promote it fully among their members. Every large European chemical company started its own REACH project, not only for the sake of compliance, but as a tool for progress in terms of better governance. In fact, despite the costs and constraints, the industry expects a number of benefits from REACH, for example: an improved reputation amongst the public, a decrease in the risk of future claims caused by the unknown effects of chemicals, and a level playing field in terms of regulations, ensuing fair competition. This positive view is most prevalent amongst large companies and some forward-looking medium-sized companies. Smaller companies with limited resources and a more short-term view may view it differently.

The environmental associations as a whole have claimed dissatisfaction, stating that the scope of the project was too limited, and its implementation much too slow. They have produced long lists of chemicals that should be banned immediately, noting that in early 2011 only approximately 50 chemicals had been identified as being of high concern and only half a dozen of them being subject to the special authorization process.

The Scope of the Regulation

REACH applies to chemical products manufactured or imported into the EU in quantities of one ton or more per year in the form of:

- individual chemicals: identified as 'substances' in the REACH terminology;

- formulations including two or more substances: identified as 'mixtures';

- manufactured goods incorporating one or more substances: identified as 'articles'.

The term 'substance' relates to chemical compounds or elements including the impurities resulting from the production process and the additives that may have been added.

The term 'mixture' relates to associations of several substances, in the liquid or solid or gaseous form, such as paints, inks, detergents, home care products or lubricants. A mixture is not registered as such, but each of the substances contained in it must be registered.

Articles are concerned by REACH if the contained substances are intended to be released during normal conditions of use. A scented candle is an example of an article that will release chemical substances during its life.

Some substances are excluded from the scope of REACH, such as radioactive substances (they are covered by the Euratom Directive), products under customs supervision, unrecycled wastes and some naturally occurring low-hazard substances (nobody will argue that water is toxic!).

While being covered by REACH, some substances are exempt from registration as they fall under more specific legislations. This is the case for medicines, food and foodstuff additives, crop protection products and biocides. Likewise some substances are subject to tailored provisions within REACH as they are used in specified conditions, such as intermediate substances used solely for the production of downstream substances, or substances used solely for research and development. Obviously all 'new' (1981 onwards) substances registered in the EINECS inventory, following a complete investigation, are not subject to a new registration file.

As it may not be so easy to decide to which extent a product is covered by REACH, the 'Navigator' tool of the ECHA website could prove particularly helpful in the process.

One key point for promoting technological development is the exemption of full registration for substances used in research and development. In fact, the previous legislation was calling for the production of a full toxicological and eco-toxicological file for any new molecule produced in quantities as small as 10 kg per year. Now a simple notification process is sufficient.

Even if a substance benefits from some sort of exemption for registration, it still must comply with the CLP Regulation on classification, labelling and packaging.

The Stakeholders, Their Role and Duties

The main actors are the European producers and importers, who must have their substances registered.

Non-European manufacturers are obviously interested in marketing their products in the EU: they cannot register their substances directly and must act through a legal European entity, appointing a European 'Only Representative' who performs the registration process on behalf of all the importers dealing with the foreign manufacturer.

All downstream users have duties under REACH, across the supply chain, from the manufacture of the initial substance to the destruction of the final product. They must:

- make sure that the substances they use have been registered (or pre-registered) by their suppliers;

- make sure that they handle each substance according to the guidelines in the safety data sheet supplied by the manufacturer;

- inform their suppliers on the uses they make with the products they receive from their suppliers and on the exposition of workers in the process;

- pass on to their customers the safety data sheets of all the substances contained in the mixtures or articles they supply;

- properly label their products;

- inform ECHA and their customers if a substance of very high concern listed by ECHA is present at a concentration of more than 0.1 per cent in their preparation or article. Upon request, the consumer must be supplied with the same information.

ECHA is coordinating the process. An abundant source of information is available on its website: basic information, guidance documents, frequently asked questions, and so on. ECHA also organizes regular stakeholders meetings and webinars. It publishes a monthly newsletter and frequent e-news addressed to subscribers (free). Data processing and communication tools have been developed for the registration process: IUCLID5 (International Uniform Chemical Information Database) is the tool available to companies to collect data and prepare their dossiers. 'Reach-it' is the online tool for companies to submit data and registration or notification dossiers.

In each country a national authority is responsible for implementing territory-wide processes and contributes to ensure further improvements in standards (HSE in the UK, Ministère de l'Ecologie in France, and so on). National helpdesks are supplying information and answering questions from companies and individuals mostly through their own websites (UK REACH Competent Authority in Great Britain; INERIS in France to name a few). The list of national helpdesks with their websites is available on the ECHA site (click HELP).

In addition, the chemical trade associations are very active in promoting REACH, either directly (CIA – Chemical Industries Association – in the UK; VCI – *Verband der Chemischen Industries* – in Germany; UIC – *Union des Industries Chimiques* –in France, and so on) or through their European federation CEFIC (European Chemical Industry Council). They carry an important task in helping the smaller companies with limited resources to cope with REACH.

Finally a large number of companies are supplying services linked with REACH in the fields of legal advice, data processing, toxicology, Only Representative service and management. Some are offering a full service in all fields.

The Registration Process

The registration process for existing substances is spread over a ten-year span, between 1 June, 2008 and 31 May, 2018.

PRE-REGISTRATION

Between 1 June and 31 December, 2008, all producers and importers of chemicals had to register with ECHA and declare the yearly quantities of existing products they were marketing. Any existing undeclared substance has been prohibited for sale since 1 January, 2009.

The pre-registration phase may be called an unexpected great success, as instead of the forecast of roughly 30,000 substances, ECHA registered approximately 150,000 substances declared by 65,000 companies, for a total of 2,750,000 filings, most of them in the last two months of the prescribed period. It was a miracle that the data processing system did not explode. However some doubts can be raised on the faith that can be given to the forecasts for the whole 2008/2018 process!

Undoubtedly some duplicate or triplicate registrations were made, especially by downstream users not being sure that their products would be registered properly by their suppliers. It seems that some distributors tried to register the full list of existing substances disregarding the quantities or the applicable exemptions (in fact distributors have no registration or notification responsibility under REACH). In any case, a very large number of existing products unknown in the EINECS inventory were pre-registered. These are mostly synthesis intermediates and so called 'reaction masses' designating the reunion, in a special way, of two or more substances that shows properties quite different from a simple mixture of the same substances.

Now any user of chemicals can consult the list of pre-registered substances (click on 'ECHA CHEM' on the ECHA website) and check the date by which the full registration is expected to be completed.

THE SUBSTANCE INFORMATION AND EXCHANGE FORUM

The REACH Regulation specifies that producers and importers of the same substance must exchange the data available to them in order to minimize toxicological tests on animals and reduce the registration costs. They also must agree on (and share the costs of) the required additional studies and on a common classification and labelling of the substance.

For this purpose, the registrants of the same substance must form a 'Substance Information and Exchange Forum' (SIEF).

Based on the pre-registration process, ECHA identified approximately 150,000 'pre-SIEFs', 93,000 of them with ten or less registrants, but also 140 counting more than 100 registrants for the same substance (some difficulties are expected in coordinating the exchange!).

Each registrant must check that his product is sufficiently close to that of the others for a common file to be submitted. Once this phase is completed, SIEFs can then be formed either by validation, splitting or merging of pre-SIEFs.

Aside from registrants, any entity claiming to own data or expertise on a substance can join a SIEF. The REACH Regulation specifies that each SIEF must designate a 'Lead Registrant' among its members, who shall coordinate the build up of the registration dossier, but it is left to the participants to choose the way they organize their work.

Each SIEF must then create an internal set of operating rules to ensure that fair trade laws are not broken (no market data can be exchanged), or to define the financial conditions for sharing available data or for splitting the costs of future studies, or to decide how new producers could join the SIEF and have access to the registration common dossier.

The goal is that the technical file dealing with the various properties of the substance, as well as its classification and labelling, be common to all registrants. The other parts of the registration dossier (uses, exposition of workers and users, risk analysis, and so on) is left to the care of each registrant.

In order to facilitate the process, registrants can organize consortia, to regroup some members of a given SIEF or members of several SIEFs dealing with similar substances. This is a voluntary procedure, as the concept of consortium is not part of the REACH Regulation.

The SIEF process is burdensome especially when the number of participants is high. A fair amount of contractual and legal documents have to be exchanged between participants, for the benefit of specialized law firms.

The SIEF system has been active since early 2009 and will continue until 2018. It started, as to be expected, with the substances to be registered in the first wave before the end of 2010, and is now mostly dealing with the substances to be registered before June 2013. However it may be risky for a producer to wait too long before entering the registration process on the ground that its substance is due for registration at a later date. He may then find that the conditions to join a SIEF have been set by the original members leaving him no choice whatsoever.

THE REGISTRATION AGENDA

The registration process is spread over a relatively long period of time to take into account the limited availability of technical and human resources to perform the enormous task of collecting and creating data for thousands of substances. Priorities were set for substances based on marketed volumes and on risk to human health and the environment.

The first wave of registration completed at the end of November 2010 involved all substances used at the rate of more than 1,000 tons per year, as well as substances classified as Carcinogenic, Mutagenic or toxic for Reproduction ('CMR 1 and 2') used at more than one ton per year and substances dangerous for the environment ('R50/R53' risk phrases) used at more than 100 tons per year. The original forecast was that over 9,000 substances should fall into this category. ECHA finally recorded only 4,700 registered substances. It may be assumed that high volume substances have largely been registered but that producers or importers may have decided to give up the production of some small volume toxic substances rather than face the cost of registration and the risk of having the substance listed as Substance of Very High Concern, on the candidate list for the 'Authorization' process. It is still too early to evaluate the effect on downstream users of the possible lack of registration of some key products for them, which according to the current rule means the end of availability.

The list of registered substances can be consulted on the ECHA site. The technical content of the dossier of a registered substance can be downloaded after confidential information on special uses has been removed to protect industrial property. By the end of April 2011, the publishable content of the dossiers of 3,400 substances was available on the ECHA site.

The technical data from the ECHA database can also be found on the international eChemPortal (echemportal.org) along with information from American, Canadian, Japanese and Australian databases.

The next wave of registration to be completed before 1 June, 2013 is dealing with substances used at the rate of 100 to 1,000 tons per year. The last wave, for substances between one and 100 tons per year should be completed before 1 June 1, 2018.

THE REGISTRATION FILE

The content of the registration dossier is a function of the volume of the substance marketed in the Union.

- For the 1 to 10 tons range, a relatively simple technical file is only required. It must contain the physical and chemical properties of the substance, its classification and labelling and any other readily available information. If the substance is suspected to be toxic to some degree, annex VII of the REACH Regulation specifies that five toxicity tests and three ecotoxicity and biodegradability tests must be performed.

- For the 10 to 100 tons per year range, six additional toxicity tests and three additional tests for ecotoxicity and biodegradability are required for the technical dossier according to annex VIII. Moreover, a Chemical Safety Assessment (CSA) must be performed, containing an evaluation of the risks for the human health and the environment.

- The requirements are further increased for the upper ranges of quantities (see annexes IX and X of the REACH regulation) for which long-term toxicity tests, including tests on animals, are now required (in the latter case, a strict procedure must be followed in order to minimize the number of tests on vertebrates).

The risk study is very elaborate: in addition to the CSA, a description of the various uses of the substance, including scenarios of exposition and procedures for safe handling and use are contained in a Chemical Safety Report (CSR), which takes into account the whole life of the product from production to final destruction and disposal. For this reason, the registrant must be aware of the uses made by the downstream users in order to advise on the proper risk mitigating procedures. At the end of the process, the registrant must produce 'extended safety data sheets' to be supplied to customers. The new safety data sheets are now voluminous documents (up to 100 pages) including the various use scenarios with their safety aspects, obtained from downstream users.

In extreme cases, when readily available data is scarce, the cost of registration, excluding internal management costs, may reach 2 million euro per substance (knowing that part of that cost may be shared among SIEF members). As an illustration, a chemical company reported that its cost for the registration of 74 substances registered before the end of November 2010 was 12 million euros.

Authorization and Restriction

The control of the risks linked with dangerous substances is based on two main procedures:

- Restriction: The substance is free for use except for what is specified as prohibited.

- Authorization: The marketing and use of the substance is prohibited unless a manufacturer or user has obtained an authorization from ECHA for a specified use.

RESTRICTION

All restrictions from previous legislation are still enforceable, and are included in the long list of annex XVII of the REACH regulation. New restrictions have been added (and will continue to be added). Member states or ECHA (at the request of the EC) can propose new restrictions, which are evaluated by the Risk Assessment Committee and the Socio-economic Committee of ECHA. Their reports are open for comments for a specified period of time and finally the Restriction decisions are made by the EC.

Most recently, the process has been used to deal with mercury, lead and their derivatives, following proposals originating from Norway and France.

In some cases, the restriction amounts to almost a full prohibition. This is the case for example for pentachlorophenol, a chemical which was once widely used as a wood preservative and is now prohibited for all marketing and use unless its content in a substance or in a mixture is less than 0.1 per cent. In other cases, the restriction is only targeting a specific use. This is the case for example for vinyl chloride that cannot be used as a propellant in aerosol, but can be freely used to make PVC plastics (provided applicable rules for health in the workplace are respected).

Let us mention that some products can be subject to both restriction and authorization. As a first step, some phthalates (plasticizers) were prohibited for the manufacture of toys and child care articles under the restriction procedure, and have now been recently included in the authorization list.

AUTHORIZATION

The Authorization is a very long and complicated procedure. This is understandable as the simple proposal from a member state to consider a substance as a potential candidate for authorization has an immediate economic impact: the producer may just decide to abandon its production and the users will have to develop a costly substitution strategy.

The targeted substances are those classified as Substances of Very High Concern (SVHC). They include substances found to be:

- Carcinogenic, Mutagenic or Reprotoxic substances (CMR);

- Persistent, Bioaccumulative and Toxic (PBT);

- very Persistent and very Bioaccumulative (vPvB);

- other highly dangerous products for the human health (such as some phthalates which have been found to be endocrine disruptors, interfering with hormone production).

Member states or ECHA, at the request of the Commission, can propose a substance for consideration as being SVHC. After an elaborate and long consultation and evaluation process, ECHA may decide to include the substance on the 'candidate list'.

The first candidate list was published by ECHA in October 2008. It contained 15 substances selected among the proposals made by member states. The list progressively expanded and contained 53 substances in June 2011. From this list, and after more evaluation both on technical and socio-economical grounds, involving the 'Member State Committee', ECHA extracts priority candidates, which are submitted to the EC for listing on annex XIV or the Regulation.

Each substance on annex XIV is given a 'sunset date' after which the production, marketing and use of the substances is prohibited. Any company willing to market the substance after that date has to submit at least 18 months before the sunset date, an authorization dossier to ECHA showing the economical interest of the substance, the inability to substitute by another less dangerous substance, and proving that the substance can be handled during production and use without any adverse effect on workers and users. ECHA will then grant or deny the authorization to the applicant on a case by case basis, and for a specified use.

The first priority list for inclusion in annex XIV was published on 21 February, 2011. It contained six products, including three phthalates, among them DEHP, a plasticizer for PVC with a yearly worldwide production of approximately 3 million tons. DEHP is thought to hinder the sexual development of male babies. The sunset date for DEHP is 21 August, 2015. The most recent consultations for future inclusion into the priority list contained seven chromium derivatives, five cobalt derivatives and trichloroethylene, a widely used solvent.

As soon as a substance is on the candidate list, the suppliers of the substance and the suppliers of mixtures or articles containing more than 0.1 per cent of the substance must advise their customers, and supply an updated SDS. Upon request, any consumer should receive the same information.

Since 1 June, 2011, manufacturers or importers of articles must also report to ECHA the presence of more than 0.1 per cent of substance on the candidate list in the products they are marketing. This will create a lot of difficulties as it is extremely difficult to make sure that any garment or object imported from Asia or elsewhere does not contain any trace of substance on the candidate list.

As of 1 April, 2011, ECHA updated its 'Guidance on Requirements for Substances in Articles', in order to inform producers, importers and suppliers of articles how to comply with the above requirements.

When a substance is suspected of being 'SVHC', wise producers and users are starting substitution programmes, as the risk of disappearance, sooner or later, of the substance from the market is high, with potential dire consequences for unprepared users. For this reason, the Member States Committee proceeds with caution, although not at the speed wanted by 'ChemSec', a Non-Government Organization-driven project aiming at the rapid inclusion on the candidate list of the 378 substances from its SIN2.0 list ('Substitute It Now').

Enforcement

Enforcement of REACH (and CLP) is a national responsibility. Member states must lay down legislation specifying penalties for non-compliance and set up an official system of controls. The role of ECHA is to host the 'Forum for Exchange for Information on Enforcement' for the coordination of the enforcement activities in the Union.

The first ECHA report on enforcement in the Union was published in August 2010. It deals with the first coordinated enforcement programme, carried out in 2009, which was targeting the compliance with pre-registration and with the availability of safety data sheets mostly at producers and importers level. The 1,600 inspections carried throughout the Union showed a 24 per cent non-compliance rate, mostly due to inadequate safety data sheets. Measures taken were mostly administrative orders and letters of appeal, with only 12 fines and three criminal processes.

The second (2010) programme has targeted the first level of downstream users (distributors and producers of 'preparations'), with a special emphasis on the suppliers of products directly used by the consumers such as paint, detergents and personal care products. Major issues are safety data sheets, labelling, unregistered substance and un-registered use of a substance.

Custom authorities are being given the task of checking that all substances entering the Union either as substance or in preparation or article are REACH compliant. At this point no case of heavy fines or imprisonment, as provided in the national laws, has been reported.

Risks for Downstream Users

It can be assumed that most producers of chemicals are now well aware of their duties under REACH and are proceeding actively with their in-house REACH project. This is probably not the case for a large fraction of the downstream users of chemicals. They may greatly underestimate their risks for non-compliance and the risk of their supplies being cut off.

According to REACH, a Downstream User (DU) is a company using a substance as such or in a mixture in its industrial activity. A distributor, who does not change the nature of the product, is not a DU. Its sole obligation under REACH is to pass on information from its suppliers to its customers and vice versa (especially concerning safety data sheets and uses). A consumer is not a DU either.

The major risk for a downstream user is the interruption of its supply chain. To manage this risk, some steps should at least be taken:

- Make sure that the needed substances are pre-registered or exempted from registration. The best way, after a full investigation to identify all substances bought as such or as a component of a preparation, is to contact the suppliers and obtain some assurance of future availability. At the same time, the list of registered and pre-registered substances should be consulted on the ECHA site. Perhaps the most difficult step is to identify all substances used directly or indirectly in the business. The fact that a substance is pre-registered is only an assurance that the product will be available until the date at which the substance has to be fully registered.

However, for cost reasons, not all pre-registered substances will be ultimately registered.

- Obtain the new 'extended safety data sheets' that your supplier must provide for recently registered substances and make sure that your own use is documented on them. If not, report it to your supplier and get advice from your helpdesk or ECHA.

- Look for potential substitutes for SVHCs, especially those already on the candidate list, and develop processes to be able to use them.

The other risks are related to non-compliance penalties, according to national laws, including fines, imprisonment and withdrawal of operating license for major offences, and are applicable (non-exhaustive list) for:

- improper use of a substance subject to restriction or authorization;

- importation, marketing or use of an unregistered substance;

- use of a substance outside the scope of the registered uses;

- failure to provide proper safety data sheets to customers;

- failure to notify customers and ECHA on the presence of SVHC in articles.

Liability suits are also to be expected from customers in case of interruption of supply contracts or for failure to provide proper information on the safe use of products.

Classification and Labelling

THE CLASSIFICATION, LABELLING AND PACKAGING REGULATION

Regulation (EC) 1272/2008, enforced as of 20 January, 2009 is the new European regulation for the Classification, Labelling and Packaging of dangerous products. The CLP Regulation replaces the Directives 'DSD' 67/548/EEC for dangerous substances and 'DPD' 1999/45/EC for preparations containing dangerous substances, and their transcription in national laws.

CLP implements the recommendations of the United Nations-driven GHS (GHS of classification and labelling of Chemicals) project, the goal of which is to harmonize the classification and labelling of dangerous products worldwide. The REACH Regulation has been amended in order to be coherent with CLP. ECHA is monitoring and coordinating the implementation of CLP for all substances and preparations, including those benefiting from exemption of registration (biocides, plant protection products, explosive articles, among others).

The CLP Regulation is not extensively described here. Only basic principles and major features are presented below. More information can be found on the ECHA site, starting with the 'basic guidance' document (direct link: http:// guidance.echa.europa.eu/docs/guidance_document/clp).

Why a new regulation when Directives DSD and DSP were considered adequate for the protection of human health and the burden on the industry for REACH compliance was already very heavy? The answer is that major progress is expected for the safety of international trade:

- Labels and hazard pictograms on chemical packaging are derived from the international GHS system. Ultimately, with the generalization of this system throughout the world, international exchanges will be facilitated and European exporters won't have to deal with a large number of different foreign regulations.

- The hazard classes as well as the pictograms are close to those existing in the international regulations for the transportation of hazardous material.

Contrary to REACH which focuses on toxicity and ecotoxicity risks, CLP includes both physical hazards (explosion, fire, corrosion) and toxicological hazards (caused by CMR substances only; persistency and bioaccumulativity are not considered). The new classification consists of nine hazard classes, subdivided into 16 categories of physical risks, ten categories of health risks and two categories of environmental risks.

The first step for producers and importers has been to reclassify their substances in the right new hazard category. They had to:

- use the classification of the substances that have been harmonized within the Union;

- use the classification of the substances which have been registered in the REACH process;

- decide on the classification of other products, based on their previous class in DSD and DSP, on their current class in transport, and on any other available data on the hazard of the substance.

Then labels and safety data sheets had to be upgraded, replacing the old 'Risk phrases' and 'Safety phrases' by the new 'Hazard statements' and 'Precautionary statements', and replacing the old 'Danger symbols' by the new 'Hazard pictograms'.

This represents a large amount of work in a short period of time, especially for companies already very busy with the REACH registration process: all substances had to be reclassified before 1 December, 2010, with proper labelling and updated SDS available. By 3 January, 2011, ECHA should have received the notifications of the new classifications of all substances on the market in 2010. It is quite improbable that the process was completed thoroughly by all actors for all substances.

The second step is concerning mixtures of two or more substances. The agenda calls for full enforcement of the new regulation by 1 June, 2015. Here the process is even more complicated as one has to combine in a proper way the properties of the various components in a mixture in order to define the hazard category of the mixture.

HARMONIZED CLASSIFICATION

As the producer or importer has the responsibility of the classification of its product, it is quite common to find the same substance with different hazard classifications in various countries. The ultimate goal is to arrive at a common understanding.

One tool for this goal is the Classification and Labelling Harmonization (CLH) process. Member states can propose to ECHA to harmonize the European classification of a given substance. The process is focused on risky substances, based on their intrinsic properties, on the volume marketed and on the potential human exposure or environmental impact. As an example, vinyl acetate was already classified as 'flammable' in all European countries, but with no classification or variable classifications for other aspects. Based on a proposal made by Germany, the Risk Assessment Committee agreed in early June 2011 to also classify vinyl acetate as 'acutely toxic by inhalation', 'toxic to the respiratory system' and 'suspected carcinogenic'. This classification is now enforceable in all member states.

The other tool is the registration process. All registrants who are members of a SIEF must agree on the classification and labelling of the substance they want to register. This means that all substances already registered have a harmonized classification, and that all substances subject to registration will ultimately be harmonized. The responsibility for self-classification by producers/importers will still remain for substances exempted from registration and for mixtures.

Current Impact of REACH and Future Developments

For the safety of the consumer, REACH is definitely a big progress. The only negative impact is the potential increase in the cost of some products, due to the replacement of dangerous products by safer ones, which could be more expensive to produce, and involve in any case a cost of development for the new preparations.

We shall therefore focus on the impact of REACH on the industry.

NEGATIVE IMPACTS AND RISKS FOR THE EUROPEAN INDUSTRY

The first immediate impact is the cost of compliance and the drain of internal resources at the expense of other market-oriented development programmes. The industry must cope with a complex regulatory system, in constant evolution. Significant difficulties are encountered in organizing SIEFs and consortia, and in setting a proper communication to and from downstream users.

More serious medium- and long-term risks are expected:

- Availability of key ingredients for downstream users:
  - Following an economic assessment, manufacturers may decide to stop the production of substances showing a reduced development potential. They shall do so if a substance shows toxic properties and may be (or already is) classified as SVHC, and if the cost of registration is too high as compared to expected future profits. But this substance, even if used in very small

quantities, may be a key ingredient for various preparations or articles. In this case downstream users will have to develop alternate solutions or go out of business. This is a key subject of concern, as the strength of the European industry is largely based on specialized high-performance, low-volume products. As an example, the European textile industry survives by offering specialized products based on a wide range of low-volume dyes and other additives.

• Transfer of activities in countries with lower health and environment standards:
    – Just as an example, the production of electronic components involves the use of a great number of chemicals, some of them toxic, all along the manufacturing process. But none of them are present in the finished part. It is obvious that it may look attractive to manufacture such components outside of Europe rather than face the unavailability of some substances and the higher cost of stringent conditions of use. Generally speaking, any end product that does not contain any of the unregistered or banned chemicals which were used during its manufacturing process is free to enter Europe.

• Closure of activities:
    – Some small- and medium-sized enterprises may be forced out of business because of the lack of resources to finance the development of new preparations (exempt of SVHC substances), not mentioning the REACH and CLP compliance costs.

• Liability litigations:
    – It is quite possible that the studies on the toxicity of chemicals could link some illnesses to the exposure to some chemicals. In this case, the producers may face onerous litigations.
    – Absence of registration, errors in the registration process or inadequate safety data sheets are other likely scenarios that may cause disruptions in the supply chain. Downstream users may then sue their suppliers.

• Legal risks:
    – A number of litigations may arise from anti-competitive behaviour in the context of data-sharing rules under REACH.

Unethical companies may face penalties for breaching competition laws by:

- using the SIEFs and consortia to exchange market data or conspire in price fixing;

- refusal to exchange technical data on substances;

- pricing the access to data on substances at an unreasonable level;

- making it difficult for a newcomer to join a SIEF or to obtain data from a consortium;

- liability insurance cost increase:
  - In view of the increased risk of future litigations, insurance companies may be tempted to increase premiums or to limit coverage. At this point, no such move has been reported. On the contrary, the chemical industry is counting on the improvement in the safety of its products to obtain favourable treatment from the insurance industry.

OPPORTUNITIES FOR THE EUROPEAN INDUSTRY

In the short term, the majority of the European industry is feeling the obligations and constraints created by REACH, but most enterprises and especially the chemical producers are expecting long-term rewards from REACH and CLP:

- Safer products:
  - The main goal is the safety of consumers and the environment. But the industry will also benefit from this increased safety and better information: accidents and professional illnesses linked to chemicals should decrease, employer's liability insurance premiums should ultimately be lower, and as a major benefit, the image of the industry as a whole, and of the chemical companies in particular should improve.
  - In fact extended reference to REACH is now included in the reports on governance of many companies, with the goal of improving their relation with stakeholders.

- Harmonized regulations:
  - This is welcome for fair competition within Europe and to some extent with foreign suppliers who must comply with REACH for the products they market in Europe. The additional benefit is the reduced cost and the simplification for the edition of various documents such as SDS and labels which had to be compliant with 30 different legislations.

- Incentive to innovation:
  - The pressure for the substitution of dangerous products in mixtures and articles, as well as the provision in REACH exempting the substances used in research from a full registration should have a positive impact for innovation in Europe.

Conclusion

The REACH process will continue to develop, with strong impact within and outside Europe.

One new area is the effective integration of nanoscale materials. They are in fact within the scope of REACH, but in part due to the absence of standardized analytical methods, their properties are not fully understood and adequate regulation is lacking. This opens a large research and development field, with the goal of understanding the specific hazard created by reducing the size of the particles of a known substance, not to mention the hazards of new nanoscale substances. Ultimately, REACH should be amended to make clear that a substance in the nano state is a different substance as compared to the same chemical in the standard state, and to include specific tests for these new products.

Meanwhile, the REACH Regulation is influencing the specific regulations for biocides, pesticides and cosmetics, with the same goal towards a better protection of the consumer. Let us mention the new European Regulation 1223/2009 on Cosmetics, adopted 30 November, 2009, which also replaces all previous national legislations and includes a registration process. It is the first Regulation which makes reference to nanotechnology, giving a definition of a nanoparticle, specifying tests for cosmetics containing nanoparticles, and making mandatory the listing of contained nanoparticles on the label of the cosmetic. This REACH inspired regulation becomes applicable in July 2013.

The REACH Regulation is also inspiring new regulations outside the EU. Countries as varied as Switzerland, the United States, China, and Turkey are now developing REACH-like schemes and ECHA is exchanging data and know-how with authorities in Australia, Japan and many other countries. Obviously foreign producers exporting to Europe, from multinational companies to large and small Indian or Chinese manufacturers, have had to deal with REACH.

Being optimistic, we can hope that the progressive implementation of GHS/CLP and REACH inspired processes worldwide will help to create a safer world for our children, without slowing technologic and economic development.

Selected Websites for Reference

European Chemicals Agency: http://www.echa.europa.eu
European Chemical Industry Council: http://www.cefic.org

SOURCE OF LEGAL EUROPEAN DOCUMENTS

http://www.eur-lex.europa.eu
http://www.europa.eu/legislation_summaries

ENGLISH LANGUAGE HELPDESKS

For REACH: http://www.hse.gov.uk/reach
For CLP: http://www.hse.gov.uk/ghs

5

Biological Risk

François Bricaire

Biological risk is defined as a risk caused by a microbiological infectious agent, essentially bacteria or viruses and, to a lesser degree, by fungi or parasites. This is a fairly broad definition of a risk that is diffuse–due to the diversity of infectious agents–permanent and potentially evolving. It is different from other major risks such as chemical and radio-nuclear risks. Attitudes about how these risks should be managed have evolved and have been embraced by the technological and sociological developments in modern societies.

Essentially, biological risk comprises the following:

- epidemic or pandemic infectious risks when they become geographically or globally widespread;

- risks caused by emerging or re-emerging infectious agents, that is, spreading extensively, whether these agents are known or unknown. The global spread of multi-resistant bacteria is one such illustration;

- the separate risk of bioterrorism, about which concerns have recently re-emerged, warranting vigilance on the part of governments.

As for other risks, plans to prepare for and fight against biological risk should be implemented and adapted on a regular basis. Updating and activating nuclear, radiological, biological, chemical (NRBC) procedures regularly and as needed is integral to their efficacy.

Description

EPIDEMIC RISKS

This risk has always existed and will always exist. We live in a world of infectious agents, some pathogenic and others not, but all living organisms are born with the aim of surviving. They therefore adapt to the conditions to which they are subjected. In other words, no matter what we do, they will survive in diverse forms. Depending on the circumstances, they can develop and create limited or more extensive infections. Infectious phenomena, in terms of form, intensity and duration, will arise depending on the infectious agent's capacity to develop, its aggressiveness, and the host organism's natural defences or artificially-aided means of defence. This is how epidemics develop; if they become geographically widespread, they turn into pandemics. Humans are contaminated either directly, via an infectious agent penetrating freely through the respiratory or digestive tract (nutrition and hydration, and so on) and overcoming the skin barrier, or directly, via an intermediary that transmits the germ (mosquito, animal bite, and so on).

In the past, notorious epidemics such as plague or cholera instilled fear and terror in populations. Today, concerns have arisen about infectious diseases that are even harder to control or fight than in the past. The risk of African hemorrhagic fevers such as Lassa, Marburg and Ebola has recently made headlines. Severe Acute Respiratory Syndrome (SARS), which emerged in 2003, prompted joint action from international bodies (WHO) and numerous governments aimed at fighting more effectively against this previously unknown and potentially severe infectious agent. Epidemics of arboviruses, essentially transmitted by mosquitoes, regularly occur in various regions of the world. Dengues are the most frequent. Recently, Chikungunya, a long-known disease, has been making headlines by spreading across various Indian Ocean zones. It continues to spread across numerous Asian territories. The West Nile virus, also known in certain geographical zones, appeared for the first time in North America in 1999. Since then, it has continued to rage across the northern part of the continent. And then there is influenza, which stems from a type of virus with multiple variants resulting from diverse mutations. The natural evolution of influenza occurs both epidemically, when a viral mutant appears in a partially protected population, and occasionally pandemically, when a major mutation of the virus creates a new variant against which the global population cannot protect itself.

After the pandemics of the twentieth century, with the most infamous being the deadly virus of 1918, more recently fears arose that a pandemic of the H5N1 'bird flu' would occur. And, in late April 2009, the recombinant virus of swine origin spread across the globe in a matter of weeks, making it the twenty-first century's first genuine pandemic. Other examples are the epidemics of Legionnaire's disease, caused by respiratory bacteria, or those caused by Listeria of food origin. These occurrences illustrate the evolution and succession of infectious agents that can result in epidemics. Some will recur and others, so far unknown or already detected but not yet developed, could become the epidemics of the future. This is why existing surveillance systems across the world need to be improved, so that they can help us anticipate and detect epidemic phenomena as quickly as possible. *However, it is extremely difficult to validate warnings given the many errors and inaccurate details that may occur, creating uncertainty and making certain responses hard to justify.*

Various elements play a role in the evolution of infectious agents or explain why it occurs. Some are natural, such as climatic factors and natural phenomena (floods, quakes), and some arise from conditions or expressions of man's way of life on his environment, such as technical progress, livestock breeding methods, food habits, means of transport, dam constructions and so on, which modify local ecologies.

Factors of globalization can accelerate the appearance and spread of epidemic infections (global events, transportation, and so on). Anything linked to the environment largely affects epidemic phenomena, in addition to the aforementioned conflict between the infectious agent and man.

The emergence in May 2011 of the *enterohemorrhagicescherichia coli* (EHEC) bacteria in the Hamburg region is a good example of the problems that can arise from emerging epidemics and their consequences. This *E. coli* 0104H4 bacteria affected over 2,000 people in the north of Germany, including a number of severe cases due to the secretion of a toxin causing renal, hemorrhagic and neurological disorders. This severe epidemic illustrates the importance of a rapid enquiry to determine the source and implement the necessary means to stop the epidemic phenomenon. These bacteria are often carried in the digestive tracts of domestic animals and can contaminate water or food products, which can then secondarily contaminate humans. It is extremely important to enforce hygiene regulations in this domain.

INFECTIOUS RISK

Infectious risk exists through the evolution of infectious diseases. Some are permanently or virtually permanently established. These are referred to as endemic phenomena, justifying regular processes intended to combat the risk worldwide.

WHO has established three essential priorities to fight:

- the worldwide spread of tuberculosis, which is linked to poverty;

- infection due to the Human Immunodeficiency Virus (HIV), which is still spreading in some countries around the globe and is kept in check more or less easily depending on the region via preventive measures and antiviral treatments;

- malaria, which is rampant in many tropical zones despite measures taken and which causes a very high rate of infant mortality.

There are many other infectious diseases such as typhoid fevers and infectious gastro-enteritis, irrespective of the infectious agent and bacteria responsible for respiratory or urinary infections.

Multi-resistant bacteria

The existence and development of multi-resistant bacteria is a highly disturbing global trend. These are bacteria that have become resistant via various antibiotics and therefore create difficult-to-treat infections. These range from staphylococcus bacteria to germs of digestive origin, such as colibacillus bacteria or Mycobacterium tuberculosis. The emergence and spread of these germs is frequently the direct consequence of inappropriate use of antibiotics worldwide. The unjustified use or inappropriate choice of antibiotics throughout the world is extremely worrisome at a time when the industry is struggling to find or develop new antibiotic molecules.

Currently, there are two main types of multi-resistant bacteria: those frequently circulating in the general population, through selection caused by pressure to prescribe antibiotics, and those currently developing to a large extent due to bacteria secreting enzymes that inhibit many antibiotics and that can become totally resistant germs. These germs, carried by individuals in their digestive tracts, can be passed on to others, notably during hospitalization. They are widespread in certain countries such as India, Israel and Greece. It is vital to detect them very quickly through a systematic examination of the stool samples of patients who have been transferred from these geographic zones. Consequently, appropriate and indispensable hygiene measures can be taken to avoid contamination via contact between patients, which potentially leads to an epidemic phenomenon.

Hence, it is essential to promote better use of antibiotics to avoid more and increasingly severe difficulties in the treatment of infections. And, while this recommendation applies to bacteria, it will also become the case for viruses and other infectious agents if care is not taken. While the resistance has a natural base, it accelerates considerably with the use of anti-infectious treatments, particularly when inappropriate.

Nosocomial risk

This risk is now more commonly known as hospital-acquired risk. It has become a modern-day concern: being hospitalized, receiving treatment and then becoming infected is a real problem and one that is hard to comprehend. However, it should be stressed that nosocomial agents are associated with microbial agents either from external sources (environment, hospital staff) or from the flora of a patient, which makes prevention more difficult. Germs present in the patient's body which are pathogenic due to the pathology that led to hospitalization in the first place are very difficult to avoid. And when a patient is frail or has become vulnerable after treatment, occurrence is more likely. The risk becomes even more serious when bacterial agents are resistant to antibiotics.

BIOTERRORISM

This risk is in a category of its own, since it arises directly from human intervention and irresponsible action that is essentially politically motivated.

The risk level doubtless ranks below chemical risk, which is easier to exploit. Biological risk is theoretically possible with numerous infectious, bacterial and especially virological agents, but on reflection it is more limited in practical terms. Indeed, it is difficult to unite all of the necessary elements. Infectious agents must be obtained, cultivated, contained, transported and released at the site of terrorism. In principle, they have to be sufficiently virulent and at the same time manageable to avoid spreading them to the aggressor or sympathetic parties. In practice, only a limited number of infectious agents can therefore be used.

Germs can be classified into the following three categories based on the probability of use (A, B, C by decreasing order of probability in Table 5.1 below).

Table 5.1   Classification of germs

Category	A	B	C
Germs	Bacillus anthracis Yersinia pestis Francisella tularensis Poxvirus (Smallpox) Filovirus (Ebola, Marburg) Arenavirus (Lassa, Machupo) Clostridium botulinum toxin	Coxiella burnetii Brucella sp Burkholderia mallei Alphavirus (Venezuela equine encephalitis) Ricin Staphylococcus Enterotoxin B Epsilon toxin of Clostridium perfringens Pathogens transmitted through food	Virus Nipah Hantavirus Tick-borne hemorrhagic fevers Tick-borne encephalitis
Characteristics	Easy to disseminate, transmission between humans High mortality Panic and social disruption ++	Harder to disseminate Moderate morbidity and mortality	Emerging potentially usable pathogens Availability Easy to produce and disseminate High morbidity and mortality

Extract from US CDC, Atlanta.

In the A category, the first germ listed is *bacillus anthracis,* which causes anthrax. It best meets the aforementioned requirements of use. Recent history has confirmed that it is clearly the easiest to use. Bacillus anthracis is highly pathogenic when inhaled, causing pulmonary anthrax; less frequently, when absorbed, it causes digestive anthrax. The secretion of a toxin is responsible for the severity of the disorder. Antibiotics are only efficient with early treatment.

Other bacteria can be used that cause septicemia, with pulmonary dysfunction in particular: *plague bacillus, tularemia bacillus.*

Among viral agents, the *smallpox virus* is the most feared. Though smallpox has been eradicated worldwide, some strains have been preserved in certain countries and, unfortunately, some have been dispersed in various parts of the world and are difficult to locate. Use of the smallpox virus is therefore possible, although it is the most dangerous for terrorists. A number of governments consider that this risk is real enough to prepare for it. The response to this virus is essentially vaccination, but it is difficult to implement since the procedure remains complicated and leads to adverse side effects for many. Because of the contagious nature of this virus and the potential severity of its effects, it is justifiably feared.

Other viruses could be used such as hemorrhagic fevers of African origin and certain influenza variants, to mention just a few of the main possibilities. However, infectious agents that have been manipulated and modified and that are therefore potentially more virulent can be more easily dispersed and are more resistant to anti-infectious agents.

In bioterrorism, a number of elements are worth bearing in mind:

- The difficulty of diagnosing initial cases, in particular when responsibility has not been claimed for the act of terrorism. Due to incubation periods for infectious diseases of variable duration, dispersion of contaminated subjects between the terrorist act and the first cases diagnosed can cause geographical dispersion, making the situation harder to control.

- Unlike chemical terrorism, which is limited, a biological attack can, depending on the infectious agent's capacity to spread, be extensive.

- Doctors have limited knowledge of these infections, since many are now very rare. Detection and diagnosis are therefore complex. Despite training, and reintroduction of the subject into medical curricula, there are still fears that diagnosis is not systematically easy.

- The speed of detection and response is directly linked to the efficiency of anti-terrorist policies. Whether stemming from terrorist organizations, diverse fanatical movements or action taken by certain countries, biological risk is not inexistent and modern means of disseminating infections rapidly can easily be envisaged.

Apart from the terrorist risk, we should not forget the similar risk of a laboratory dissemination accident. This can be caused by infectious agents or the numerous diseases on which researchers are working. Recently, epidemics caused by the SARS coronavirus occurred, but fortunately these were reported rapidly. Because of these incidents, extremely strict precautions need to be implemented and complied with. High-level biosafety laboratories (P4 category) have been built to optimize response capability and ensure a high level of safety standards.

Risk Responses

Responses to infectious risk have existed for a long time and have evolved thanks to massive progress in medicine and infectiology. For example, surveillance of infectious diseases, hygiene regulations, vaccinations, anti-infectious therapies, treatment aimed at stimulating the organism's means of defence and improved means for detecting infectious agents are all basic elements in the fight against infectious risks. However, recently, approaches and responses to infectious risk have evolved, changing the way in which we envisage the fight against epidemic and contagious phenomena.

CHANGES IN THE FIGHT AGAINST INFECTIOUS RISK

The fight against constantly evolving infectious phenomena, which can occur in epidemic surges and which are more or less foreseeable, is conducted on a regular and permanent basis using the aforementioned responses. Results are more or less efficient depending on the agents under attack, the phenomena observed and local conditions for fighting the infectious risk. Efforts will grow and improve to reduce risks and risk occurrence and confront all individual and collective infectious problems.

Likewise, the fight against nosocomial infections has become a priority. Tougher hygiene regulations, updated written procedures, and compliance with regulated and verified technical measures should prevent this type of infection from occurring insofar as possible. And, thanks to improvements in the architectural conditions of healthcare structures, highly qualified personnel and adequate staffing levels, this risk has been lowered. This risk not only has potentially serious individual consequences, it can also become extremely costly for society.

PREVENTIVE APPROACH

In addition to the aforementioned basic elements, a new concept has gradually emerged and is starting to take shape and acquire a structure. The objective is to foresee the risk and organize ways of preventing an epidemic and contagious phenomenon before it occurs. Failing this, the aim is to stop it, or at least slow it down and diminish the consequences. This concept is aimed at protecting both individuals and the community as a whole, with actions that are therefore both individual and collective. Its development has been made possible by a number of factors: thanks to technical progress, the surveillance and detection of infectious phenomena have greatly improved. Anticipation is more targeted and new means of microbiological diagnosis exist, but they still do not provide the level of detail needed for more adapted implementation by policymakers. Due to globalization, needs have perhaps grown and the desire to tackle the problem has increased. This desire has been expressed by the global organization WHO and relayed by many of its members. In our changing societies, particularly those in rich countries, new demands have arisen: negative phenomena like epidemics are no longer acceptable. Not so long ago, epidemics were endured and at best fought, with reports compiled ex-post facto. Today, many countries either no longer accept this approach or accept it a good deal less. Since forecasts can be made, measures are therefore demanded. Policymakers are expected to react more or less responsively. And the principle of precaution is a response to these demands.

IMPLEMENTING RESPONSES TO INFECTIOUS RISKS

Some responses in the fight against infectious risk are complementary to existing procedures, while some have been established to tackle a specific infection and others are aimed at tackling a defined set of risks. In the hospital sector, these are expressed in emergency 'white' plans. In particular, we will discuss recently established plans made in response to the emerging infectious phenomena and new risks we have described. They have been progressively constructed around older versions but draw on more recent warnings and experiences. Events such as the African hemorrhagic fevers of some years ago, bioterrorist acts, envelopes possibly containing anthrax, the SARS epidemic, the H5N1 influenza pandemic alert in 2003, and the A (H1N1) influenza pandemic of swine origin have helped to build on and update these plans. This is why, in addition to plans aimed at individual risks, there is a shift towards a globalization of plans. Over time, measures need to be harmonized and adapted. As well as developing awareness of the measures taken by individual countries, there is an international dimension to consider. Through discussion, decision making and reports, harmonization can gradually be achieved. Taking into account the reflections of all parties is indispensable if these measures are to be drawn up and implemented both efficiently and reasonably.

Over the years of constructing these plans, objectives and approaches have evolved. For example, the idea of stopping transportation to reduce epidemic transmission was deemed unrealistic given the need to maintain business as usual. The closure of schools was also logical in theory, but would have to be modulated according to the circumstances. Hospital services also have to modify their approach based on their experiences of epidemic events. Hospital reception services and decisions to place infected patients according to sectors, whether specialized or not, need to be adapted, amended or possibly corrected.

These plans need to be established not only at the domestic level, but also at the level of service providers in both public and private enterprises. Business continuity planning (BCP) measures must also be requested and established. Individuals must feel involved and able to apply the measures described as essential, and the community must continue to function. The aim is to limit, insofar as possible, inconveniences caused by the measures envisaged. Adaptability, flexibility and fluidity based on the epidemic's characteristics and evolution, are the keys to success.

Plans need to allow for management of the infectious phenomenon. They should channel and reduce collective and individual concerns and prompt a sense of civic responsibility.

PRACTICAL APPLICATIONS OF RISK RESPONSE RESOURCES

France was one of the first countries to devise plans to implement these procedures. The Ministry of Health, aided by experts, has been responsible for restructuring plans and organizing the fight against infectious disease. Thanks to the campaign against influenza, progress has been made not only in the response specifically aimed at this infectious agent, but also in the overall approach, the necessity of which we have stressed.

The main elements in the fight against infectious disease can be summarized as follows:

Basic structure: defence zones

Though the French Ministry of Health is the main organization involved, numerous other government structures also have a role to play, including Ministries of the Interior, Justice, Employment, Defence, and so on. The need for an inter-ministerial co-coordinator soon became obvious and the *Délégué Interministériel pour la Lutte Contre la Grippe Aviaire* (DILGA) was set up to tackle bird flu. The defence zone is the optimal base unit. In each defence zone, one or two referral centres have been designated, with the east and west zone having two referral centres. For these infectious problems, the referral centre is attached to a university hospital centre with an infectious diseases service. The referral centre is in charge of organizing all elements inherent to the epidemic phenomenon, both locally and for the entire zone.

In addition to the central government organization headed by the Ministry of Health and backed by both the Ministry of the Interior and ultimately the Prime Minister, the referral centres are overseen by administrative authorities (*préfectures*). The executive structures are the hospitals, with the *service d'aide médicale d'urgence* (SAMU) emergency service upstream, which can be contacted via the emergency phone number (15). These services regulate and, at the start of an epidemic phenomenon, they transfer suspected or confirmed cases to the referral services. Cases are then isolated, necessary samples are taken and, with the referral laboratories, the first cases are detected. They allow the authorities to take the necessary steps. Subsequently, systems are extended, as needed, to other hospital structures and the local physician is consulted. Depending on the characteristics, intensity and gravity of the infection, various actions deemed necessary are launched at the appropriate moment. Crisis units at various levels are there to regulate action in a timely and appropriate fashion. For the Ile de France Paris region, the referral service is *Assistance Publique – Hôpitaux de Paris* (APHP), which then set up the *Coordination Régionale du Risque Epidémique et Biologique* (COREB) centre to conduct practical operations, linked to the SAMU 75 emergency services and referral hospitals, with four for adults, one for children.

For bioterrorism, after detection, the response is based on activation of the Biotox plan in a defence zone, under the authority of the *préfecture*, along with the SAMU and referral centres, with the latter co-coordinating actions that are adapted to needs: the type of infectious agent, number of cases and how the phenomenon has evolved.

Plans for patient care

Each hospital has been asked to prepare a plan for the care of infected patients (admission and safety) approved by public authorities, with hospitalization according to the variable resources and the organization of supplies. Likewise, deprogramming measures for certain activities must be planned to manage all medical activities and more specialized care linked to the epidemic phenomenon. It has been proposed that sectors be split into High Viral Density for infected patients and Low Viral Density. This can be modulated by giving priority to the care of infected patients in a particular sector of the various specialized services (cardiology, maternity, and so on). These measures could concern public and private healthcare structures.

Likewise, care from the local physician is structured around medical practitioners, supported by directives specified in the plans. The priority of keeping infected patients at home to avoid taxing the hospitals, which must be reserved for severe or complex cases, can only be met via well-structured and vigilant surveillance services in towns. Coordination and collaboration between the hospital and the local authorities are therefore indispensable.

Business continuity planning (BCP)

These plans aside, public and private enterprises (transport, energy, banking, food, and so on) also have business continuity plans aimed at optimizing staff protection and maintaining activity. They are developed in collaboration with occupational health and safety medical services. The company needs to be organized, protect itself, adapt to circumstances and be proactive.

In brief, the plan should include a means of organizing activity (impacts, responsibilities, key jobs, and so on) and work measures, of taking preventive measures (updating the unique document and the professional risk prevention plan), of communicating on these measures and of consulting staff and staff representatives.

Collective measures

Without going into further detail on the means used, the fight against infectious epidemic phenomena requires compliance with collective measures that could involve implementing restrictions in meetings and public gatherings.

- Hygiene measures:
  - Washing hands, use of hydro-alcoholic solutions and cough and sneeze management are examples. Barrier measures include the use of masks to reduce airborne transmission of disease, surgical masks and FFP2 protection masks. They should be used during periods of contamination risk. This type of protection entails a change in habits and behaviour. It also requires organizing supplies, distribution, the means of distribution, rules of use for anti-infectious agents (antibiotics and antiviral substances such as the famous Tamiflu in the treatment of influenza) and inventory renewal.

- Vaccination:
  - Vaccination is a crucial element in fighting an epidemic, particularly one of viral origin: it involves managing orders once vaccinations have been developed, establishing strategies for use, managing instructions and the means for delivering vaccinations, potentially defining priority populations, ensuring the traceability of applications and potential incidents or accidents and verifying efficacy. Should it become necessary to organize a mass vaccination programme, a number of difficulties may then arise. As an example, preparing vaccinations against smallpox or the A influenza pandemic turns out to be a difficult and complex task.

This set of non-exhaustive means is the basic toolbox for best practice at the appropriate time. Best practice entails not using all tools simultaneously and ensuring that they can be modulated to meet circumstances, the infectious agent and how the epidemic is evolving. Accordingly, measures must be adaptable and flexible.

It is essential to ensure optimal protection for the population faced with the infectious phenomenon rather than trying to maintain normalcy at all costs. Keeping everyday life as normal as possible means determining many practical points to the best of abilities. However, solving one element often sparks several other problems that all require solutions and so on.

Our final comment on these practical aspects concerns the role of the media, which is often criticized for being excessively focused on the source of concern. Instead, media should provide calm, complete and objective information. It is important to be able to help in these circumstances by giving the best possible information, prompting a rational and responsible response. Positive participation by the media should involve working with the relevant authorities and passing on the best possible messages to the population in the fight against the epidemic risk.

Critical Observations of Systems

All responses set up for the good of the population should be open to criticism. Permanent and uncontested vigilance could lead to decisions that will be considered inappropriate or excessive. For instance, measures imposed by the discovery of listeriosis could seem excessive and have potentially serious consequences for third parties or companies finding themselves in difficulty.

For nosocomial infections, legitimate steps very often result in the risk of medical malpractice suits, which may be appropriate in some cases and not at all in others. This risk could potentially lead to fear in health workers. Reducing risks also means avoiding excessively bold or complex action. And it would be an unfortunate outcome if medical teams were loath to undertake new techniques or actions which, though potentially life-saving, are audacious and therefore risky.

In terms of responses to epidemics, policymakers may find themselves systematically saying they are doing too much or not enough. The principle of precaution is excellent, but should be applied judiciously and cautiously. It should always be applied for the good of all and not for political ends. It must be applied in a measured fashion and be relative rather than absolute.

The announcement of an epidemic phenomenon should not incite fear and anxiety in populations. This is difficult to achieve and appropriate and efficient communications are therefore essential. A global response that excludes nobody who is or feels concerned is therefore crucial. Preparatory measures should be permanently conducted to adapt civic attitudes to the possibility of such an event. This is clearly the best way to avoid fear – a bad advisor – which is more likely to prompt criticism and rejection. A series of announcements that raises the risk of appraisal error may discredit all parties involved. If policymakers cry wolf, citizens will no longer react when it is really necessary. Also, plans and measures cost money, and some may consider the cost excessive. While possible for wealthy countries, these investments may seem disproportionate, particularly when they concern virtual risks, whereas the real and serious risks are in developing countries that do not have the means to combat them.

Should we look backwards and tackle epidemics as we did in the past? While theoretically possible, this seems very difficult. It would constitute a step backwards. Forecasts, precautions and preparations have become the acceptable responses in today's demanding societies. Risks are no longer acceptable in themselves. And even costly investments can be considered valid responses since they offer reassurance. In terms of the lives saved and the economic losses avoided, a set of diverse responses will be highly profitable at the end of the day. Doubtless, more changes are needed, such as confirmation of organizational means. More flexible, fine-tuned plans should be possible in the future, making them more efficient and credible and more likely to be followed.

It is essential to offer explanations to the public via improved communications and to provide citizens and professionals with better training in this new approach to managing biological risk.

As a result, it should be possible to gradually adopt better and more flexible responses with relative calm, less media hype and fewer drawbacks for society. But there is still work to be done by governments, international policymakers, professionals and individuals.

References and Bibliography

Bricaire, F. La grippe: une infection nosocomiale (A hospital-acquired infection). *Presse Médicale*, 35 (10), 2006: 1415–1416.

Bricaire F., Bossi P. *Bioterrorisme (Bioterrorism)*, Elsevier Editions, Paris, 2003.

Bricaire F., Bossi P. Infections virales émergentes (Emerging viral infections). *Bulletin de l'Académie Nationale de Médecine*,190 (3), 2006: 597–609.

Bricaire, F.,Saldmann, F. *Les Nouvelles Épidémies: comment s'en protéger? (How to protect yourself from the new epidemics?)*, Flammarion, Paris, 2009.

DerenneJ.-P., Bricaire F. *Pandémie 'La Grande Menace (Pandemia, the Great Fear)*, Fayard, Paris, 2005.

Derenne J.-P., Bricaire F. Preparing for the next influenza pandemic. *Revue des Maladies Respiratoires*, 23, 2006: 17–21.

Franz D., Jahrling P., Friedlnder A., et al. Clinical recognition and management of patients exposed to biological warfare agents. *Journal of the American Medical Association*, 278: 399–411.

Goossens H., Ferech M., Vander S.R., Elseviers M. Outpatient antibiotic use in Europe and association with resistance: a cross-national database study, *Lancet*, 365, 2005: 579–587.

Henderson D., Inglesby T., Barlett J., et al. Smallpox as a biological weapon, consensus statement.*Journal of the American Medical Association*, 281, 1999: 2127–2137.

Inflesby T, O'Toole T., Henderson D., et al. Anthrax as a biological weapon, 2002: updated recommendations for management. *Journal of the American Medical Association*, 287, 2002: 2236–2252.

Ippolito G., Puro V., Heptonstall J. Hospital preparedness to bioterrorism and other infectious disease emergencies. *Cellular and Molecular Life Sciences*, 63, 2006: 2213–2222.

Lee N., Hui D., Wu A., Chan P., Cameron P., Joynt G.M., et al. A major outbreak of severe acute respiratory syndrome in Hong Kong. *New England Journal of Medicine*, 348, 1986: 1986–1984.

6

Supply Chain Risks

Eric Wieczorek

Supply chain disruptions have been at the forefront of many newscasts, magazines and newspaper editions for over two decades now.

Your grandfather's supply chain was very different from today's complex way of manufacturing a product or rendering a service. In the past, most companies manufactured everything under one roof or sourced their components from local, or geographically close, suppliers.

Today, competition and innovations have allowed organizations to source products and services from geographical areas, which were previously deemed as inaccessible.

One may then ask, 'But what are the costs? And do they outweigh the benefits?'

The benefits have been steep and dramatic. Companies have been able to reduce lead times, improve services and bring innovative products to the marketplace, often at cheaper prices than they could produce on their own by procuring from a third-party supplier. It is easy to envision how economies of scale work in the favour of a component manufacturer who can serve many different customers rather than the customer itself building its own components. The components manufacturer, thanks to the sheer volumes and possibly favourable labour costs, is able to produce better, faster and cheaper, allowing you the customer to reap the benefits and compete better.

The 'costs' on the other hand have also been steep for some companies, so steep that they have ceased operations. Market globalization, today, means that many companies are sourcing their products and services from third parties and in turn sell those products and services to other third parties and even to their own suppliers. At the beginning of the chain your company may be your supplier's customer, while at the end of the chain, once your product or service is ready for sale, your supplier maybe your company's customer. Take the example of a computer chip manufacturer who sells their chip to computer manufacturers. That computer manufacturer may very well sell its finished product to the chip supplier. There is a multitude of examples like this one in almost every industry.

We understand that nowadays virtually all goods and services one uses are relying on a web of suppliers and customers; goods which are end products in one industry are mere components in another and there goes the supply chain!

The impact of supply distribution is now easier to conceptualize and we realize that its ramifications can be vast and leave virtually no organization immune to disruption.

As risk managers or risk professionals, what are we to do to manage the risks of our companies supply chain(s)? If 'knowledge is power' we must begin to understand all aspects of supply chain risks. We must be prepared to answer the seven basic questions: 'What, where, when, who, how, how much and why.'

The goal of this chapter, focused on supply chain risks, is therefore to begin educating ourselves, as risk professionals, about the risks inherent to our companies' supply and demand chains. After all, and in my personal opinion, what greater risk is there to an organization than its inability to sell its products or services? (I am sure there are exceptions, but at the time of writing I am unable to think about 'what' in the world could be a bigger risk to a company than its supply chain).

Throughout this chapter we will refer to the 'Organization', the 'Company', the 'Enterprise' or any synonym which we will capitalize. By using such capitalized words, our intent is to refer to the organized business (publicly or privately held) for which its risk professional(s) is/are in charge of the supply chain risks evaluation.

Definitions

THE SUPPLY CHAIN

'Googling' the words 'supply chain definition' would surely bring out many very different definitions of the same concept. It seems as though everyone understands what a supply chain is but everyone has his or her own definition. There does not seem to be an official definition of what is a 'supply chain', therefore, I will attempt to produce my own:

> *The Supply Chain [of a company] is the process and network, which enables a company to manufacture, sell and deliver a product or service to its customers. Its network is comprised of retailers, distributors, transporters, manufacturing or service suppliers. Its process involves the planning, procurement, manufacturing, delivery of goods and services and handling of the returned goods.*

The Supply Chain Council SCOR Model defines the supply chain process as five subprocesses:

- *Plan*: The process which evaluates supply and demand in order to best meet requirements for production, sourcing and deliveries.

- *Source*: The process or procuring goods/services in order to meet planned or actual demand.

- *Make*: The process which transforms products to a finished state to meet actual or planned demand.

- *Deliver*: The process which brings the finished goods or services to the end customer in order to meet actual or planned demand.

- *Return*: The process which handles customer-returned products.

THE SUPPLY CHAIN RISKS

Here too, there are many definitions of 'supply chain risk' but no 'real' consensus or official definition. For the purpose of this chapter, we will define supply chain risk as 'a threat, which could result in the inability of the Organization to supply its current and/or future customers and/or jeopardize the current and/ or future demand for its products'.

There are many ramifications to this definition; some obvious ones are loss of market share and customers, loss of current and future revenues, reduction in shareholder values and possible disappearance of the Company all together. For the Organization to survive, it must understand what factors affect the supply chain risk and where the threats are coming from.

Real 'Life' Examples of Supply Chain Disruptions

The most widely-used example of supply chain disruption in the industry is the case of Swedish company Ericsson Telecom. It has been the object of many news articles and cited at countless risk management, supply chain and business continuity presentations I have had the opportunity to attend.

- *The Phillips/Ericsson case*: In 2000, a small ten-minute fire started at a Phillips plant in Albuquerque, NM. The plant had to shut down for weeks. The Philips plant manufactured cellular phone chips for two customers, Nokia and Ericsson. Ericsson had no backup supplier. The shortage of parts cost Ericsson US$1.7 billion in the quarter and four years later revenues were still less than 50 per cent of the pre-fire levels. The company is now known as SonyEricsson.

- *The Toyota case*: The 1995 Kobe earthquake closed Japan's largest port for two months and created about US$100 billion in physical damages. As a result of damage and lack of transportation, Toyota, amongst many other world auto manufacturers, was unable to produce more than 20,000 cars on schedule.

- *The port of Los Angeles case*: In 2002, the port of Los Angeles, CA closed for ten days as a result of strikes. The US economy suffered a reported US$1 billion to US$2 billion loss per day. This not only stopped delivery of goods but also paralyzed many industries due to supply shortages.

Other cases:

- *US Northeast blackout*: In 2003, the US Northeast suffered a blackout. This affected many residents and companies in the transportation, water and power supply, and telecommunication industries.

- *Mattel and Fisher*: In 2007, Mattel and Fisher-Price recalled millions of toys made in China due to lead-containing paint.

- *Bayer*: In 2008, a Bayer Pharmaceutical plant suffered an explosion in West Virginia. Besides the production shutdown and loss of profits, a federal investigation revealed that the lack of response from the company had exposed members of the first response unit and the entire local community to extremely serious risks. Bayer's reputation was tarnished.

- *Nestlé*: In June 2009, Nestlé was forced to recall its Toll-house cookie dough brand from the market as a result of E-coli being found in its manufacturing plant.

- *Iceland volcanic eruption*: In April 2010, a volcanic eruption over Iceland resulted in the melting of massive amounts of ice and flooding destruction in the country. The ensuing ash cloud contributed to the paralysis of the European airspace and the complete or partial closure of many airports. It was estimated that the air transportation industry was impacted to the tune of £130 million per day.

- *Japan earthquake*: In March 2011, an earthquake followed by a Tsunami hit Japan creating the biggest natural disaster in Japan's history. Many industries (automobile, information technology, power generation and so on) were affected by crippled buildings, shortage of parts, unreliable electrical supply and manufacturing plant shutdowns.

The above examples demonstrate how devastating a supply chain disruption can be. It also indicates that there are many sources of disruption; some within the control of a company and some driven by acts of nature.

Between 1989 and 2000, Professors Singhal and Hendricks of the Georgia Institute of Technology and The University of Western Ontario conducted a study of more than 800 companies, which publicly announced supply disruptions during that period.

The study found that, over the three-year span after the disruption and across all industries, companies experienced 33 to 40 per cent lower stock returns compared to their peers. Their share price became 13.5 per cent more volatile as those companies suffered dramatic drops in operating income, return on sales and assets. The study also evidenced the lasting effects of such disruptions. It reported that most companies still reported negative changes in operating income, sales and inventories two years after the first report of an event.

Supply Chain Risk Factors

Supply chain disruptions can have many shapes and impacts. The first step in evaluating a risk is understanding its possible sources. While the examples above show us that disruptions may arise from the misfortunes of a partner or a supplier several layers removed from our supplier, they can also result from the Organization's own failures, and external factors which cannot be controlled. There are many reasons why a supply chain may fail and seeking the eradication of all supply chain risks are often impractical, costly, time and resource consuming or even impossible. We can categorize, however, all types of supply chain risks based on four factors (Figure 6.1). Let us look at those factors in order of the most controllable by the Organization to the least.

THE ORGANIZATION ITSELF AS A SOURCE OF SUPPLY CHAIN RISKS

Natural and man-made disasters

From the Bayer example above, we realize there are hazards associated with manufacturing goods or services. Fires, flood, explosions, equipment and machinery breakdowns are potential events which can easily lead to the temporary or permanent loss of use of a company's assets or employees. The usual causes for such events are related to people or engineering but may also result from natural catastrophes such as flood, typhoon, hurricane, or earthquake, or both human and natural as in the case of the recent 2011 Japan earthquake; the nuclear disaster resulted from the inability to cool off towers

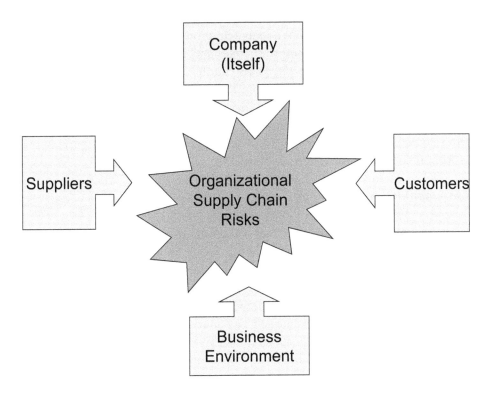

Figure 6.1   Supply chain risk factors
Source: Eric Wieczorek

because the back-up power generation was impacted by the tsunami that flooded the power plant location. Had the generator been elevated above the height of the wave, likely power supply would have been available.

Employees and labour

Many organizations are forced to stop their production because of employee and labour disputes. The example of the port of Los Angeles in 2002 illustrates how employees and labour contract can put an entire region and its economy on its heels. The port of LA lost revenues and profits but the brunt of the impact was felt by all those businesses which depended on goods arriving from Asia and other continents to the West Coast.

Foreign and homeland political environment

In their quest to produce faster, better and cheaper, companies are also exporting their skills and technology to countries where labour is cheaper but where the legal system does not adequately protect their intellectual property or where governments and political changes may affect their ability to produce goods from the infrastructure within the country.

Meanwhile, back in the country where the company has its headquarters, laws and regulations are also changing and companies may face restrictions from doing business or importing and selling goods from certain parts of the world forcing to re-route or create new supply chains.

Management decisions

Globalization has changed the face of doing business in virtually every industry. In the early century, most companies embraced vertical integration and manufactured most of the goods they needed to produce their products. The level of control over supply, costs and risk was higher than today as the company had oversight over the entire chain. For the most part though, those companies sold their products in their own markets.

In the 1980s, companies began to take note of the challenging issues of globalization. To become more competitive they started to adopt 'just-in-time' inventory, lean manufacturing and outsourcing techniques to achieve economies of scale. Today the most world-renowned shoemaker does not manufacture any shoes but merely sells its designs. As in the above-mentioned Ericsson case, other companies can end up in situations where they have no back up supply or not enough inventory to face a potentially devastating and long disruption.

Business model

Some companies, because of the way they generate their revenues, are more prone to business interruption (BI) than others. The business model, in evaluating BI, is a critical piece of the puzzle.

We can illustrate such a fact by taking the example of a manufacturing entity versus a company whose sole business is to sell auto insurance policies.

The first is likely to rely on a physical location (owned or third party) to manufacture its products. In the absence of any business continuity plans and any stocked finished inventory, our manufacturer is vulnerable to many man-made or natural perils which could immediately disrupt 100 per cent of its expected incoming revenues as well as many other potential repercussions. The financial impact is sudden, immediate (because it has no inventory) and will last until manufacturing operations can resume and the first finished product is available for sale.

On the other hand, the insurance company sells an intangible product and collects its premium either up front or throughout the policy period. It may be organized with geographically-dispersed sales agencies or may sell its product via the Internet.

A disruption affecting its agencies or its Internet-based business would not affect the portion of periodic premium payments to be collected on policies already in force. Such type of business model diminishes the impact of supply chain disruptions since a likely, large portion of revenues would continue to be collected.

Business systems and information technology

Rare are the companies today which do not rely on computers and data management systems. The supply chains of a large number of companies have been positively impacted by innovations in computer technologies. These technologies have enabled the Company to collaborate with suppliers and customers and improve its ability to plan procurement activities and forecast demand. Such need for supply chain visibility has also increased the Company's dependence on computer systems while reducing the ability of human response to a critical situation. A computer error or malfunction is then likely to have quick and direct repercussions on the Company and beyond.

SUPPLIERS' RISKS/CONTINGENT SUPPLY RISKS

As demonstrated above, the organization's supply base is an important factor in evaluating the risks inherent in the Company supply chain. Supplier risk will emerge whenever the Organization's ability to continue delivering its products and services are jeopardized by a disruption encountered at suppliers or, in a cascading effect, at the suppliers of the supplier.

The word 'supplier' refers to either the direct suppliers (that is, the supplier from which a finished product/service becomes a component or raw material of the Organization's products or services) or the suppliers supplying your direct suppliers.

Like the Organization under evaluation for supply chain risks, the supplier faces many, if not all, of the same risks. The supplier itself has its own internal procedures, policies, business environment, employees, management and customers affecting its ability to bring to market the products/services needed by the Organization.

The cases of sole or single sources of supply are mainstream, either because it is not possible to source from another supplier or because the supply chain goals have dictated that more economies would be extracted out of the concentrating procurement activities with one supplier. In a similar situation, in 2001, the French aircraft carrier Charles De Gaulle was impacted by the breakage of a propeller. Only one company had the technology to make the specifically designed propeller and the company had to be rescued from bankruptcy.

While controlling the Organization's own risks factors may be a challenge for most risk professionals, evaluating and managing contingent risk is an integral part of managing supply chain risks.

CUSTOMER RISKS

At the other end of the supply chain spectrum is the customer. Often predicting our customers' demand is a challenge and thus a source of potential disruption. An unanticipated decrease in demand can result in lengthy and expensive reshuffling of the supply chain, the potential shutdown of manufacturing lines, write-off of considerable inventory (see CISCO US$2.1 billion inventory write-off in 2001), or the idling of manufacturing plants. Such changes in demand can result from sudden changes in customer tastes, and need for new technology which may render an entire supply chain obsolete if it were not anticipated.

The Company's customer landscape is another source of worry. The number of customers the Organization deals with is directly tied to the likelihood and severity of supply chain disruption. The risk professional must realize whether the Company's customer base is concentrated within a particular industry or geographical area and anticipate the facts that the industry may change or that a natural disaster could affect multiple customers at once. Following Hurricane Katrina, many residents of the city of New Orleans were physically displaced throughout the USA and subsequently made the decision to never go back. It resulted in a large loss of customer base to many companies and the city of New Orleans.

THE COMPANY'S BUSINESS ENVIRONMENT

The business environment undoubtedly bears an impact on the company supply chain. By business environment, we include such risk as currency exchange, political risks, laws, regulations and even culture in the home, supplier and customer countries.

Currency fluctuations, from a supply perspective, affect the Organization by, on one hand, either increasing or decreasing the ability of delivering goods at competitive prices to customers. Similarly, from a demand perspective, it affects the customer's ability to buy goods or services.

One implied consequence of political risks is the inability to deliver goods or services within or from a country as a result of political instability, war or strifes or even sanctions or tariffs imposed by host governments.

The laws and regulations of a particular country may give some indications as to the oversight and procedures in place to protect the Company. In certain countries, the land belongs to its people and the implantation of an office or subsidiary may result in the complete loss of control of the goods or services emanating from the location. It may also mean that potential trade secret, technology and know-how are not adequately protected from piracy and counterfeiting. Counterfeit goods cost companies enormous amounts of sales and profits and are sources of great potential damage to brands and company reputation.

In the United States, the Food & Drug Administration (FDA) governs the landscape of pharmaceutical and food manufacturing for humans and animals. The regulation developed over the years has made it more difficult for companies to bring new products to market or even continue manufacturing products based on methods that had been used years ago. Companies must abide by the regulations of 'Current Good Manufacturing Practices' or face potential government-imposed shutdowns and possible sanctions.

The FDA, in 2010, warned Johnson & Johnson of possible legal action and injunction, should the quality issues in manufacturing its Tylenol brand remain unsolved. The risk the company faces in such a case is not only the cost of a recall, but also the loss of future market share, the possible indefinite shutdowns of certain plants (which may affect other products) as well as severe to irreparable damage to its reputation.

The Supply Chain Risk Within the Context of Enterprise Risk Management

The recent economic downturn has really highlighted the need for risk professionals to begin managing risk at the organization level. The function is increasingly becoming a true risk management approach as opposed to, in its purest form, an insurance purchasing function. The Company needs to manage risk at the 'enterprise level' and demonstrate a willingness to manage even 'currently' uninsurable risks.

The mortgage crisis has had worldwide ramifications, which for many companies belonged to the above category of 'business environment risks'. Most companies were hit as their own customers were impacted by the crisis and, in a snowball effect, ended up affecting industries otherwise far removed from the original customer.

By the time the crisis was uncovered it was too late and many governments were trying to find out how to keep 'things afloat'. The next step in such a situation is to find out why it happened in the first place and what can be done to prevent it from happening again. The warning signs were there and scandals like Enron and others were just the premise for governments and companies to realize that more transparency, governance and risk management is necessary. In such situations, employees, shareholders, suppliers and customers are systematically the ones affected. Credit agencies, whose sole purpose is to evaluate the creditworthiness of those companies, had egg on their faces; they did not have the procedures and processes in place to foresee the warning signs.

In contrast, it is important to also realize that the very Company takes risk everyday in its course of doing business. Most investors understand the concept of 'no risk no rewards' and demand a premium in the form of interest rate or return on investment when making risky investment decisions. The investor wishes to be able to make well-informed decisions and is now asking for 'transparency' through enhanced risk disclosure by the Company.

The Enterprise Risk Management (ERM) movement we are currently witnessing is an attempt to systematically address and communicate what risks are inherent to a company and establish a process to either manage the risk or make conscientious decisions to live with the unmitigated risks. The supply chain risk is one of them; albeit, an important one!

CONTRASTING THE ROLE OF THE RISK MANAGER VS. THAT OF THE SUPPLY CHAIN MANAGER

As seen in the past, companies looked for vertical integration and controlling all aspects of their supply chain; from raw material to finished products. For the risk managers, the stakes were also simpler; he or she had visibility or authority over an organization that spans a larger range of the manufacturing process.

Today, the competitive environment has driven the supply chain towards maximizing the efficiency and externalizing most of the costs out of the network. Strategies such as off-shoring, outsourcing, just-in-time inventory, vendor-managed inventory (VMI), supplier consolidation, sourcing from emerging economies, lean manufacturing, all aim at reducing short- and long-term costs out of the Company's balance sheet and income statements.

The risk professional is somehow now responsible for managing the safeguarding of the company assets and for enterprise-wide risk management.

The strategies for managing the supply chain goals and managing its risks imply that both risk manager and supply manager have very contrasting goals. Finding that enterprise balance means the supply chain must mind its risks while risk management must mind the goals of the supply chain. In the end, both organizations work to ensure the survival and future of the Company.

Let's illustrate how each organization drives that goal in a way that is often conflicting (Figure 6.2). To the supply chain manager 'survival' may mean availability of finished goods or services and the lowest cost possible, while to the risk manager survival means emerging out of a critical situation with the least harm done. In essence, what separates the functional goals and their impact on the company survival are the philosophies pre and post supply chain disruption.

The Supply Chain Risk Management Framework

As with most perils, the framework for managing the risks of the Company's supply chain is based on their identification and quantification so as to determine initially where the risks are and what could be their impact to the company. The next step is deciding whether the risk can be reduced. Some risks can be mitigated

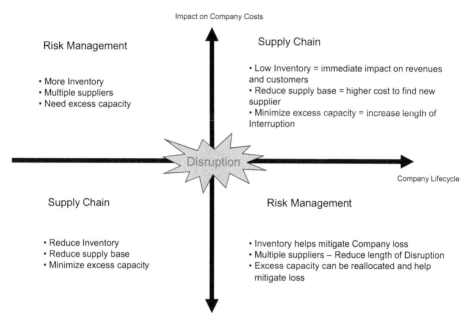

Figure 6.2   Roles of the risk manager and the supply chain manager
Source: Eric Wieczorek

and some cannot; an organization may decide not to do business within a certain country because of political instability, however it may be unable to secure a second source of raw material supply due to intellectual property rights.

If after mitigation a potential financial impact still remains, the Company would then need to decide how to finance the risk. Ultimately as the company changes, its supply chain also changes and the risk 'du jour' may not be that of tomorrow; a different strategy may then need to be devised. The Company must monitor the risks and periodically review whether yesterday's assumptions are still valid and whether the potential financial impact has changed.

IDENTIFICATION

The four sources of risk to our supply chain were identified and detailed in the above-mentioned supply chain risk factors section. Internally most companies are organized with employees, in-house process or a collection of processes as well as physical infrastructure to manufacture or produce a service. Externally, they rely on suppliers and customers to make and sell their products. Collectively, suppliers, Company and customers are subject to the risk associated with the local and global business environment. As defined above, supply chain risk is a threat which could result in the inability of the Organization to supply its current and/or future customers or jeopardize the current and/or future demand for its products. Let's analyze each of the products and services the Company produces and answer the following questions (Figure 6.3):

- What internal factors can affect our products?

- Which suppliers contribute to the production of our products?

- Who are our customers and how many are they?

- What are the environmental factors affecting all three relationships of the chain?

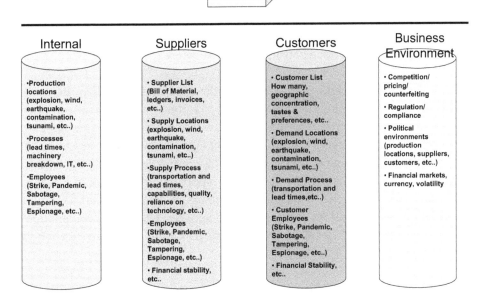

Figure 6.3   The four pillars of risks
Source: Eric Wieczorek

QUANTIFICATION

Quantifying a risk is giving it the dimension of 'importance' to the Organization. Some risk may be catastrophic but relatively infrequent while some others could happen often but have low severity.

We could look at the probability of a particular plant within our manufacturing network burning down to the ground or being the victim of a devastating earthquake; but what information will that really provide to our efforts of managing the supply chain risk?

Say the complete loss of a plant will result in a financial impact of US$1 million and the probability of it happening is 10 per cent:

- Does that mean we should insure the plant for US$100,000?

- Does that mean we should put aside US$100,000 every year and expect to pay US$1,000,000 once every ten years?

- What if the probability figure is wrong and such a loss happens more than once in ten years?

- Where would I even find a probability figure I can rely on within my organization? I most likely do not have such history. I may never even have had such an event before.

As a risk manager (and this is my personal opinion) I am much more interested in evaluating what is the maximum impact my potential loss/event can have on the company rather than taking the chance that it may or may not happen. If it does not happen, perfect! But if it does, at least I know how much with 100 per cent probability or close. The concept of Maximum Foreseeable Loss (MFL) is better suited to my needs. At least I can report the 'true' value of a risk to my management and say 'the business interruption risk of an earthquake/or devastating fire to plant XYZ is somewhere between US$0 and US$1 million' with a relatively high level of confidence every time the quantification is performed.

Based on this philosophy, we can focus on quantifying the severity of a risk or its MFL rather than its probability.

With every supply chain disruption, the Company faces the following potential simplistic financial impacts:

1. loss of profits;

2. continuing expenses for the duration of the event;

3.   expenses incurred to implement mitigation plans and recover from a disaster as soon as possible;

4.   loss of market share, reputation, customers and/or suppliers for short period of time or even forever;

5.   loss of capitalization, shareholder base and/or credit rating;

6.   the snowball effect of all of the above, which can ultimately contribute to the bankruptcy or acquisition of the Company.

It will be challenging to any company to quantify the loss of reputation and market share following a major disruption. If bankruptcy ensues, it then becomes evident that, ultimately, expenses have outweighed the remaining earning power of the company. Such a situation is highly dependent on customers and shareholders' behaviour after the event. That behaviour will undoubtedly be affected by the speed with which the company can recover and by how much it can financially absorb from the hit of the disruption.

As a result, our intuition is that there is a correlation between the quantification of impacts 1 through 3 above and the effect on the potential recovery of the company. The higher the immediate impact on profitability of the Company is, the more likely it is to lose significant market share and shareholder value, and the less likely it is to survive.

The ability of the Company to overcome the financial impact from lost profits and expenses immediately resulting from a disruption is thus an indicator of its ability to ultimately survive.

For simplicity, we will refer to 'lost profits and expenses' as 'business interruption (BI)' (items 1, 2 and 3 above) as opposed to the 'indirect' potentially less immediate effect of items 4 to 6 above.

The factors affecting the BI value are as follows:

•   The products/services affected by the event. Is it a range of products or the entire portfolio? What is the relative contribution of those products and services to the overall financial health of the Company?

- The ability of the company to mitigate the lost profits and how fast that mitigation can be implemented.

- The cost of expenses which it might incur in order to implement the mitigation plans and those expenses which might continue during the interruption.

Business Interruption Quantification Illustration – A Supply Chain Break Example

The following example (Figure 6.4) envisions the scenario of a Company which suffers a disruption at its Italian plant. The main assumption is that the plant is rendered obsolete in the chain. The supply chain diagram below tells us that raw materials are made in either Puerto Rico or France. The manufacturing is handled at a third party in Germany which then sends the semi-finished goods for final packaging to either Italy or Mexico. Our Italian plant supplies the European and Asian markets while our contractor in Mexico supplies the American markets.

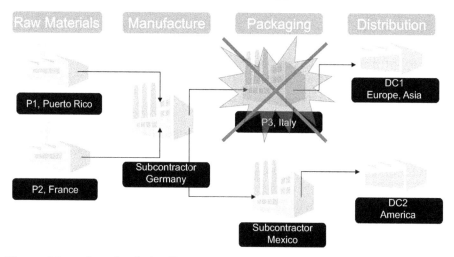

Figure 6.4   Supply chain disruption
Source: Eric Wieczorek

How do we quantify the potential loss of use of our plant in Italy and its resulting impact on the financials of the Company?

The following facts about the supply chain of this product are developed through a careful review of the Company's business model, financials and contingency plans.

- A disruption at our Italy location implies that Distribution Centre DC 1 is idle after it runs out of inventory on hand for the duration of the event and until Italy is able to resume operations and send finished goods.

- DC 1 has on average two months of finished stock.

- The plant in Italy is not capable of supplying goods for a period of three years.

- The product annual profit margin is US$1billion.

- Europe and Asia represent 30 per cent of the annual profit margin.

- Italy continues bearing some expenses at the rate US$10 million per year.

- The Company's contingency plan is to implement packaging operations at its Mexico subcontractor.

- The Mexican contractor has the packaging capacity to absorb normal demand requirements to supply Europe and Asia but it will take six months to ramp operations, bring in machinery and add an additional shift to the production operation.

- The implementation of the Mexico contingency plan will cost a total of US$5 million to the Company.

- DC1 will incur US$5 million of expenses until Mexico can resume supply for Europe and Asia.

Based on the example above, we can develop the following visual representation of the various factors and steps in the evaluation and their impact to the Company's bottom line (Figure 6.5).

It is clear from this example that the Company benefits here from the existence of a Contingency plan, since it has the ability to implement Mexico as a back-up supplier. The same methodology can be used to evaluate the loss of the German subcontractor in the chain. Based on our diagram, the subcontractor is a bottleneck in the chain and the loss of this supplier could mean the entire

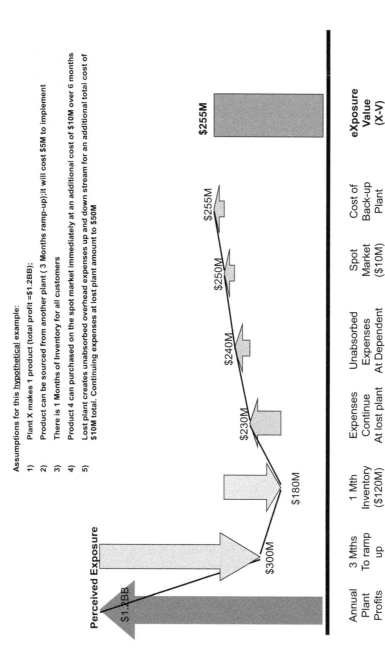

Figure 6.5   Factors and steps in the evaluation

Source: Eric Wieczorek

product and profit margin are at risk while the company would continue to incur significant unabsorbed costs at the plants downstream and possibly also jeopardize its relationship with the Mexican subcontractor.

Quantifying the supply chain risks for this Company would entail repeating this process for each and every product or services in its portfolio, each and every manufacturing location including third-party location until an enterprise-wide view of the risk can be depicted. Subsequently the decision-making process of managing the supply chain risks can begin within the organization. The risk management professional and Company management can then make decisions about risk control and risk financing activities.

The Role of Insurance

The role of insurance is to transfer the financial risks associated with specific perils from the insured to an insurance or collection of insurance companies.

While various traditional types of insurance policies do protect against risks which can be categorized as supply chain risk, the availability of broad coverage for such risks is rather limited at this point compared to the numbers of risks which can trigger a supply disruption and cause financial harm to the Organization.

Political risk and traditional property insurance policies do offer elements of response to BI but on a limited basis. Business insurance coverage is triggered by political unrest (such as confiscation, embargo, closure of borders, and so on) or physical damage to the insured or its supplier's property. Additional limitations are typically placed on the policy wording to address possible geographic or industry risk accumulation or interdependency between suppliers and customers who may be insured and reinsured by the same insurers. As such, property policies limit the amount of financial coverage for contingent BI or for physical locations which are not named under the policy. Loss of market share and reputation are also hazards which are not addressed.

Today we are observing the emergence of supply chain insurance products. The coverage tend to address a broader range of risks, however the availability tends to be very limited and can be somewhat unattractive for companies already accustomed to large deductibles.

The supply or value chain is like the blood or a vital organ of the company. Without it, or because of a significant disruption to it, the organization faces many risks affecting its ability to generate revenues all the way to the possibility of jeopardizing its very survival.

Conclusion

The supply chain risk management is vital to the company but so are its efficiency and its ability to deliver the highest quality product or services at the optimal costs. The organization must decide between acceptable levels of risk versus efficiency of its vital organs. History has shown that vertical integration was not the solution for achieving lean manufacturing and extracting most costs out of the supply chain. Recent history has also shown that the techniques utilized to achieve optimal efficiency and remain competitive in today's global marketplace have generated new risks unheard of so far and which turned out to be outside the control of the organization implying lower levels of control.

As the emergence of those risks has now become evident and a number of real-life examples are resurfacing every day, the industry is taking note. Organizations are beginning to realize that there needs to be a certain balance to be achieved between risk and efficiency. Today the concept of vertical integration is coming up again on the strategy agendas of senior executives. Since every organization is unique in what and how it produces its products and services, the strategic and tactical solutions to managing the supply chain and its risks must be unique as well. The solution probably lies somewhere between vertical and horizontal business models.

The balance between those two models is the answer to the strategy of managing risk while risk quantification is key to the tactical decisions to be factored accordingly into strategy formulation.

References and Bibliography

Supply Chain Operations Reference (SCOR) Model – Supply Chain Council Reference or the SCOR 90 Overview – http://www.supply-chain.org.
Food & Drug Administration (FDA) – http://www.fda.gov.

7

Country Risk

Olivier Hassid and Lidija Milasinovic

The assertion of global economic logic was accompanied by several crises. The first and second oil shocks of the 1970s, the various country crises between 1994 and 1999 – Mexico, Asia, Russia and Brazil – and, more recently, the subprime crisis in the United States. These successive crises shook the economic sphere and revealed that the notion of country risk is rather poorly factored into the development of economic strategies. While there is no doubt that opening up borders has contributed to economic growth,[1] it is equally clear that it has also been instrumental in increasing threats, fears and vulnerabilities. For this reason, we are justified in asking how this notion has evolved with each successive economic, political and social hazard, and what its place is in the current context.

We shall begin with a discussion of the research in this area, which has in fact led to a redefinition of the contours of the notion of country risk, as it responds to external changes that are themselves linked by new variables. In theory, the economic–financial angle[2] is a less predominant aspect, while the consideration of social, political, ideological and cultural factors is given greater weight in the analysis. Our intention is to compare this speech with reality and see how well it holds up to scrutiny.

Then, we will present the country risk as a support function for various management tools. Our goal is to confirm its strategic positioning within the economic, commercial and political development of the business.

---

1   Historically, the rise in trade coincides with global economic growth. Between 1948 and 1992, the value of global trade went from US$57.5 billion to US$3,600 billion. Over the same period, the volume of global trade multiplied six-fold. Simultaneously, the planetary revenue was multiplied by a factor of three. This dual development suggests that the increase in global trade is related to growth in global revenue (Rainelli, 2003).

2   '*Regardless of the domain of human cultural manifestations, reducing them to their economic causes only is not exhaustive in any sense whatsover, even in the case of economic phenomena properly speaking.*' Translation from the French, Max Weber's *Essai sur la Théorie des Sciences*, Plon, Paris, 1917, p. 10.

The Country Risk

Knowledge of the 'country risk' is a relevant indicator for businesses, which face increasingly varied and numerous risks. Treatment of country risk first implies a structured analysis of the current situation, and this in turn requires to outline the concept of country risk and highlight its evolution to redefine the position of each developed or developing country, on the international scene.

The first part of this chapter focuses on a general presentation of the country risk, while part two addresses the impact of globalization on the country risk.

GENERAL FRAMEWORK OF THE COUNTRY RISK

The country risk is characterized by its definition, its identification, its assessment and its management role.

Definition

There are three approaches to the 'country risk', depending on whether we are looking from the perspective of the risk creditor and type of risk, the foreign debtor entity and the nature of the risks, or the risk generating events, that is, the type of possible crisis (Gautrieaud, 2002).

These approaches are intended to address the numerous questions that an investor, a business or a bank may ask. These questions mainly concern the nature of the risk, as well as the return on each investment/transaction, which are relatively different between a developed country and an emerging one.

Definitions of the notion of country risk are many and at the present time we do not have a universally accepted one. Over time, they tend to become more precise, as they further factor in the mutations surrounding the risk.

In 1975, country risk was defined as *'the uncertainty linked to the political and economic environment of a business and its effects on the business organization'* (Brewer, 1975).

In the 1990s, country risk was defined in the following manner:

> *The country risk can be defined as the risk of the materialization of a*
> *loss, resulting from the economic and political context of a foreign state*
> *in which a business carries out some of its activities (Marois, 1990).*

Today, it is defined by a more complete approach:

> *The country risk is defined as the occurrence of observed or latent*
> *volatility in business conditions in a country over the expected return*
> *on investment. It encompasses economic and financial elements, but*
> *also sociopolitical, ideological and even regional ones, linked to all types*
> *of transactions in a given country (Bouchet and Groslambert, 2002).*

This definition, by including factors other than economic and political ones, shows the multidimensional nature of the notion of country. We will use this definition in the present chapter.

The pillars of country risk

As the definition above suggests, the country risk is polymorphous. This polymorphous nature may take a variety of forms: the economic risk, the political risk, the judiciary–legal risk and the regional risk.

- The economic risk 'arises from the volatility of economic and financial aggregates. It is analyzed and anticipated by factoring in the decisive principles of macroeconomic growth (balance of payments, price, investment, monetary and budgetary policy, and so on). After examining the economy's internal and external competitive strength, which includes observing the quality of its infrastructure and institutions, a map of the country's structural and situational strengths and weaknesses can be drawn up' (Bouchet and Groslambert, 2002).

- The political risk 'encompasses the threat of destabilization and submission to the arbitrary and disregard for the rule of law in the foreign country. The risks of volatility, both internal (coup d'état, civil war, and so on) and external (terrorism, regional conflict, and so on), are analyzed on the basis of the probability of their impact, over the short and medium terms, on the volatility of return on investment'[3] (Bouchet and Groslambert, 2002).

- The judiciary–legal risk 'affects the stability and the transparency of the regulatory and hence of the business environment' (Bouchet and Groslambert, 2002).

- The regional risk: 'the globalization of markets entails an interdependence of the economies of various regional blocs, with heightened risks of contamination of financial crises. These are linked to the gregarious instinct of private investors, who consider the emerging markets as just one more asset class in their portfolio' (Bouchet and Groslambert, 2002).

The risks mentioned above are considered to be major due to their higher likelihood of occurrence. They can be contrasted to so-called minor risks. It should be borne in mind that this list can be supplemented by two other risk categories.

The first is social. Very often, as the definition suggests, it is attached to the notion of political risk. But this amalgam results in an incomplete or even truncated picture of the social risk, which is much more than just a component of political risk. It is a factor of instability that can have serious consequences for the company's productivity and corporate image, especially if it has a high media profile. Therefore, it is critical for the company to be able to deal with the social risk, which is an indicator of the prevailing climate (the relationship between management and labour unions, for example) within the business, particularly during crisis periods: 'social strategies need to be revisited with the aim of factoring in the existence and actions of newcomers. It would be an error to limit it to the management of relations with representative labor unions, which are the company's usual interlocutors' (Landier, 2001). Social players may include community organizations, media organizations or even political groups.

The second is societal, by which we mean the convergence between the political, economic, human, cultural, sociological, geopolitical, scientific, philosophical and psychological environment. This tendency varies from one

---

3   It is important to specify that the sovereign risk is often confused with the country risk. The sovereign risk corresponds to the risk attached to the state/government and to the public administrations of a given country and its capacity to repay its debts and honour its obligations, while the notion of political risk is much broader.

country to the next. Companies need to adopt a humble and respectful attitude towards the local traditions and customs of the host country they are doing business with.

The set of risks mentioned are highly interdependent. Their juxtaposition opens up new risk categories, such as corruption and debt. The Asian crisis of 1997 is just one of many examples: the political crisis caused a high degree of economic instability that was encouraged by a high degree of corruption, debt and so on.

The notion of country risk also covers ecological, product, industrial, human, IT risks, and the like. As the list is long and common to each business organization, it is important to organize and prioritize the risks. Once they have been identified, they can then be assessed.

Measuring country risk

There are various approaches to assessing country risk. All of them have one point in common: they run up against the inherent difficulty of assessment due to the fact that political and social environments are in perpetual motion and hence potentially unstable. Among the rather large number of methodologies that exist, we have chosen to present three.

- The first is the technique known as rating. This method consists of rating and then ranking countries on the basis of various indicators, such as per capita Gross Domestic Product (GDP) and political parties. The countries are ranked from most to least risky. The rating may be global, or it may concern only one specific variable of the risk. In this case, the analysis focuses on economic and financial instability following currency depreciation problems, payment default or any other event that may impair financial or commercial transactions. As an example, the rating system enables us to assess the issuer's capacity to honour its obligations to creditors and/or the capacity of a security to generate capital and interest payments in accordance with the agreed-upon schedule of maturities, due dates or dividends. The advantage of this method lies in its simplicity and low cost. Conversely, its reliability has been criticized, since the objective assessment of risks has not been convincingly demonstrated. Moreover, this rating system does not provide any indication of the possible future return on an investment, or on the volatility of the issued securities, or on the liquidity of a particular security. Nor does this method offer any way of predicting crises and conflicts (the invasion of Kuwait by Iraqi soldiers, revolutions in Arab countries, and so on). Lastly, the assessment criteria can rapidly become obsolete.

- The second technique is dynamic segmentation. It entails a qualitative analytic grid-based method that consists of identifying the most representative socio-cultural or socio-professional segments of a country in order to measure its level of political stability. This level is then used to monitor political, economic or social events that could represent a risk for a foreign business present locally. Current users of this approach include Coface, the World Bank and BNP Paribas.

- The third and last is the probabilistic method, which involves imagining as many scenarios as possible – primarily political and social – that could occur, in order to measure the consequences of occurrence on local investments. As an example, certain decisions and measures taken by local policymakers or by the government of the country may set off negative events such as nationalizations, coups d'état, strikes, wars, riots, bombings, kidnappings, and so on.

Today, businesses cross these different approaches in order to arrive at the most complete and the most refined possible analysis prior to envisioning a system for managing the risks they have detected. As this complementary approach illustrates, businesses have become aware of all the decisive factors governing a society (or in any case a significant number of them).

Managing the country risk

The country risk is a 'theory of the diagnostic' (Meunier and Sollogoub, 2005). The diagnostic serves as a role and the country risk as a function. It should enable companies in general and investors in particular to identify and treat the risks they will be confronted with. Analysis enables us to define the diagnostic that will be used to treat the risk or risks in question. The role of country risk management comes into play at this stage in the process, the goal of which can be summed up as follows: '*The fundamental role of risk management is to transform the company's risk profile by reducing or even eliminating undesired risks and encouraging the taking of other risks, those that are desired and knowingly and willingly accepted, in order to transform them into opportunities'* (Paris and Aubin, 2002). The dual goal, therefore, is to reduce risks to a maximum and to transform them into opportunities. Looked at in this way, risk management boils down to creating value.

Organizing the country risk management process is a long and complex task, and the efficiency of the outcome is contingent on the adoption of a robust structure and a disciplined methodology. First and foremost, a set of objectives must be drawn up. This requires asking a certain number of questions, such as: How important is the risk? How should the complete set of detected risks be managed as a whole? What resources should be used? Should these risks be centrally managed from corporate headquarters or directly onsite? Who should manage the risk? What level of corporate management should the country risk manager report directly to? How should the team be assembled? How should the company's ability to manage risks be assessed? And so on.

As a general rule, the risk organization model corresponds to the business or organizational model, that is, it is a function of its size, its business lines and its strategy. The risk organization will be implemented at the Group level before being adjusted and adopted at the subsidiary level, much the same as business units are. This dual interpretation offers the advantage of providing a global vision combined with an expert perspective, mobilizing all players around a plan of action. The whole must be supported by effective internal communications in order to fully leverage all available information and knowledge.

Properly speaking, there is no country risk management process per se. As a general rule, we are more likely to refer simply to risk management. The methodologies are numerous and respond globally to the following organization:

1.   Identification, assessment and ranking of risks. Generally presented in the form of a map, this step is the most important one in the process. It requires information for input that is precise and timely.

2.   Risk treatment. The options for risk treatment are adapted depending on the risk and determined on the basis of corporate strategy.

3.   Monitoring evolutions of risks and risk treatment applications
      in the form of reporting. This step allows us to oversee all of the
      actions carried out.

4.   Leverage and feedback.

The country risk is no longer thought of as simply a notion; it has become a genuine
diagnostic, analytic and management tool that is gradually being adopted by
business organizations. The country risk is becoming a credible value. To preserve
this credibility, the country risk – like changes in society – has to constantly evolve
in order to remain in alignment with a world that is in a state of perpetual motion.

TOWARDS A NEW WORLD

The country risk has become more complex with globalization. Its evolution is
related to a number of different factors, as set out below.

Emerging countries

The concept of emerging countries, or of emerging markets, was born in the 1980s
as a way of talking about developing countries that offer economic and business
growth opportunities for investors and businesses alike. This concept harkens
the notion of 'new industrialized nations', whose development has accelerated
in the past ten years. Currently, use of the term emerging countries varies with
the institution and the economist. The list of countries that qualify as emerging
is not official. Here are a few examples. In 2005, the bank Goldman Sachs listed
Brazil, Russia, India and China, collectively referred to as BRIC (the bank is
credited with coining this acronym), plus ten 'major developing economies'
(Bangladesh, Egypt, Hungary, Iran, Mexico, Nigeria, Pakistan, The Philippines,
Thailand, Turkey). In 2007, the World Bank devised its own category, known
as the 'emerging economies', to classify China, India and the 'other countries'.
In 2008, Ernst & Young borrowed this term to refer to the BRIC plus Argentina,
Mexico, Saudi Arabia and South Korea. The same year, the Boston Consulting
Group, PriceWaterhouseCoopers and Crédit Agricole created their own lists. In
April 2011, the BRIC group became BRICS with the addition of South Africa to
the club, whose members comprise the planet's major emerging countries.

While the term developing country characterizes a country in terms of its
economic and human development, the term emerging country tends to focus
primarily on the economic aspect of development.

The emerging countries have gradually acquired a significant position in the global economy, through their growing role in the capital markets as well as in markets for goods and services. On a collective level, they have become important for the global economy and for global stability. On an individual level, the pace of growth varies from one country to the other. The BRIC group, China in particular, stands in sharp contrast to the others. This difference is well illustrated in a document entitled Overview on Country Risk (BNP Paribas, 2010). According to the BNP Paribas economic research department, the catch-up phase is thought to be over for the Asian countries and is nearly so for the countries of Latin America (excluding Venezuela and Argentina). Conversely, for the countries of Eastern Europe, there is still much catching-up to do, because of weak growth in Western Europe and financial instability within the Eurozone. The other emerging countries are not represented. Despite a certain degree of economic recovery for them, they remain synonymous with high instability. Their social imbalance is an obstacle to the development of a middle class which, among other things, allows for the emergence of steady consumer spending levels. In addition, an excessive disparity between social classes can lead to unrest and revolt among the poorest classes or to a certain degree of attraction for political leaders who are able to represent them but to the detriment of certain key moral/ethical values. The example of Thailand, with the rise to power of Prime Minister Thaksin Shinawatra in 2001 speaks for itself. Other examples of instability resulting from various interconnected risks could also be added to this dark picture. There is no lack of negative examples, and they are often the source of various risks: corruption, political, social and so on. Financial instability can be characteristic of the economic instability of a country, related to a corruption risk that in turn is related to a poor justice and legal system.

Nonetheless, and whatever the risk, an emerging country – because it is emerging – remains an opportunity in and of itself. In fact, it happens that investors or entrepreneurs find it more profitable to take a risk even before they have taken the time to improve the management of strategic transactions or operations. In this case, the notion of country risk is only integrated as a last resort into its development axis. Agreeing to assume the risk is similar to what a business would do in any developed country, except that the risk is being taken in an emerging country and hence a country at risk. Obviously, this comment does not hold for every emerging country, and this is precisely where the distinction between them is reinforced. This change in behaviour with respect to certain emerging countries is worth reflecting on in our attempt to rethink the country risk. Should the notions of both emerging country and country risk be revisited? If so, on what basis and using which criteria? Are economic and financial criteria sufficient?

Systemic risk

Systemic risk is defined in terms of the systemic crisis that it generates. We speak of a systemic risk when a specific and unexpected event leads to negative impacts on the entire system, thereby provoking a crisis in its ability to function. Let's take, for example, event X, which affects the financial markets and prevents the delivery of capital. When this situation arises, businesses and investors stop investing, which in turn has economic consequences that are more or less serious, all the way up to recession. The systemic risk is a reflection of the interconnectedness between markets and economic agents, and the result is widespread instability that can produce panic-induced chain reactions which overturn traditional systems and, at the same time, impact the real economy. International institutions have given a common definition to the phenomenon of systemic crisis: *'a systemic crisis is a risk of disruption to financial services that is caused by an impairment of all or parts of the financial system and has the potential to have serious negative consequences for the real economy. The systemic risk is hence the risk that this disruption to financial services will occur and that it will be capable of affecting the entire sector as well as the real economy'* (IMF-BIS-CSB, 2009).

Hence, systemic risk is the result of a multiplication of risks, often inherent in the financial and banking system, and which have been poorly anticipated by risk management, regulatory or internal control structures in place for the financial sector in question. For example, an accumulation of poorly estimated risks, of the macroeconomic imbalance type, can lead to the disruption of a financial institution or a market, giving rise to a shock that leads to the emergence of the systemic risk. In the words of Jean-François Lepetit in his report on systemic risk prepared for the French Minister of Economy and Finance, *'Systemic risk should not be reduced to the sum of the individual risks assumed by financial players. Analysis of systemic risk should be broad, because it concerns all of the activities that go on in the market. Systemic risk concerns every player'*, institutions as well as governments and economic agents. Moreover, systemic risk, by materializing systemic crises, also provokes repercussions beyond the country in question: *'These crises go along with the extension of financial liberalization in the developing countries'* (Aglietta, 1999).

Systemic crises have become more severe since the advent of globalization: they are both increasingly frequent and have greater impacts on a global scale.

The financial systems of some countries have provoked major economic and financial crises. In 1994, the Mexican economic crisis began with the devaluation of its currency, the peso, which then spread to the real economy of the country before sending shock waves around the world, especially in Latin America. The following year, Mexico's GDP shrank by 7 per cent. The Asian economic crisis began in 1997, hitting Southeast Asia first and then spreading to other emerging countries: Russia, Argentina and Brazil. All of these countries then experienced very high rates of inflation.

By the same token, bank collapses have also steadily multiplied, going from an average of ten failures annually between 1945 and 1980 to more than 200 at the end of the 1980s for the United States. In the early 1990s, the banking crisis that hit Norway, Sweden and Finland cost between 4 per cent and 11 per cent of those countries' GDP. The subprime crisis, which began in the summer of 2007 in the United States, arose because the world was awash in liquidities and loans were being granted at very low interest rates. Currently, the public debt crisis affecting Greece, Portugal and Ireland is destabilizing the Eurozone but also significantly impacting the United States.

In light of these examples, it is fair to ask if the systemic risk has not called into question the notion of 'country at risk'. It is true that the systemic economic crises we saw earlier are attributable to emerging countries. However, we have a number of counter-examples that also assign responsibility to the developed countries. In this context, it is clear that the notion of country at risk needs to be revisited.

So-called countries at risk: are they the ones we think they are?

Unlike the 1980s and 1990s, the emerging countries did not cause the current crisis, which began in the United States. In fact, we might well wonder today if the country risk is not primarily attributable to the developed countries. The deal has changed and, with it, the way in which we look at developed and emerging countries. This observation was forcefully made by the research team at BNP Paribas. According to its survey entitled 'Overview on Country Risk', a new country risk map came into focus with the end of the acute phase of the crisis. This map enables us to distinguish among the emerging countries with, on the one hand, those countries that are at the forefront of the global economy and, on the other, those that are behind in terms of international integration, reforms and governance. In addition, this survey promotes the idea that some developed countries should be examined from the perspective of the country risk without being considered a country at risk.

This new panorama implies a reconfiguration of international relations, influenced by the new hierarchical levels of tension between developed and emerging countries.

The various scenarios envisioned by the economic powerhouses to work through the crisis can be the source of tension between them and the emerging countries. The research team at BNP Paribas subdivided them into four categories. These categories concern the squeeze on credit that can trigger a slowdown in growth. They also concern the risk of pressure on production capacities, the rise in commodity prices and hence signs of inflation. In addition, there is the risk of volatility in the global capital markets. The entire mix is subject to issues that arise when monetary policy decouples. To summarize, what emerges is a high risk of financial and currency market reversals. Once again, the tensions are only mentioned with respect to the economic, financial or commercial angle. We think it is important to incorporate other parameters: the social risk and the societal risk.

The social risk is common during a financial crisis, with the following consequences: higher unemployment, decline in purchasing power, impoverishment of the population, rise in existing social tensions, development of an underground economy, and so on. In countries that are already fragile economically and socially, the situation can become explosive when the economic context deteriorates. As an example, we might mention the main oil-producing nations (Iran, Nigeria, Iraq and Venezuela), which frequently fall prey to civil and military unrest, and/or acts of terrorism. The same holds true for countries that are experiencing strong growth despite bad management by the government of natural resources (Russia). In particular, political instability has an impact on the risk of disruption in the supply chain for agricultural goods (certain Asian countries, such as India, Indonesia and Thailand). In addition, some investments are called into question as a result of armed conflicts or an arbitrary decision made by the authorities that deprives the country of economic growth, and deprives its population of the chance to find work. In the area of sovereign risk, the level of debt for some countries leads to late payments on government contracts. Another example would be the exposure to the natural catastrophe risk. In a country that has been hard hit by an economic recession the risk of disaster only exacerbates an already critical situation. Panic, famine and revolt exacerbate the violent behaviour of citizens. The risk of insecurity is very frequent in this type of situation and can take different forms (physical violence, sequestration, and so on).

Even though the new panorama of countries at risk provokes changes in the relations and tensions between developed and emerging economies, we observe that the risks and consequences that are internal to a country do not change.

The societal risk can be an aggravating factor. The variables related to the cultural–historic context and to the composition of the society must be taken into account. When a company chooses to set up a business in another country, it has to take its operating environment into account. As an example, any deterioration in sanitary conditions, such as the lack of access to health care in some countries; the global rise in serious organized crime, mafias and other terrorist activity; the worldwide water problem. When a hotel complex opens its doors in a country where these issues have raised concerns, it must ensure the comfort and safety of its guests but also make sure that it acts with care and caution and that it adapts to its environment rather than imposing the rules of its own personal and business culture locally. Taking the societal factor on board can help to limit and/or manage possible incidents of unrest, piracy, violence, and so on. Through local integration the hotel transforms these potential risks/threats into genuine opportunities for development with the natives. In addition to gaining a certain degree of peace of mind, the hotel business will have the added benefit of acquiring a socially responsible image (Pellerin, 2010).

The growing importance of the country risk demonstrates the extent to which it is sensitive to disruptions. It isn't enough to merely take it into account. It is vital to include the notion of country risk into the strategic development of businesses in order to offer solutions that factor in every level of risk.

The Strategic Function of the Country Risk

The thorough analysis of an ecosystem is decisive in maintaining the competitive strength of the business. The analysis of the country risk, as it was presented in the first part of this chapter and considered here as a key variable of this ecosystem, becomes a strategic pillar in the competitive game. In addition, the business must integrate the country risk into its strategic management principles in order to improve operations. From among the numerous management support functions of any business, we have selected four management tools on the basis of their importance on the human level and the ease with which the country risk analysis can be integrated: project management enables the business to coordinate all of its development related activities; crisis management; sustainable development and security/safety.

The aim of the second part of this chapter is to cross these management tools with the analysis of the country risk and demonstrate that the latter increases the efficiency of each of these tools.

PROJECT MANAGEMENT

The strength of a business is highly dependent on its ability to successfully carry out all of its projects. Project management is standard practice in businesses today. It encompasses all of the actions that need to be completed in order to respond to the needs and actions defined by an organization. It is a diverse and varied activity that may concern – among others – innovation, strategy or construction. To conduct these projects, businesses adopt an approach to project management that helps them structure and organize the project from start to finish. There are two objectives that it must successfully meet.

The first is related to duration: a project is a temporary action that has a defined beginning and end.

The second is related to the cost, due to the mobilization of human and material resources required to carry out the project.

Like the business itself, project management has also become increasingly international, complex and long tail. The project's decision makers must ensure that it meets a certain number of requirements. First of all, project management must meet a set of contractual commitments in terms of quality, performance and technicity. Secondly, it must have a mechanism for ensuring that the various risks associated with the project do not disrupt its smooth rollout. This means taking into account the environment in which these risks could emerge.

Decision makers have to integrate the project's country risk–return tradeoff into their project approach, and ask how they can best manage the country risk related to whatever project they are concerned with. The challenge is to identify all the risks that could have a negative impact on the cost and deadline objectives before considering the range of possible actions to take. The risks to which it may be exposed are multiple. They may come from the internal environment: organizational, operational, commercial, human, financial, technical and so on. They may also be external: socio-economic, geographic, natural, institutional, regulatory and so on. Once they have been identified, the risks can be classified on the basis of their effects, impacts, likelihood of occurrence, detectability, weightings and their criticality indices. Apart from identification, all other aspects are subject to a system of measurement than can either be defined by a score, a scale or a financing weight. Once the classification process is complete, risk treatment action plans should be developed; the residual risk will then be determined once this phase is over. The action plan, through thorough identification of the country risk, will enable the business to convert aggravating risks into acceptable ones. Any global approach to country risk that is associated with a project must include feedback, which is also a very important step that allows the organization to capitalize on experiences within the structure. It will be that much easier to update the approach if there is a change in the phase of the project. In any case, it is highly recommended to monitor risks and update the risk map accordingly on a regular basis.

CRISIS MANAGEMENT

Corporate executives have to start from the principle that, regardless of the nature of the market where their company operates, the environment can become unstable at any time and they can be confronted to a crisis without warning. By crisis, we mean any disruptive and destabilizing situation that can lead to disorder (political, social, economic, geopolitical, climatic and so on) with serious consequences. Crises cause major disruptions, especially if they get widespread media coverage, and can in extreme cases lead to the disappearance of the business. But if the crisis is handled correctly, then a return to business as usual is the expected outcome.

Many works deal with the subject of crisis and the concept of crisis management. There are numerous definitions of the term as well. Our preference is for that offered by Roux-Dufort, which has the advantage of being a complete definition.

> *A crisis is a dynamic process which, in reaction to a triggering event, reveals a series of organizational dysfunctions and inadequacies in terms of management practice. It sets in motion a non-virtuous circle that will degenerate, while at the same time mobilizing multiple*

stakeholders, some familiar with the company and some not (Roux-Dufort, 2003).

Working from this definition, it is possible to build management tools. The main objective of crisis management is to deal with the appearance of a crisis and, in order to do so, it has to have a particular modus operandi. The methodologies are also numerous and varied, and generally entail the following steps:

- The first step concerns the period prior to the crisis. This is an organizational phase that consists of recognizing the risk profile, exploiting the early warning signs, preparing a response with one or more plans of action and structuring the role of each individual in the aim of getting prepared to deal with the crisis.

- The second step takes place during the crisis. It consists of acknowledging the crisis and activating a crisis unit charged with handling the crisis and communicating proactively, both inside the company and out.

- The third step is post-crisis. It consists of a full debrief of all events, soliciting the perceptions of team members and using this feedback to make adjustments to the system and the organization.

The first step is decisive. It implies that the company has asked itself the key questions and has obtained the responses needed before beginning the process of identifying the major risks. These risks have been classified according to different families of possible crises (reputation, financial, health, information, assets, human resources, industrial accidents, natural disasters, crime and so on) associated with risks whose origin implies a strong likelihood of occurrence (for example, media scandal, stock price collapse, product contamination, erroneous information, significant production interruption, loss of a key executive, oil spill, earthquake, hostage taking and so on). The higher the profile of a company – in terms of name recognition and media coverage – the higher its risk profile.

Regardless of the methodology applied, information remains the fundamental component of any crisis situation. The need to be informed is not sufficient; the information in question must be as relevant, precise and transparent as possible. In crisis management, the quality of the diagnosis, the organization and the communication hinge on the quality of the information.

Its efficiency also depends on the manager's ability to obtain this information as rapidly as possible. In addition to providing this insight, the country risk analysis offers the manager information on the local decision-making circuits and hence on the different procedures and conditions for intervention that exist. This aspect is critical when a company has to manage a crisis that occurs in another country, which happened recently to a British oil company with operations in the United States. The country risk should also be based on a solid and in-depth analysis of the media in order to protect the company's image against various ethical crises.

This analysis is done upstream and entails the elaboration of a process whose aim is to restore balance after a defined factor has shaken it. In other words, the country risk analysis has several aims, three of which seem to us to be particularly important for crisis management.

- First of all, it allows us to draw up a risk profile for the business and to position it with respect to the likelihood of occurrence of the latter.

- Secondly, it helps us to prepare the business behaviourally; that is, it prepares the business to act and react. This aspect is fundamental, as it protects against the risk of improvisation. However, improvisation is not totally avoidable; even the most imaginative amongst us find it very hard to imagine every possible scenario. On the other hand, it is possible to reduce the consequences that can rapidly aggravate a challenging situation.

- Lastly, it will enable the business to adapt, revise its judgment, reassess its response strategy and hence protect itself in a context that is changing, anxiety provoking and disruptive.

Analyzing the risk is thus necessary, although a delicate process, since it is part of crisis management as a decisional tool that will enable the business to reduce the impact of the crisis before trying to work through it.

SUSTAINABLE DEVELOPMENT

It is difficult to reconcile economic issues and those inherent to ethics and social responsibility. At the same time, businesses have no choice. On the basis of the definition of sustainable development that was put forth by the

French Ministry of Ecology, Energy, Sustainable Development and the Sea, *'No development will be possible if it is not economically efficient, socially equitable and ecologically tolerable.'*[4] The concept of sustainable development arises from this postulate and was enunciated in 1987 by then Prime Minister of Norway Brundtland during the World Commission on Environment and Development: *'Development that meets the needs of the present without compromising the ability of future generations to meet their own needs.'*

Held once a decade, the Earth Summit brings together world leaders to develop and enrich the concept. The Rio Summit of 1992 was a genuine success, since most of the participating governments agreed to draw up a national sustainable development strategy. The Johannesburg Summit, which was held in 2002, was just as important. It provided an opportunity to assess and supplement the programme that had been launched already. A plan of action containing 153 articles was presented in 2002, covering high priority themes such as water, energy, agricultural productivity, biodiversity and health. In addition, this Summit served as a demonstration that the war against terrorism is not the world's only current problem.

In France, according to the Ministry of Ecology, Energy, Sustainable Development and the Sea, initiatives that need to be undertaken to right the balance between economic issues and social and ecological imperatives are the following:

- 'Government decision-making practices need to change.'

- 'The Government is not the only party responsible for sustainable development. The involvement of all socio-economic groups is needed.'

- 'It is necessary to rebalance the economic power relationship between the Northern and Southern countries.'

- 'It is necessary to create an international institution responsible for ensuring that Government obligations are respected.'

Rising to these challenges and requirements, businesses have opted to adopt a responsible and engaged approach. Corporate Social Responsibility (CSR) intervenes at the global, community and national levels.

---

4   http://www.developpement-durable.gouv.fr/Definition-du-developpement,15067.html.

Sustainable development has become a necessity today, addressing as it does the need to preserve the planet. It is also a source of opportunities for the economy and society. Currently, taking sustainable development into account means balancing three objectives for the business and for society – they are economic efficiency, social equity and preservation of the environment.

This concept has become a corporate priority in the past few years. Businesses are no longer judged only on the basis of their financial and commercial performances: they must have core values and conduct business ethically and responsibly. It will have escaped no one's notice that application of the fundamental principles of sustainable development has allowed some multinationals to acquire a new and virginal image.

Country risk analysis must integrate the issue of sustainable development. It is important, for example, to ensure that the company's presence in a particular country does not disrupt its ecosystem or biodiversity.[5] It also has to verify that its local partners (suppliers, producers and so on) respect their sustainable development charter. For instance, the company must make sure that its suppliers and producers employ adults, ensure normal working conditions and use eco-friendly non-polluting materials.

Today, businesses are obliged to take sustainable development on board if they wish to pursue their own development. Failure to adopt a sustainable development policy can have negative consequences, from product boycotts to investor refusal to accept the risk of being associated with the company. In any case, the business can lose its competitive edge. Accordingly, new assessment criteria are being adopted with increasing frequency. This is sometimes referred to as the intangible dimension, a term that encompasses everything that touches upon image, reputation, ethics, and so on. Ignoring the sustainable development dimension is tantamount to putting the company in jeopardy and running the risk of placing the ethical risk, among others, as a potential risk that should be added to its risk map.

---

5   As Pellerin rightly notes (2010),'A business has to strive to preserve local ways of life and disrupt the day-to-day life of the surrounding community as little as possible. For this reason, respecting specific local cultural practices becomes a factor in long-term stability, starting from the observation that these cultural specificities preceded the arrival of the business and will subsist after its departure. On Madagascar, the Canadian mining company Sherritt had to deal with the persistence of customary rites that prevented the passage of the pipeline across certain regions (…). [To get around this problem], the company had no other choice but to consult the various communities living along the pipeline several times' (p. 104).

The concept, by striking fear in the hearts of businesses while also being positioned as a lever of development, has met its challenge and become by the same token a formidable tool of influence.

SECURITY

> *Ensuring security in the business is another way to plan for and protect the company against risks. Before pursuing this thought, it is necessary to define the concept of security. The English language draws a clear distinction between issues related to malevolence and deliberate action, for which the word security is used, and those related to accidents, for which the word safety is appropriate. In French, conversely, there is confusion between the words sûreté and sécurité. This is partly because both notions refer to the prevention of the consequences of a risk or sector-specific features (nuclear safety refers to the prevention of nuclear accidents, while IT security refers to the protection of networks against acts of malevolence). This explanation supports the observation that the words sûreté and sécurité are still sometimes used interchangeably, to evoke risks related to malevolence as well as those related to accidents (Hassid and Masraff, 2010).*

As is the case with the content of Hassid and Masraff's book, *La Sécurité en Entreprise*, the two words refer to the prevention of acts of malevolence.

Efforts undertaken by businesses in connection with their bid for global development may lead to numerous security problems. When the inequality gap between rich and poor countries widens, acts of malevolence may increase against multinationals as a result of a feeling of injustice on the part of the local population. The list of these events qualified as insecurity risks includes staff security and the security of material goods and financial assets. In addition to threats related to the increasingly global reach of businesses (kidnapping, hostage taking and so on) they may be a result of the increasingly financial nature of economies (money laundering, fraud and so on), the information society (cybercrime, boycotts and so on) or economic competition (counterfeit, corruption and so on). Security and safety must be ensured to comply with regulatory obligations. Directive no. 89/391/CEE dated 12 June, 1989 sets forth the fundamental principles of worker health and safety. It places the assessment of occupational risks at the top of the list of general principles of prevention, in cases where risks were unavoidable at source.

The consequences for businesses are of a different kind. The repercussions go well beyond corporate reputation. The risks related to malevolent acts against people are of a more serious nature. They attract more attention than those that threaten funds, property and other financial assets. Consequently, neither the management of security and safety nor budget allocations is the same. For instance, a business can use extraordinary means to protect itself against armed guerillas or acts of terrorism. This may entail providing armed guards or military units for certain people when they travel. While there is no such thing as zero risk, the goal has to be next to zero when it comes to protecting human lives.

The challenges of security are multiple, and go well beyond the direct protection of people and property. Developing effective prevention policies is an issue of economic importance for businesses. Indeed, the cost of prevention, regardless of what it is, will always be lower than the losses incurred, not to mention the significance of the psychological impact on the population when loss of human life is involved. In addition, the existence of a security system in and of itself is reassuring for the refractory individuals and helps retain the best talent; it also provides greater comfort to investors and shareholders. In light of these elements businesses can organize and reinforce their security accordingly.

Security is driven by country risk analysis to identify and understand threats. Deep knowledge of the various threats requires the development of a full global vision of the insecurity risks the business may be exposed to. Once again, how can the importance of the country risk possibly be overlooked? It is true that security is a full-fledged management function just like project or crisis management. However, analyzing it as a preliminary step supplies all the information that is needed for its accomplishment. It is also fundamental to ensure that the country risk analysis is completed for the tenets and goals of good security management to be fully appreciated.

Conclusion

Using the country risk as a tool of analysis for the prevention and management of risks is a solution that an increasing number of theorists and practitioners support and are adopting. Still subsumed under the more general category of risk, the country risk is slowly emancipating itself and becoming a stand-alone model in its own right. This observation is in part related to the evolving nature of its definition, use and acceptance. The country risk began its career as a negative notion that was thought to be an obstacle to the global development of businesses. Little by little, its position has evolved dynamically, such that it is now conceived of as an opportunity. In becoming a tool that aids in decision making, the country risk is also becoming a strategic issue for businesses and their decision makers.

Nonetheless, country risk analysis has been undermined by the current crisis. Whether the problem is the financial crisis in the United States that spread to the rest of the world (systemic crisis); the Greek, Irish and Portuguese debt crisis, which has destabilized the entire Eurozone; the societal crisis that was revealed with the Arab Spring revolt; or the nuclear disaster at Fukushima that struck Japan, we must ask ourselves what the relevant territory for analysis is and where its limitations lie. And while the country risk is quantifiable in terms of probability, the success that we expect has more to do with uncertainty, which is not. This distinction, between risk and uncertainty, introduced by Knight in 1921, leads us to relativize the efficiency of country risk analysis, which is not an exact science.

We have surpassed the era of pure mathematical speculation and statistics. These considerations serve as supports for thinking and not as means. The country risk cannot be summarized in a simple equation, and socio-cultural factors must be added into this analysis. We know this, but do we really take it into account? Do we perhaps limit ourselves to the realm of the certain? The unstable aspect of what is human, the difficulty of planning or predicting actions and reactions cannot be measured with the help of rating techniques. Up to now, the country risk has been taken into account only by economists, entrepreneurs, bankers, shareholders and investors. Where are the sociologists, the historians, the philosophers and the geographers? At what point should the human sciences be integrated? Isn't the leading actor in country risk the country itself? That which is characterized, in particular, by its territorial space, its people who write their own history one day at a time...

References

Aglietta M. *L'économie Mondiale 2000 (The World Economy)*, La Découverte, Paris, 1999.

Bouchet H., Groslambert B. Comprendre et gérer les risques (Understand and manage risks) in *Le Risque Pays: complexe, multicritère et volatil (The Country Risk: complex, multicriteria and volatile)*, Éditions d'Organisation, Paris, 2002.

BNP Paribas, *Overview on Country Risk*, Paris, 2010.

Brewer T. *Political Risk in Business: New direction for research, management and public Policy*, Praeger, New York, 1975.

Gautrieaud S. *Le Risque Pays: approche conceptuelle et approche pratique (The Country Risk: Conceptual approach and practical approach)*, Université Montesquieu de Bordeaux, 2002.

Hassid O., Masraff A. *La Sécurité en Entreprise (Corporate Security)*, Maxima, Paris, 2010.

Knight F. *Risk, Uncertainty and Profit*, Boston, MA: Hart, Schaffner& Marx; Houghton Mifflin Company, 1921.

Landier H., *Se préparer à l'imprévisible, Management social (Preparing for the unpredictable, social management)*, point de vue n°613, 2001.

Marois B. *Le Risque Pays (Country Risk)*, PUF, Paris, 1990.

Meunier N., Sollogoub T. *Économie du Risque Pays (Country risk economics)* La Découverte, Paris, 2005.

Paris J.-M., Aubin C. L'organisation de la maîtrise des risques (Risk managment organiation) in *Comprendre et Gérer les Risques (Understand and Manage Risk)*, Éditions d'Organisation, 2002.

Pellerin M. La responsabilité sociétale des multinationales: un engagement éthique au service de leur sécurité (MNC social responsibility: ethical engagement applied to their security), *Sécurité & Stratégie*, Hors-Série, Juin–September, 2010.

Rainelli M. *Le Commerce International* (International trade), La Découverte, Paris, 2003.

Roux-Dufort C. *Gérer et Décider en Situation de Crise: outils de diagnostique, de prévention et de décision (Manage and Decide in a Crisis Situation : diagnostic, prevention and decision tools)*, 2ᵉᵈ, Dunod, Paris, 2003.

Sionneau B. *Risque Politique, Risque Pays et Risque Projet (Political Risk, Country Risk and Project Risk)*, Cahier du Lips, 1996.

Further Reading

Ansoff H.-I. *Stratégie du Développement de l'Entreprise (Enterprise Development Strategy)*, Éditions d'Organisation, Paris, 1989.

Benhmansour H., Vadcar C. *Le Risque Politique: dans le nouveau contexte international (The Political Risk: in the new international context)*, Dialogues, Paris, 1995.

Dripaux B., Aubin C. Gestion de projets and gestion des risques (project management and risk management in *Comprendre et Gérer les Risques (Understand and Manage Risks)*, Éditions d'Organisation, Paris, 2002.

Fontugne M., Kervern G.-Y., Hunter M. Gestion de crise: préparation, anticipation et action (Crisis management: Preparedness, anticipation and action), *Comprendre et Gérer les Risques (Understand and Manage Risks)*, Éditions d'Organisation, Paris, 2002.

French documentation, *Le Financement de l'Économie (The Financing of the Economy)*, Paris, 2006.

van Greuning H., Brajovis Bratanovic S. *Analyse et Gestion du Risque Bancaire: un cadre de référence pour l'évaluation de la gouvernance d'entreprise et du risque financier (Banking Risk Analysis and Management: A reference framework for the evaluation of the business governance and financial risk)*, ESKA, Paris, 2004.

Gond J.-J., Igalens J. *La Responsabilité Sociale de l'Entreprise (The Corporate Social Responsibility)*, PUF, Paris, 2008.

International Monetary Fund – Bank for International Settlements, Central Statistical Bureau, 2009.

Lagadec P. *La Gestion des Crises: outils de réflexion à l'usage des décideurs (Crisis Management: Decision support tools for decision makers)*, McGraw-Hill, Paris, 1991.

Lagadec P. *Apprendre à Gérer des Crises: sociétés vulnérables, acteurs responsables (Learn How to Manage Crises: Vulnerable societies, responsible actors)*, Éditions d'Organisation, Paris, 1993.

Lepetit J.-F. *Rapport sur Le Risque Systémique (Report on Systemic Risk)*, Paris, 2010.

de Larosière J. Le rôle croissant des pays émergents sur la scène économique mondiale, 2008. http://www.canalacademie.com/ida2724-Pourquoi-les-pays-emergents-sont.html

OECD, Economic Outlook, 2002 and 2009.

Porter M.-E. *L'Avantage Concurrentiel (The Competitive Advantage)*, InterÉditions, Paris, 1986.

Pras B. *Les Firmes Multinationales Face au Risque (Multinational Firms Faced with Risk)*, Economica, Paris, 1980.

Stephens J. *Managing Commodity Risk*, John Wiley & Sons, Chichester, 2001.

The Financial Times and PriceWaterhouseCoopers, The Art of Crisis Management, *Les Échos*, Paris, 2001.

The French Labor Code, Articles L 4121-1and following, and Article R 2121-1.

Weber M. *Essai sur la Théorie des Sciences (Essay on the Theory of the Sciences)*, Plon, Paris, 1917.

Webography

Coface – http://www.cofacerating.fr

Ernst & Young – http://www.ey.com/fr

Ministère du Développement Durable – http://www.developpement-durable.
  gouv.fr

PriceWaterhouseCoopers – http://www.pwc.fr

The World Bank – http://www.worldbank.org

United Nations – http://www.un.org/fr

PART II
Strategic Management

8

Strategic Management

Anne Barr, Catherine Antoinette Raimbault,
Patrick Leroy and Jean-Noël Guye

Detecting emerging risks must be an integral part of the risk management process. According to ISO 31000:2009 (Risk Management – Principles and Guidelines), 'The organization's monitoring and review processes should encompass all aspects of the risk management process for the purposes of… identifying emerging risks'.

This task of identification appears to be invaluable with respect to:

- The magnitude of emerging phenomena, as illustrated in the preceding chapters: a major turning point in the technical and industrial development of the twenty-first century in the case of nanotechnologies, the third industrial revolution in the case of information and communications technologies, acceleration of the rapidity and the extension of epidemic infections, multiplication of applications that are the source of electromagnetic fields, significant regulatory changes, heightened vulnerability due to the extreme complexity of supply chains, the mutation of financial and political environments, and so on.

- The interdependency of many of these risks.

- The changing nature of our relationship to risk and how it is perceived by the public.

For some of these phenomena, research on related risks has had a hard time keeping up with the accelerated pace of technological breakthroughs, contributing by the same token to a certain degree of mistrust or even distrust with regard to the impacts and an often negative perception of these trends.

As liability exposures and the importance of public opinion and image grow, this subject becomes unavoidable. In a publication entitled 'Electrosmog – A Phantom Risk', the Swiss reinsurance firm Swiss Re wrote, of these fields, that they represent, 'A prospective hazard, the magnitude of which cannot be gauged and which perhaps does not even exist, but which is nonetheless real – if only in that it causes anxiety and provokes legal actions.'

The integration of these emerging issues into a risk management process can occur at several different levels:

- reassessment of a risk that has already been identified, for which the likelihood of occurrence and/or the magnitude of the impact should be modified;

- identification of a new risk, which then enters into the traditional cycle of opportunities and threats analysis, assessment of the stakes in terms of both strategy and operations, and finally the decision on whether or not control measures are required;

- integration of emerging issues into the decision-making process for strategic projects.

The Process of Managing Emerging Risks

The emerging risk management process is identical to the conventional risk management process, but with a few features that are specific to it: the process entails identifying risks (the term detecting is more frequently used for emerging risks), measuring them (work is more likely to be done on the basis of scenarios than risk modelling due to the lack of reliable available statistical data) and managing them (pooling with other risks and prevention are more frequent, in the absence of tried and tested techniques for transferring emerging risks).

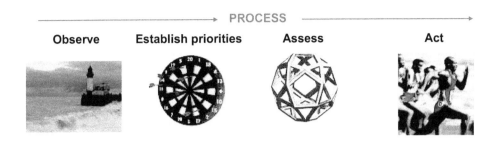

Figure 8.1   Early detection and monitoring of emerging risks
Source: AXA Group

EARLY DETECTION AND MONITORING OF EMERGING RISKS

Paradoxically, since we can only look for that which we have designated, the detection and monitoring of emerging risk trends require that we have identified them by name beforehand! Accordingly, we have to compare the risk factors (industrial or financial sector, market trends, socio-economic environment, and so on) that may impact the enterprise with the pursuit of its strategic objectives, which allows us to draw up an initial list of risks (this approach is generally done on the basis of expert opinion).

Once this list of risks has been established, it is time to assign a level of priority to each risk. The level assigned will be based on the appetite of the enterprise for risk (or its risk tolerance) as defined by executive management.

The next step is to ensure that this list of emerging risks is kept up-to-date (as well as the related priorities). Accordingly, this list will be subject to ongoing review and will evolve over time to reflect scientific and technological breakthroughs, the degree of media attention the various risks receive, changes in jurisprudence, including what is known as soft law in English-speaking cultures… in other words changes in how the risk is perceived by all stakeholders.

The enterprise's risk management division – if it exists – or the entity or employee designated to manage risk within the organization, in the absence of a dedicated department, may submit a list of the main emerging risks that are deemed relevant. It is then up to executive management to make the necessary choices and trade-offs, taking into account the resources available to the enterprise as well as the various competencies required to study these risks in depth. The resulting short list of emerging risks will thus be limited to subjects considered to be in need of the most urgent attention or to be the most important, and these are the risks that the risk management unit or manager and the operational teams will then have to assess.

ASSESSING EMERGING RISKS: QUALIFICATION AND QUANTIFICATION

First of all, the risk is clearly defined; its probable causes are identified; and its consequences for the business of the enterprise are described. In addition, it is necessary to determine if the risk is one whose impact is more or less circumscribed geographically, or if there is some possibility that it will extend regionally or even globally.

Due to the paucity and lack of reliability of what little statistical data exist, a scenario-based approach is preferred, taking into account certain thresholds as well as the sectors and divisions of the enterprise that could potentially be impacted.

If the qualification of a risk reveals the existence of a potential threat, a quantified assessment is needed and will be carried out on the basis of various scenarios that are envisaged. It will also be necessary to consider the direct impacts (damage to facilities, damage claims filed by third parties, and so on) and the indirect consequences (operating losses due to business interruption, adverse impact on image, impact on reputation, and so on).

The data thus obtained across the business and for all facilities will be consolidated and then submitted to executive management for comparison with the appetite for this type of risk.

EMERGING RISK MANAGEMENT

General remarks

When the quantified direct and indirect impacts, after the scenario or scenarios have been applied, is close to or surpasses the risk appetite of the enterprise, it becomes necessary to implement actions for either reducing or transferring this type of risk, such that the upper limit of what is deemed by executive management as tolerable is not exceeded.

Strategies for reducing emerging risks are quite diverse. First and foremost among them is the diversification of risks, which seeks to prevent the over-exposure of a product line, in a specific industrial sector or within a single geographic region. But there are also other ways to reduce emerging risks: prevention and communication, authoritarian reduction (the decision to stop producing or selling a product line or to pull out of a market, and so on), and solutions that involve the partial or total transfer of the risk in order to return to within acceptable exposure limits (recourse to the capital markets, insurance, and so on). However, these methods of transfer are often not an available option for emerging risks.

Warning thresholds or levels are validated and then put in place, in order to anticipate the successive levels of evolution of the risk and to avoid moving too quickly from an acceptable to an unacceptable level of exposure. As each threshold is surpassed, specific responses are triggered, from business as usual to watch to rollout of a monitoring process for a particular risk to a warning level that would require the triggering of an authoritarian reduction in the level of these risks. The usual solutions for transferring risk must be put in place *before* these thresholds are surpassed, as risk management departments should be able to anticipate future developments and prepare stress testing scenarios as well as emergency back-up plans that are required to ensure business continuity in critical situations.

Due to the specificity of emerging risks and the difficulty of detecting them, it is necessary to link early detection tools with the implementation of these warning thresholds.

A few preventative approaches

Each problematic issue that could have an impact on the business calls for specific preventive measures and resources, over which a watch system is needed. In view of the level of uncertainty linked to these risks, prevention will most likely take the form of applying the set of best practices suggested by the appropriate experts and regulators. For many subject areas, these resources will be transversal, like the exposures themselves. They will touch on Quality, Health, Safety and Environment (QHSE) aspects as well as on areas such as procurement, selling, contracts, the protection of material goods and so on.

With nanotechnologies, for example, and although research still needs to progress in a number of subject areas, a conservative approach is already recommended, particularly when it comes to professional exposures, encompassing situations of production, handling, storage, work with nanomaterials but also cleaning and maintenance. These situations can also involve subcontractors, which would then require special treatment in terms of prevention, training, monitoring and possibly special contractual clauses. Protecting premises against the risk of possible explosion as well as against environmental impairment risks must also be considered. In situations where product liability could come into play, and in addition to the need for compliance with the REACH regulation for chemical substances, a preventive approach could take inspiration from the nanomaterials approach contained in the recent directive on cosmetics (identification, product sheets, consumer information, and so on).

Some emerging problematic issues generate a potential for crisis, such as biological risks (pandemic), supply chain risks (critical supplier), info-technologies (a major viral attack) and nanotechnologies (explosion and resulting pollution). Every organization must identity these potential crisis points and make sure that the related emerging risks are included in their usual process of crisis preparation, along with the appropriate scenarios, and specific response studies.

The preventive approach could also be considered from the perspective of the criteria developed in connection with corporate social and environmental responsibility, which already lies at the heart of issues related to corporate image and reputation, specifically taking into account the interests of stakeholders and the levels of responsibility attached to the sphere of influence.

Supervision and Governance

ORGANIZATION

To ensure that the process of detecting and monitoring emerging risks is carried out efficiently and reliably over time, it appears necessary to specify the responsibilities connected to these activities and processes.

In light of the multiplicity and the potential severity of the related issues, the responsibility for monitoring cannot be placed in the hands of just one employee in the organization. Risk managers, because they operate within the professional realm of risk, will nonetheless be among the pivotal players with respect to these issues due to the significant contribution they can make in terms of detecting and monitoring emerging problematic issues within their organization. To play this role effectively, risk managers must have access to high-quality information on various subjects, and communications relays should be set up between scientists and operational staff to facilitate access to this information. Vigilance with respect to the quality of the information flowing in will remain in and of itself an issue, due to the subjectivity risk that attaches to these issues.

The process of analysis, assessment and possibly the control or management of these risks could be carried out by multi-disciplinary committees set up specially for this purpose and composed of representatives from R&D, production, procurement, sales, contracts, legal affairs, health and safety, environmental issues, and so on – much like the REACH or Genetically Modified Organism (GMO) committees created in the past by many businesses to gain a transversal view of these problematic issues. For companies whose reach is international, the presence of representatives from subsidiaries may offer added value, to the extent that the criticality of some emerging issues may vary from one large geographic region to the next. If this kind of transversal approach is adopted, the risk manager could serve as the information relay and advisor/expert, enabling the players who own the risks to appropriate the emerging risks being studied and the approach selected for managing them. Educating the owners of the risk on these issues could be improved by adopting a simple and positive approach to such risks.

Involving top management in the conception and implementation of the organizational management framework for these emerging risks appears to be indispensable. Top management involvement is equally necessary in the application of the global risk management process of the organization, in the spirit of ISO 31000. Taking these risks into account when formulating the enterprise's strategy will also be a fundamental point, as it will ensure that decision making allies both possible opportunities and potential threats.

WHICH TOOLS FOR MANAGING THESE RISKS?

Risk mapping, available today in a number of organizations, can be an important asset for understanding emerging risks, to the extent that risk maps presuppose that risk criteria have been defined by the organization, with its scales of impact and likelihood of occurrence.

Different types of impact will have to be assessed: in the case of nanotechnologies, for example, the impacts may touch on strategic matters

(product orientations), personnel – workplace health and safety – the
environment, product safety, liability and responsibility pledges, production,
and so on. Like the Chinese company that was mentioned in the press as being
the cause of the first deaths as a result of on-the-job exposure to nanoparticles
in a paint factory, the impact on reputation should not be ignored. In the case
of biological risks, exposures inside the organization can have an impact on
its personnel, dependent processes and employer obligations in the area of
health and safety. Outside the organization, the supply chain is also likely to be
impacted, with possible ruptures in supplier deliveries and in the organization's
deliveries to its own clients.

Positioning the criticality for the enterprise of these various problematic
issues in the form of a risk landscape can prove to be a useful educational tool
that can benefit in-house communications.

Example (Figure 8.2): Emerging risks landscape for a company that specializes in the
manufacture of cathode ray tubes, with a subsidiary in Asia and in the United States,
integrating numerous components from Asia, with a high level of automation and IT
integrated at the group level.

The company is considering the possible acquisition of a Chinese company
specializing in the production of electronic components.

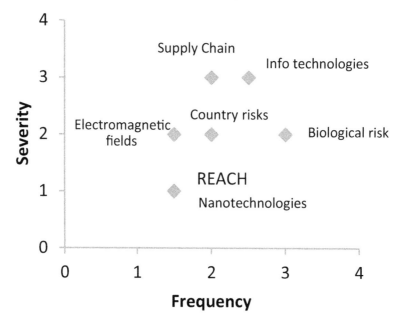

Figure 8.2   Emerging risks landscape
Source: Anne Barr

In this example, the contemplated acquisition could have an impact on the criticality of the nanotechnologies risk, among other things, given the significant increase in the number of exposed employees.

Once this landscape of emerging risks has been sketched out, existing general risk maps could be updated to include the most critical new risks, or changes could be made to the risk criticality indicators of risks already mapped, as the case may be.

FEEDBACK ON AN EXAMPLE OF EMERGING RISK STEWARDSHIP
(With the participation of Mr. Patrick Leroy, Risk Management, Roquette Frères)

Some companies have already set up structures designed to monitor emerging risks. One such company is Roquette Frères, questioned on its experience in managing the CMR risk, that is risks linked to carcinogenic, mutagenic and reprotoxic products. Stress was laid on the following points:

- Thinking needs to be done transversally, in project mode, with a steward who owns the risk (for example, a manufacturing manager).

- The risk owners must appropriate the approach and become aware of their driving role as project players (see ISO 31000).

- Impacts must be analyzed to reveal the critical issues and stakes.

- It is important to raise awareness through an approach that is positive and with information that is clear, simple, accurate and concrete.

- Today, access to this information remains difficult, though it is critical for shedding light on the debate and must be reliable and accurate to be credible.

- Seek measurable results through a truly structured approach: a specific and pragmatic action plan, major efforts to educate, train and raise awareness targeting operational staff, specified avenues of improvement, a best practices guide, regulatory watch function in place.

GOVERNANCE

The mutation underway in the framework for corporate governance should step up the pace of the process of integrating emerging risks into organizational executive management strategy.

This mutation traces its origin to the occurrence in recent years of a series of crises and financial scandals that have shaken the economic and financial world and the capital markets to the core, leading to the gradual appearance of legislative and regulatory frameworks and compliance guidelines that are more adapted to organizations. Both the Sarbanes–Oxley Act (SOX), passed in the United States, and various European directives (2006/46/EC amending the 4th and 7th directives and 2006/43/EC, known as the 8th directive), are key steps in the development of these regulatory approaches.

- Sarbanes–Oxley Act of 2002
  - The Sarbanes-Oxley Act, passed in 2002, placed new responsibility on management, boards of directors and audits committees. It is said to be 'the most far-reaching reform of American business practices since the time of Franklin Delano Roosevelt'. The Act mandated a number of reforms to enhance corporate responsibility, enhance financial disclosures and combat corporate and accounting fraud (*Source:* US Securities and Exchange Commission).

- Directive 2006/46/EC specifies that a company shall provide a corporate governance statement in the annual report, which should include a description of the main features of the company's internal control and risk management systems (*Source*: Official Journal of the European Union).

- The 8th European directive on company law Directive 2006/43/EC (Article 41) requires that public-interest entities shall have an audit committee, and states in section 2b that this audit committee must monitor the effectiveness of the company's internal control, internal audit and risk management systems (*Source*: Official Journal of the European Union).

- FERMA, the Federation of European Risk Management Associations, and ECIIA, the European Confederation of Institutes of Internal Auditing, have jointly published a practical guidance to assist organizations with the implementation of article 41 of the 8th European Company Law Directive (*Source*: FERMA).

Boards of directors and supervisory boards are now responsible for the oversight of risk management via their audit committees, and they are responsible for ensuring that risks are factored into strategic thinking and decision-making processes. Among these risks, emerging risks should be taken into consideration based on the importance of the stakes attached to them, as well as the utility of a global approach. Their positioning at the heart of the strategy of the business will represent a lever of growth and value creation and will, in so doing, give the organization a competitive edge.

Emerging Risks and Insurance

DEFINITIONS, CHARACTERISTICS AND DEGREE OF UNCERTAINTY

The task of taking emerging risks into account is one of the most complex in the risk management process for insurance groups. Paradoxically, it is also one of the most stimulating, since it allows them to expand beyond the horizons, necessarily short term, of the usual management of risks and engage in a longer-term reflection on risks for which the catastrophic impact on all of the portfolios in a single line of business may not be revealed for at least 15 years or so.

Within insurance companies, it is the risk department that is responsible for ensuring that the risks the business has to or will have to face are correctly identified (at the source), anticipated, measured and then managed dynamically. Generally, this department does not manage the risks directly itself: its role is to ensure that the operational echelons of the company, those that are in daily contact with the actual risks, are well aware of them and that they have the tools (possibly provided by the risk division) to manage them. In some respects, the risk department is the second line of defence, upstream from operations, thinking not only about the undesirable developments of known risks, but also about trends in new risks whose potential consequences are not yet known or are difficult to quantify.

The detection of emerging risks is important but it does not appear to be urgent; the responsibility that an insurer assumes in the name of its policyholders is analyzed over the long term, although this long-term responsibility is not in any way synonymous with small claims: AM Best has estimated (4 December, 2009) that remaining exposures linked to asbestos claims in the United States alone could cost US insurers 75 billion dollars after having led to the bankruptcy of 89 businesses in the United States in the last 28 years!

The insurance industry currently and frequently uses the following definition of emerging risks: they may be new, developing or already existing risks, but they can lead to potential losses that are difficult to quantify in terms of frequency and severity.

By way of example, we may cite new risks like nanotechnologies, risks that have been detected but that remain hard to quantify, such as those related to climate change, certain risks, like the longevity risk (linked to longer life expectancy that will require insurers to pay out on annuities for longer periods) or old risks that re-emerge, such as pleural plaques related to asbestos exposure.

What are the principal characteristics? We can mention their high degree of uncertainty, their potential for catastrophic accumulation (see Figure 8.3), and the initial difficulty in establishing an explicit relationship of causality – which is why they are so important for the insurance industry.

We have observed that knowledge of these risks is in a state of perpetual evolution, that it is based primarily by scientific and technical breakthroughs but that, more than the risk in and of itself, it is the perception of those concerned with respect to the risk that has changed, due to changing socio-economic criteria, case law or the media gaze.

As a result of the globalization of trade, the withdrawal of a product that is global in scope contains the seeds of a non-negligible potential for catastrophic accumulation. The resulting shock could be compared to the passage of a sudden storm over a small percentage of the totality of the portfolios of an insurance group that is diversified globally, with an impact on both sides of the balance sheet (assets and liabilities). Imagine one component in a food product that is sold worldwide and that suddenly turns out to be carcinogenic.

Immediately, we see the dilemma between early detection of emerging risks, which allows for more efficient action, but which also comes with a high degree of uncertainty (When can we accept some uncertain pieces of information as reliable?, Claude Henry 'Decision-Making under Scientific,

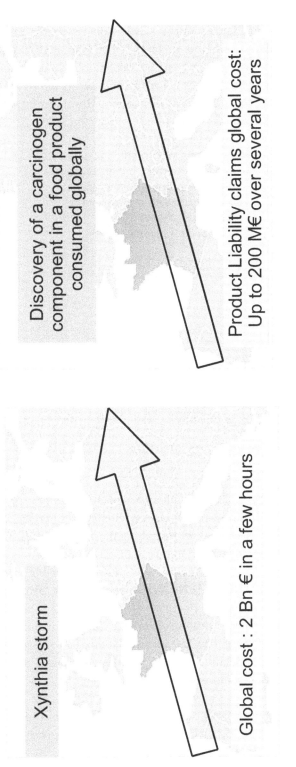

Figure 8.3 Catastrophic accumulation potential
Source: AXA Group

Political and Economic Uncertainty', Cahier de la chaire développement durable EDF-Ecole Polytechnique, n° DDX-06-12, June 2006). In practice, we see that in the emerging phase, when risk detection is low, the possibility of action is great, and that the further we advance in terms of our understanding of the risk, the lower the possibility of action – dramatically in the case of asbestos – (see Figure 8.4).

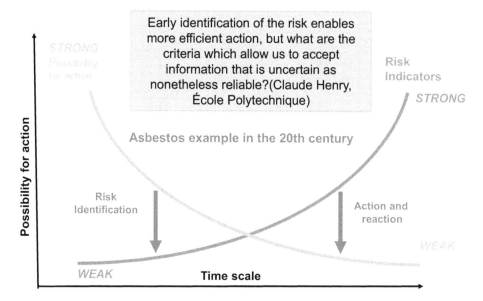

Figure 8.4   Detection and scope of action
Source: AXA Group

The insurance industry is increasingly aware of the potential for catastrophic loss experience that could arise in connection with emerging risks. Accordingly, the industry has set up processes for managing these risks that go hand in hand with the state-of-the-art tools used in risk management today.

EMERGING RISK MANAGEMENT WITHIN THE AXA GROUP

The list of emerging risks is drawn up on the basis of expert opinion. It is currently composed of more than 150 risks subdivided into 30 risk families that belong to four sectors of origin: technological risks, legal and regulatory risks, environmental risks and socio-economic risks.

This list is updated in light of recent developments in the four sectors of origin cited above. Operational networks take part in the process by providing feedback and information on new risks. The rest of the data comes from various research findings in scientific reviews or on the Internet, used to capture a representative idea of the perception of risks.

The process of monitoring the emerging risks on this list is organized on the basis of quantitative tools that measure the Internet buzz on the risk, track trends and send warnings when thresholds are surpassed.

Qualitative tools of analysis are used to verify that the trends and the surpassing of thresholds truly correspond to a change in the risks and not to an Internet distortion.

A synthetic report (Figure 8.5) is then drawn up to warn of and disseminate information related to these risks.

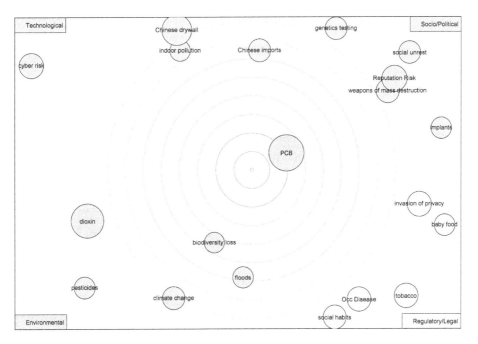

Figure 8.5   A risk mapping example

This data is provided indicatively and does not represent the opinion of AXA.
Emerging risks are classified on the basis of their sector of origin: Technological – Environmental – Socio-political – Regulatory/Legal.
Dangerous aspect of the risk: The closer the bubble is to the bull's eye, the stronger the increase (in speed and in intensity).
Insurance weight of the risk: The higher the insurance weight is, the larger the bubble's diameter is.

Source: AXA Group

All operational networks are then informed and educated, and the subjects that could have the greatest impact are studied in depth by work groups comprised of various experts.

The conclusions of these work groups are then shared and both best practices and recommendations are disseminated. In some cases, these give rise to the rollout of new insurance products and services by improving our knowledge of these issues. The exchange of information with our clients also helps to implement prevention strategies.

CONSIDERATIONS FOR THE INSURANCE INDUSTRY

As part of its mission to facilitate economic development and innovation, the insurer's role is to pool risks with its clients, allowing the latter to unload the risks they cannot or do not wish to assume.

Over the years, insurers have developed a vast array of data and expertise with respect to all of these types of risks, and can share this information and expertise with its clients, offering them a better understanding of these risks.

Because prevention is one of the most basic aspects of the insurance business, the dissemination of the methods and techniques of prevention will enable a first step in the process of risk reduction through a better comprehension of the risks themselves.

Better knowledge of emerging risks should lead, after they have been quantified, to a greater degree of risk transfer, a process that is currently difficult to achieve due to the lack of reliable and exploitable statistical data.

Risk is the raw material of the insurer; accordingly, it is not a question of systematically ruling out the consequences related to the potential appearance of these emerging risks; rather, it means rolling out a process (tools and metrics) and cultivating a culture for the selection of these risks that will allow the insurer to choose those risks that it wishes to retain after having assessed and priced all of them using the most reliable and complete information available.

References and Bibliography

ISO 31000:2009 (Risk Management – Principles and Guidelines).

COSO, Committee of Sponsoring Organizations of the Treadway Commission. Guidance 'Enterprise risk Management' – http://www.coso.org/guidance.htm.

Swiss Reinsurance Company publication 'Electrosmog – a phantom risk' – http://www.swissre.com.

REACH Regulation on chemical substances – http://ec.europa.eu/environment/chemicals/reach/reach_intro.htm

AM Best Company – http://www.ambest.com.

Sarbanes–Oxley Act of 2002, US Securities and Exchange Commission.

European Directive 2006/46/EC, Official Journal of the European Union.

The 8th European directive on company law, Official Journal of the European Union.

Guidance on the implementation of article 41 of the 8th European Company Law Directive by FERMA/ECIIA – http://www.ferma.eu/about/publications/eciia-ferma-guidance/.

Conclusion

Alexei Grinbaum

The scope of humankind's technological capability is immense. Man is closer today to the dream of omnipotence than he has ever been, although this dream was attested well before the age of modern technology: as Horace said,[1] '*nil mortalibus ardui est*'. At the same time modern society is a risk society.[2] In our age, political thought, which used to be guided by the idea of revolution, is led by a vision of future catastrophe. The heuristic that governs our technological choices is one of fear.[3] There is an apparent tension between this boundless power and this bottomless fear, which indeed lies at the very foundation of the ethics of science and technology.

With regard to technological change, the future always seems uncertain and moral indifference leads to the paralysis of action. We do not easily believe that tomorrow can be radically different from today. What is new is that our ability to forecast correctly and to foresee the future has stayed well behind our capacity of action powered by emergent technology. This fact alone is *the* ethical problem of technology. What kind of discipline does it call into existence? Ethics is an attempt to create, and to use, tools that enable *thinking* about technology at the time when human action often precedes thought and the understanding of its results comes, alas, far too late. In the 1950s Hannah Arendt clearly stated what this separation of technology and thinking would imply for the human condition: 'If it should turn out to be true that knowledge (in the modern sense of know-how) and thought have parted company for good, then we would indeed become the helpless slaves, not so much of our machines as of our know-how, thoughtless creatures at the mercy of every gadget which is technically possible, no matter how murderous it is.'[4] Arendt's

---

1   'Nothing is impossible for humankind.' Horace, *Odes* I, 3.
2   U. Beck, *Risk Society: Towards a New Modernity*, Sage Publications, 1992.
3   H. Jonas, *The Imperative of Responsibility: In Search of an Ethics for the Technological Age*, University of Chicago Press, 1985.
4   H. Arendt, *The Human Condition*, University of Chicago Press, 2nd edition, 1998.

dubious hero here is not Eichmann, but the almighty engineer, who was a positive protagonist of the social fiction of her time. From the point of view of this archetypical engineer, anything that is technically possible must and will be made; as Richard Feynman said, 'What I cannot create, I do not understand'[5].

Ethics is concerned with uncertainty and studies technological action that begets a future meaning of the human condition. However ethics cannot be reduced to prudence, cost–benefit analysis, or any of the following types of uncertainty:[6]

Risk: we know both the probabilities of possible harmful events, and their associated kinds and levels of damage. The various techniques of risk assessment are directly applicable.

Uncertainty: we know the types and scales of possible harms, but not their probabilities. Risk evaluation techniques aren't applicable, except if probabilities are understood subjectively as mere degrees of belief. In this case the precautionary principle applies and prescribes further research that would determine the values of the various objective probabilities.

Ambiguity: the problem at hand is not one of the likelihood of different forms of harm, but where the measurement, characterization, aggregation or meanings of the different issues are themselves unclear, disagreed among specialists or contested in wider society.

Ignorance: we don't have complete knowledge over all the possible forms of harm themselves. We 'don't know what we don't know' – facing the possibility of surprise. This renders problematic even the questions that we ask at the outset in risk assessment.

Indeterminacy: the possibilities for different social 'framings' depend 'reflexively' on complex interactions and path dependencies in the coevolution of social, technological and natural systems. In other words, not only do our commitments and choices depend on what we know, but what we know is conditioned by our preferred or expected commitments and choices.

On the basis of numerous examples, English researcher David Fleming identified what he called the 'inverse principle of risk evaluation': the propensity

---

5   J. Gleick, *Genius: The Life and Science of Richard Feynman*. Pantheon, New York, 1992. p. 437.
6   U. Felt (rapporteur), B. Wynne (chairman), *Taking European Knowledge Society Seriously*, Report of the Expert Group on Science and Governance to the Science, Economy and Society Directorate, Directorate-General for Research of the European Commission, 2007, p. 36. J.-P. Dupuy and A. Grinbaum, 'Living With Uncertainty: Toward the Ongoing Normative Assessment of Nanotechnology', *Techné* 8 (2), 2004, pp. 4–25.

of a community to recognize the existence of a risk seems to be determined by the extent to which it thinks that solutions exist.[7] Cognitive psychology provides tools that partly explain, or at least unravel the motivation of, what appears as perfectly irrational risk assessment. Contrary to psychology, ethics does not study the motives of human action. It poses hard questions about the human condition, its meaning and their evolution under the influence of technology. Ethical reflection broadens the analysis provided by the quantitative models of risk assessment, potential harm or exposition to danger. The contexts of ethical reflection can include narratives that belong to the collective memory of humanity and yet help us think about technology. For example, the biblical myth of Tobias and the fish addresses the problem of uncertainty created by a new, emerging phenomenon:

> And he [Tobias] went out to wash his feet, and behold a monstrous fish came up to devour him. And Tobias being afraid of him, cried out with a loud voice, saying: Sir, he cometh upon me. And the angel said to him: Take him by the gill, and draw him to thee. And when he had done so, he drew him out upon the land, and he began to pant before his feet. Then the angel said to him: Take out the entrails of the fish, and lay up his heart, and his gall, and his liver for thee: for these are necessary for useful medicines.[8]

How could it be that the fish had so frightened Tobias, who was not so young, for he would marry a girl during the same trip? At the same time, how could the boy so easily take the fish out of water and draw it upon the land? If the fish were small, then why such fear? Was Tobias frightened just because he had never before seen such a fish, and its sheer novelty sufficed to make him cry with a loud voice? When 'in absence of certainty and given the best scientific and technological knowledge,'[9] Tobias chose not to do anything but to cry for help, was he applying the precautionary principle or was he simply paralyzed by fear?

With the fish hidden from eyesight in the water, Tobias couldn't know its true size; he believed that the fish would decidedly swim up to where he stood and kill him. The size of the fish was enhanced, not by natural fact, but by the fear that it provoked.

---

7   David Fleming, 'The Economics of Taking Care: An Evaluation of the Precautionary Principle', in David Freestone and Ellen Hey (eds), *The Precautionary Principle and International Law*, La Haye, Kluwer Law International, 1996, p. 148.

8   Tobit 6: 2–5.

9   Formulation of the Precautionary Principle in the French law called 'Loi Barnier'.

However, once the angel had taught Tobias how to seize the fish, he could put it to use and make useful medicines. Uncertainty and fear dissolved after Raphael's words. Like Tobias, we shall certainly undergo a similar change with regard to new technologies. Time will modify them and better adapt to our needs; but it will change and adapt us too, so that *in fine* emerging technology will be perfectly integrated to the new human condition. However, there is a significant difference between this case and the story of Tobias: while the latter could ask the angel for guidance, we cannot hope to resort to divinity or take technology 'by the gill'. Fear and paralysis will continue while we have not found an equally effective alternative.

Addendum

For further information please refer to 'Toolkit for ethical reflection and communication'of the project ObservatoryNano sponsored by the European Commission: http://www.observatorynano.eu/project/catalogue/4ET/.

Appendix 1

Selected Organizations and Benchmarking Committees

International organizations and benchmarking committees have been set up to track the status of knowledge, organize educational efforts aimed at governments and the public at large, provide technical and financial support, and issue both recommendations and warnings on new and emerging risks. It is worth drawing up a panorama of the principal organizations, their respective roles and their work. The list below is not exhaustive, however, and the reader is urged to expand the scope of research to include other sources.

European Agency for Safety and Health at Work (EU-OSHA)

Established in 1996 by the European Union and based in Bilbao, Spain, the EU-OSHA constitutes the principal reference point in the area of workplace health and safety at the European level. Its central role is to *contribute to improving the workplace across the European Union.*

The agency has a tripartite organizational structure: it works with governments, employers and personnel representatives. It is a single reference point for technical, scientific and economic information related to workplace health and safety (WHS).

The agency also plays a role in educating workers and promoting a risk prevention culture in the workplace, providing information on the methods and tools designed to help roll out preventive measures. It also disseminates best practices in the area of WHS.

The European Risk Observatory (ERO), which is part of OSHA, was set up to identify new and emerging risks and to serve as a platform for debate among decision makers. The results of its research were published in December 2009, in a study entitled 'New and Emerging Risks in Occupational Safety and Health'. This survey identifies as new factors of risk 'technical innovations (nanotechnologies, biotechnologies) as well as social or organizational changes (poor working conditions associated with work migration, jobs in the informal economy, emerging forms of work)' (*source:* European Risk Observatory).

The study on new and emerging risks to occupational safety and health associated with green jobs has just ended its first phase with the publication of a report in March 2011, and has entered into its second phase, which entails identifying the major emerging technologies in green jobs by 2020 and their potential impact on worker health and safety.

European Food Safety Authority (EFSA)

The EFSA has set up a unit dedicated to emerging risks called EMRISK. The Emerging Risks Unit is responsible for establishing procedures to monitor, collect and analyze information and data in order to identify emerging risks in the field of food and feed safety with a view to their prevention.

French Agency for Food, Environmental and Occupational Health & Safety (ANSES – *Agence Nationale de Sécurité Sanitaire de l'Alimentation, de l'Environnement et du Travail*)

This Agency is the result of the merger effective 1 July, 2010 of two former agencies, the French Food Safety Agency AFSSA (*Agence Française de Sécurité Sanitaire des Aliments*) and the French Agency for Environmental and Occupational Health Safety AFSSET (*Agence Française de Sécurité Sanitaire de l'Environnement et du Travail*).

The Agency's mission is to help ensure human health and safety with respect to the environment, work and food. It is also responsible for protecting the health and well-being of animals, protecting plant safety and assessing the nutritional and functional properties of food.

By merging these two agencies into one, a stronger pool of expertise is created: its scientific competencies (intelligence and research) and its expertise in the assessment and management of risks.

To cite just one example of its work, AFSSET issued an opinion in 2009 on radio-frequency identification (RFID) systems, recommending the pursuit of the scientific watch and research on the biological effects of RFID waves.

In 2011, ANSES made radio frequencies one of its priority themes, creating a standing work group on Radio Frequencies and Health.

International Agency for Research on Cancer (IARC)

The IARC is part of the World Health Organization (WHO).

The mission of the IARC is to coordinate and conduct research on the causes of human cancer and the mechanisms of carcinogenesis, and to develop scientific strategies for cancer prevention and control. The Agency is involved in both epidemiological and laboratory research, and disseminates scientific information through publications, conferences, courses and fellowships.

International Organization for Standardization (ISO)

ISO is the world's largest developer and publisher of international standards. It is a Non-Government Organization (NGO) with a network of the national standard institutes of 162 countries.

It enables a consensus to be reached on solutions that meet both the requirements of business and the broader needs of society (*Source*: ISO).

Standards such as ISO 31000 relating to risk management, ISO 26000 providing guidance on social responsibility, ISO/TR 12885:2008 on health and safety practices in occupational settings relevant to nanotechnologies, ISO 28004:2007 on security management systems for the supply chain or ISO/IEC 27000:2009 on information security management systems, are examples of ISO contributions to the debates in emerging risks and their management.

The National Institute for Occupational Safety and Health (NIOSH)

NIOSH is the US federal agency responsible for conducting research and making recommendations for the prevention of work-related injury and illness.

Through its Research to Practice (r2p) Initiative, NIOSH works closely with partners to transfer and translate research findings, technologies, and information into prevention practices and products (*Source*: NIOSH).

The agency has developed a partnership programme on occupational emerging risks through the National Occupational Research Agenda (NORA) to raise the status of knowledge on those issues and improve workplace practices.

National Research and Safety Institute (INRS – *Institut National de Recherche et de Sécurité*)

INRS is a key link in the French system for the prevention of occupational risks, exercising its activities for the benefit of employees and businesses that fall under the scope of the basic social security system in France.

INRS is supported by the CRAM regional health insurance funds (*Caisses Régionales d'Assurance Maladie*) and the CGSS general funds (*Caisses Générales de Sécurité Sociale*). From the toxic risk to physical and psychological well-being, INRS conducts missions, programmes of study and research aimed at gaining a better understanding of occupational risks, as well as at analyzing their effects on workplace health. It also offers means of prevention. Studies are carried out from the research centre located in the Lorraine region.

The Organisation for Economic Co-operation and Development (OECD)

Established in 1961, the OECD is an international economic organization whose members include governments that are committed to the principles of democracy and the market economy. The OECD is not just one of the world's most important sources of statistical, economic and social data; it also deals with global economic, social and environmental issues and is a trailblazer in the area of identifying the future challenges facing modern society, in particular emerging risks.

The OECD's International Futures Programme is particularly interesting in this regard. For decision makers, it represents a tool for defining strategies and action plans through in-depth and far-reaching analyses on major possible future developments, key emerging challenges and trend break factors (*Source:* OECD).

For all foreign investors, the OECD offers many tools, including a country risk classification system, breaking news on emerging economies and best practices in the area of internal control and ethics in the fight against corruption.

The publication entitled *Emerging Risks in the 21st Century: An Agenda for Action,* which was published by the OECD in 2003, deals with emerging systemic risks. It offers a forward-looking and holistic vision of the risk in order to 'capture the interdependencies and interactions among forces of change, among hazards and systems'.

In the area of nanotechnologies, the OECD Council has established a working party on manufactured nanomaterials to study the practices of OECD member countries concerning nanomaterials safety and to develop the required assessment methodology (*Source: Emerging Risks and New Patterns of Prevention in a Changing World of Work,* World Labour Organisation (2010)).

Scientific Committee on Emerging and Newly Identified Health Risks (SCENIHR)

Instituted in 2004, SCENIHR advises the European Commission and formulates opinions on issues related to emerging and new health and environmental risks, and on broad, complex or multidisciplinary issues requiring a comprehensive assessment of risks to consumer safety or public health (*Source*: SCENIHR).

The areas of activity that fall within the scope of SCENIHR include, for example, the potential risks associated with the interaction of risk factors, synergic and cumulative effects; antimicrobial resistance; new technologies such as nanotechnologies; medical devices, including those that integrate substances of animal and/or human origin; tissue engineering; blood products; fertility reduction; cancer of the endocrine organs; physical hazards, such as noise and electromagnetic fields (cell phones, emitters and electronically controlled domestic environments); and methodologies for assessing new risks.

United States Environmental Protection Agency (US EPA)

The mission of the US EPA is to protect human health and the environment. To meet this goal, the agency is committed to developing and enforcing regulations, providing funds for specific programmes, conducting leading-edge research on environmental issues, training and publishing information.

EPA Partnership Programmes address a wide variety of environmental issues by working collaboratively with companies, organizations, communities and individuals.

The agency manages a growing number of emerging issues as the focus of environmental protection broadens to creating a greener, more sustainable economy as a whole (*Source*: US EPA).

The World Economic Forum (WEF)

The WEF is an independent and international non-profit organization that was established in 1971. Its annual risks report is based on an analysis of global risks as well as on information that is supplied by working groups, corporate executives and experts from around the globe.

The 2011 Global Risks report highlights the fragility of world economies, exacerbated by the financial crisis, the growing complexity of global risks and a system of world governance that is ill-adapted to the new planetary shocks and challenges. Against this backdrop, the report issues a warning that places global governance and economic disparity failures as the two most serious threats weighing on the world today. This year, the report lays particular stress on the high level of interconnectedness between risks, the consequence of which is an increase in systemic risks.

What emerges from this observation is the need to instill a culture of risk management in organizations. At the same time, risks will have to be approached differently, from a more global and strategic perspective, and head-on with the future challenges of the organization and its environment.

World Health Organization (WHO)

The Geneva-based WHO is the international directing and coordinating authority for health matters within the United Nations system.

It is broadly empowered to handle such matters as chronic and infectious diseases as well as mental health issues, nutrition, food safety, accidents, biological risks, the economy of healthcare and health prevention. The WHO is in charge of directing global action in the area of health, financing research in this area, setting standards and criteria, putting forth political options based on persuasive data, offering technical support to countries and also tracking public health trends (*Source*: WHO).

In the area of climate change, the WHO conducts research on its health effects and provides technical and financial support for action plans aimed at reduction and adaptation. It also participates in efforts to raise awareness of the risks, particularly in the Asia–Pacific region (*Source: Protecting Human Health from the Effects of Climate Change in the Asia-Pacific Region*, WHO).

Webography

ANSES	–	http://www.anses.fr
EFSA	–	http://www.efsa.europa.eu/
EPA	–	http://www.epa.gov
IARC	–	http://www.iarc.fr/indexfr.php
INRS	–	http://www.inrs.fr
ISO	–	http://www.iso.org
NIOSH	–	http://www.cdc.gov/niosh/
OECD	–	http://www.oecd.org
OSHA	–	http://www.osha.europa.eu
SCENIHR	–	http://www.ec.europa.eu/health
WEF	–	http://www.weforum.org
WHO	–	http://www.who.int

Appendix 2

Climate – A Brief History of Climate-related Pledges and Their Potential Impacts

The sixteenth United Nations Climate Change Conference, held in Cancun, Mexico in December of 2010, gave rise to a certain degree of new hope in multilateral negotiations just one year after the Copenhagen Summit meeting, which had underscored the difficulty for various governments to reconcile economic development and the dual issue of scarcity and the environment.

The Cancun Agreements call for a series of breakthroughs aimed at fighting against the phenomenon of global warming, including the creation of a Green Fund for developing countries, the adoption of a mechanism designed to fight against deforestation called REDD (Reducing Emissions from Deforestation and Degradation), and maintaining the pledge to limiting global warming to 2° C compared with the pre-industrial era.

A number of critical questions are still pending, however, in particular that of how these various measures will be paid for and the extension of the Kyoto Protocol in early 2013. These and other key issues will be discussed at the next conference, which will be held in Durban in late 2011.

Although the results have fallen far short of the initial ambitions, one positive outcome has been to raise general awareness of the fact that nature can no longer be considered merely as an exploitable object, that governments must make efforts in addition to their formal commitments, and that sharing clean technologies is absolutely necessary to ensure responsible economic development and to protect our environment.

A SHORT REVIEW OF THE VARIOUS COMMITMENTS

In 1972, the first international conference on the human environment was held in Stockholm, resulting in the creation of the United Nations Environmental Programme (UNEP).

In 1987, the concept of sustainable development made its first appearance, in the Bruntland Commission report.

In 1988, the United Nations created the Intergovernmental Panel on Climate Change (IPCC) to impartially assess available international scientific, technical and socio-economic information on climate trends.

In 1992, the Rio Earth Summit unveiled a global programme for fighting the effects of climate change, resulting in the Rio Declaration on Environment and Development, a set of guidelines for better management of the planet. A total of 150 countries adopted Agenda 21, an international UN action plan offering a blueprint for the twenty-first century structured around four key areas: the economy, the environment, social issues and ethics. Three conventions were also signed: the convention on the fight against desertification, the convention on biodiversity and the United Nations Framework Convention on Climate Change (UNFWCC).

The Kyoto Protocol (also known as the Kyoto Agreement) of 1997 went into effect in 2005, strengthening the framework convention by adding legally constraining objectives that require the world's most industrialized nations to achieve an average reduction in the greenhouse gas emissions of 5 per cent up to 2012 (8 per cent for Europe).

EU Climate and Energy Package

For the European Union, the fight against global warming has been ongoing. In December of 2008 the EU adopted the Climate and Energy Package, a host of measures, directives and decisions that seek to achieve the so-called '3 times 20' objective by the year 2020:

- reduce greenhouse gas emission by at least 20 per cent;

- decrease overall energy consumption by 20 per cent;

- increase the percentage of renewable energies in the overall mix to 20 per cent.

Caring for Climate, the Business Leadership Platform

A commitment supported jointly by the UN's Global Compact, the World Business Council for Sustainable Development (WBCSD) and the UN's

Environmental Programme (UNEP), the platform was designed to promote practical solutions and influence both public opinion and public policymakers.

This initiative enables business leaders to make proactive commitments related to climate change, on an individual as well as a collective level: the signing parties agree to set objectives, roll out strategies, adopt appropriate practices and annually disclose the emissions of their business in connection with their commitment to transparency under the United Nations Global Compact.

Carbon Disclosure Project

This report provides an annual snapshot of the threats and opportunities related to climate change facing listed corporations worldwide.

Since February 2010, the SEC (Securities and Exchange Commission, which regulates the US capital markets) has been requiring businesses to make disclosures on their climate risks (greenhouse gas emissions and disaster prevention measures).

The European Commission has published a White Paper on adaptation to climate change, the aim of which is to roll out a full-fledged strategy of adaptation between now and 2013. One of the actions related to the strategy involves the implementation of a centre for exchanging information on the effects of climate change.

As this deadline approaches, business enterprises find themselves facing significant strategic and operational challenges, and need to integrate the consequences of global warming into their strategic thinking processes. Doing so in turn entails identifying trends, challenges, risks, medium- and long-term impacts and interactions with other global changes. The complexity of the subject makes this task all the more difficult for decision makers given the tense economic context, made even more so by resource-related tensions.

Admittedly, the new energy, socio-economic, health and safety, societal and ethical issues, and the new and more stringent regulations represent fantastic growth opportunities. But it is also important to factor in the risks that are related to this change. Climate conditions and rising temperatures give rise to the emergence of infectious diseases and the risk of a pandemic, and extreme weather events can disrupt resource supply chains. Chain reaction on a grand scale is a genuine risk for supply chains, with the potential to impact the systems of one or more countries at the same time.

A clear understanding of the magnitude of the risks related to climate change is necessary at the highest level in the business organization, that is, boardrooms and shareholders, so that an explicit strategy with respect to climate change can be developed and supported. The image and indeed the long-term survival of the business are at stake.

Index

For Product Safety Concerns and Information please contact our EU
representative GPSR@taylorandfrancis.com
Taylor & Francis Verlag GmbH, Kaufingerstraße 24, 80331 München, Germany

9 781138 271784